M000311251

SAVING FOR THE FUTURE

SAVING
FOR
THE FUTURE

My Life and the Alaska
Permanent Fund

DAVE ROSE

as told to Charles Wohlforth
Foreword by Arliss Sturgulewski

Epicenter Press is a regional press publishing nonfiction books about the arts, history, environment, and diverse cultures and lifestyles of Alaska and the Pacific Northwest.

Publisher: Kent Sturgis
Acquisitions Editor: Lael Morgan
Editor: Kent Sturgis
Jacket Designer: Elizabeth Watson, Watson Design
Text design: Victoria Michael
Proofreader: Susan Ohrberg
Indexer: Sherrill Carlson
Printer: Lightning Source

Copyright ©2008 Frances Rose
No part of this publication may be reproduced, stored in a retrieval system, or transmitted in any form or by any means, electronic, mechanical, photocopying, recording, or otherwise, without the prior written permission of the publisher. Permission is given for brief excerpts to be published with book reviews in newspapers, magazines, newsletters, catalogs, and online publications.

Library of Congress Control Number: 2007909858

ISBN 13: 978-0-9790470-5-3

First printing March 2008
10 9 8 7 6 5 4 3 2 1

Printed in Canada

To order single copies of this edition of SAVING FOR THE FUTURE, mail $17.95 plus $6.00 for shipping (WA residents add $2.80 state sales tax) to Epicenter Press, PO Box 82368, Kenmore, WA 98028. Orders also may be placed 24 hours a day by calling 800-950-6663, or placed online at www.EpicenterPress.com.

CONTENTS

FOREWORD

S trangely enough, when I think of Dave Rose, the image that often comes to mind is of him as a leprechaun. Dave gave me that mental picture at a St. Patrick's Day party when he cheerfully mocked his own round shape and mischievous spirit by dressing up all in green complete with a hat, shoes, and vest. The joke captured a unique aspect of his personality. Like many people in public life, Dave was intelligent, accomplished, and confident. You don't make contributions like his without believing in yourself. Yet, unlike most people I've known in public life, Dave could laugh at himself. He knew how to connect compassionately with all kinds of people. His integrity was total, even at the most difficult moments.

All of those qualities shine through in Dave's memoir. His pride is evident as he shares memories, funny stories, and lessons he learned from his role in major events that shaped Alaska. His humor is ever-present, as is the caring for others that seems to have driven him as strongly as his powerful ambition. As for his integrity, readers will see it in Dave's actions and in the way he accounts for himself.

I have known Dave since we served together on the Anchorage Municipal Assembly. My background was in public policy rather than politics and I may have been naïve about getting things done. Dave was more experienced politically, but he shared my interest in good government and became an invaluable ally and teacher. He cared passionately about enacting the right policy and had the political know-how to turn good ideas into law. We enjoyed working together and I learned from him.

Dave went on to the Alaska Permanent Fund and I went to the Alaska State Senate, a good vantage point from which to watch Dave develop a deserved reputation as a financial wizard and as an icon for thousands of Alaskans collecting dividend checks. His achievements at the Fund and his subsequent personal financial success did not affect the good humor and compassion I had come to respect. Despite struggling with his health the last two decades of his life, Dave remained steadfastly optimistic and cheerful amid adversity. His optimism surely was a key to his success in life, but he also must have had hidden reserves of strength to maintain his positive spirit through years of dialysis, a kidney transplant, heart surgeries, and related difficulties. I never heard him complain.

Weeks before his death, Dave asked me through an intermediary to write this foreword. I am sad to say he didn't live to read my comments, or to receive the praise that surely will come with the publication of this entertaining and important work.

Dave's death and the completion of his book call for an appraisal of this remarkable man. As I think of him in his leprechaun costume, his core of humanity sticks with me. Dave was a devoted and caring husband who enjoyed a wonderful marriage to Fran and raised two exceptional sons, Evan and Mitch, whose success in business and politics was a great source of pride. He offered rock-solid friendship to hundreds, perhaps thousands, of Alaskans and gave generously even to those he barely knew. His mischievous smile and large heart brought warmth to everyone with whom he worked. Dave was not only a great Alaskan, he was a whole person. This book is a chance to rejoice not only in the success of Alaska's Permanent Fund, but also to drink in the details of a good life, well lived.

Arliss Sturgulewski

INTRODUCTION

I was a small Jewish kid with a round face and horn-rimmed glasses sitting in the back of a Catholic church in Queens Village, waiting for mass to end so I could get into the gym and shoot baskets, maybe win a little money playing basketball. No one would have picked me out as a kid who would help build Alaska. Ours was a neighborhood with gangs, Irish against Italian, and teens carrying zip guns made of one-inch iron pipes. Fights were commonplace. I was a boy growing up without a father, without anyone to ask about the facts of life or to invoke as a protector in the rituals of schoolyard conflict. My school, PS 109, promised nothing special and expected little. I didn't rise above the expected. All signs pointed to a life on a well-worn path, close to home.

Yet I left that path and ended up going somewhere completely new. Alaska in the 1960s was a place of exploding possibilities. By good fortune and some personal ambition, I found myself there, helping build a new state, fighting for tolerance and equality as a political leader, and shaping some of the unique fiscal institutions that have made Alaska the richest state in the union. I learned construction skills to help build Anchorage's first synagogue and financial skills to run a bond bank that helped build Alaska's public facilities.

In 1982 I took over the Alaska Permanent Fund Corporation, which at that time amounted to a cardboard box of files and a money-market and mortgage portfolio of $3.5 billion. The fund was something fundamentally new, created by Alaska's voters to convert a portion of their natural resource wealth into financial assets to be saved in perpetuity. No model existed for managing it or avoiding the pitfalls of handling money on behalf of a diverse populace of opinionated citizens. Other oil-rich governments had attempted such programs without success.

Ten years later, with a solid staff, a thoughtful board of trustees, and built-in checks and balances to prevent corruption, the fund had become an unassailable institution and a long-term source of financial strength for Alaska, and contained almost $13.3 billion. At this writing, it had surpassed $40 billion, and the lessons learned were ready for export to other resource-rich governments.

I have a lifetime of extraordinary experiences and exciting challenges to look back on. There's a good story in my journey from Queens to Juneau. It's a story about Alaska and the opportunities it gave me. The turning points are decisions made in the frontier spirit under the guidance of common sense. Yet I am not a hero in this tale, only the main character. My life story isn't one of overcoming impossible odds or dedicating superhuman effort. It's about having good mentors and making the most of good breaks—and about where those breaks came from along the way.

While the circumstances of my life may have been unique, the forces of upward mobility and opportunity that helped me should remain available to others for the good of society. My greatest good fortune is that my potential was never wasted. Prejudice never defeated me, and the people and institutions I worked for gave me room to succeed or fail. The U.S. Army was my ticket out of New York and it gave me the managerial skills I needed. The voters of Anchorage and leaders of Alaska put faith in me and taught me, by trial and error, how to survive in politics. By the time I reached the permanent fund, I had a combination of managerial, financial, and political skills that made me fit for the job. For that I thank Alaska and America.

Whatever I owe to my place and time, however, my deeper and more profound debt is to three exceptional women who molded and saved me. First, my mother, left on her own with two children and a marginal business for which she was unsuited, making envelopes on a narrow street in downtown Manhattan. She persevered with grit and an elegant style that never left her. Surely whatever strength of character I gained as a child came from her.

My wife, Fran, was a companion and foil through the years. Our relationship was born in a political disagreement—and we've never stopped debating—but she is my indispensable guide and helpmate. At critical times in our life together, she made the sacrifices necessary to allow my career to advance. Everything I have now belongs at least half to her.

And finally, a special woman who has chosen to be anonymous, a good samaritan unrelated to me. She gave me the kidney that kept me alive, and did so without expectation of compensation or recognition. To benefit from a gift of such pure goodness is an overwhelming honor and a responsibility that often has brought me to tears.

My health has been a problem for the last one-third of my life. My most noteworthy professional challenges came after my diabetes was diagnosed and I began losing my eyesight. My guidance of the formative years of the Alaska Permanent Fund and the creation, with Fran, of Alaska Permanent Capital Management—our successful institutional investing firm—occurred as my health declined. I spent four years on dialysis and was told by my doctor to put my affairs in order because I wouldn't have much time left to live unless my heart's diseased pacemaker leads could be replaced in a risky operation. With a donated kidney, my condition stabilized but as I worked on this text I again faced open-heart surgery. I have a great sense of the limit of our time on earth. Now is the time for me to reach back over my life and draw out the lessons that may help others—and to tell some funny stories one more time.

The value of what I learned about protecting and harnessing public assets has proved of interest to political leaders in Russia and the Middle East as resource-rich, emerging governments seek models for managing and protecting their wealth. As director of the Alaska Permanent Fund Corporation, the Alaska Municipal Bond Bank, and the Alaska Industrial Development Authority, I participated in building institutions that saved the bulk of the state's wealth while using a responsibly limited portion of it to leverage economic growth and construction of public facilities. Alaska's story is unique in this respect. Many pitfalls face a government sitting on top of valuable natural resources. Most have stumbled, wasting their money or damaging their private sector economies. In Alaska, a different pattern emerged: We transformed non-renewable resource wealth into hard financial assets, producing a renewable stream of income. That singular achievement—turning oil into securities—set Alaska apart and made the state's financial history important far beyond its borders.

How this would happen wasn't obvious to anyone at the start, but today we can see the pieces that brought about Alaska's successful experiment in saving. The creation of the fund came about at a perfect moment, when Alaskans were concerned with avoiding waste of oil dollars. The fund's founders cleverly avoided defining its goals or function, allowing the idea to be all things to all people. Once the fund was in place, its early history involved extensive debate to set its purpose, an essential process that cleared away key hazards. My own role as the first executive director was fortuitous because I brought a combination of political, managerial, and financial skills to the job that helped me steer through diverse challenges that we met early on.

More fundamentally, the Alaska Permanent Fund survived because it was insulated from day-to-day political pressures by other institutions that provided for the needs that politicians might otherwise have expected the fund to cover, including industrial and community development projects. I call these other institutions "blockers" because they blocked those who craved funding for public needs—often legitimate ones—and who otherwise would have looked to the permanent fund.

Strong public support also protected the fund. The payment of an annual dividend to Alaskans was the most obvious source of this political cover, but managerial philosophy also made a difference. Public confidence grew from the fund's operational transparency and stringent ethical standards; from steady, common-sense management that was easy to understand; and, perhaps most important, from its *success*.

As I think back on that kid in the church waiting to play basketball, I realize that while the distance traveled is great, some aspects of my personality remain the same. One of my chores as a kid was to mow the enormous lawn at a summer house my mother owned in upstate New York, four acres that would take two days of sweat with a push mower. I negotiated with Mom for a better deal. She agreed to pay thirty-five cents an hour toward the purchase of a power mower. I kept working, but before I had saved enough, I reopened the negotiation and she agreed to match my contribution. With the money in hand, I marched into Sears and bought a mower with a Briggs and Stratton engine for something less than $200. I still have a picture of myself next to that mower, beaming with pride. I had stuck with the job, but I'd also used some skill leveraging my work into something better. I ended up getting a lot of my summertime back that would have been spent pushing a mower.

That may not be a heroic story, but it is how I got from Queens to Juneau. To the extent that my personality fit the needs of the Alaska Permanent Fund in its early years, it was that same mix of politics, finance, and simple drive that made it work.

PART I

MY LIFE BEFORE THE PERMANENT FUND

CHAPTER 1
A single-parent childhood

I remember in clear detail the night my father died, but exactly what happened and how it shaped me remains as much a mystery to me today as sixty years ago when I was nine. My mother thought I was asleep, but I could hear my father's voice coming from the bathroom. I never found out what was wrong with him—perhaps he was diabetic, as I came to be in later life. Certainly he was overweight and overworked. Earlier that night, he had left our house in the working-class neighborhood of Queens Village for an ice cream. He went into the bathroom, belching.

My mother asked, "How are you feeling?"

My father said, "Not well." Then I heard him say, "It hurts. It hurts."

Mom stayed with him, and then he passed out on the floor of the bathroom. I could hear her trying to revive him before she called a doctor. "Hurry, he's passed out," she said.

I waited silently in bed.

The doctor bustled up the stairs, examined my father, and coldly declared, "This man is dead."

When the doctor and my mother dragged my father's body from the bathroom to the bedroom—I could hear a scraping noise in the hallway—I pretended to wake up. My mother sent me to sleep with my older sister, Amy.

We were lying awake together when my mother came in and told us, "Well, your father is dead." She told us that he had gone to heaven.

The truth is my father hadn't been around much before he died. I have almost no warm memories of him—he simply was present. I remember being spanked after I threw a book at my father because he wouldn't read to me—I broke his glasses. Edward William Rose was a printer whose skills landed him a job during the Great Depression. By the time of his death at age fifty, he co-owned a small envelope factory at 35 Wooster, a narrow street a block off of Broadway in the downtown Manhattan neighborhood of Soho, primarily producing custom work for large clients, earning a modest income. It was enough to buy us a house and adjoining lot in Queens, but not in a particularly desirable neighborhood, and a summer place on nine acres with a creek in what was then the Catskills farming community of Lanesville, about 130 miles north of the city.

My single warm memory of my father arose from an episode at the old farm we called Rosebrook, which he bought a few months before he died. My mother had sent Dad shopping for mayonnaise or some such thing in Phoenicia, the neighboring town, where, it turned out, the grocer was trying to sell an old, swaybacked horse. My father impulsively bought the horse, parked his car, and rode the horse home. He knew nothing about horses. Unsure how to tell my mother what he had done, Dad took his time getting home, stopping for a few beers at Tony's Bar and Grill on the way. (Later, whenever the horse ran away, we usually found her at Tony's, which must have made a favorable impression on her.)

I had rarely seen my mother in such a panic as when Dad arrived home with the horse. She feared being left with this balky equine most of the week while he worked in the city. My father said he would find someone to help, but not long after that he died. For Mom, the prospect of life on her own must have seemed overwhelming. Oddly, she focused on the horse rather than raising two children and running an envelope factory by herself. How could she ever manage such an animal?

At first, my feelings about my father's death were mostly feelings of sympathy for my mother, not sadness for him. Born Mary Nadelstein, the daughter of immigrants from Romania, she called herself Marion. The name fit better with the intellectual persona she made for herself. In younger years, she wrote poetry, some of which was published in the New York newspapers and was included in an anthology at Columbia University, where she took some classes. She hung out in tea rooms in Greenwich Village, where she heard some of the century's most famous poets read and was pursued by Maxwell Bodenheim, king of the Village bohemians. She never lost her elegant manners and somewhat aristocratic bearing. She could hardly have been worse suited for running an envelope factory.

My father's partner, Ernest Harper, became her partner, and my father's consuming job of marketing, bookkeeping, and managing business affairs became her job for the next thirty years. Harper fixed the machines and tended to the mechanical side of the business. The factory in Manhattan was ninety minutes from Queens on a bus and two subway lines. Basically, it was a small sweat shop, full of women from Spanish Harlem who spoke little English. Sheets of paper twenty-two by thirty-four inches were printed, cut to shape by dies, and inserted into a machine for folding and gluing with a tapioca-based adhesive. Most of the fifteen machines were dangerous, and we kids weren't allowed to operate them. The repetitive action could mesmerize a worker into dozing and catching her hair in a powerful mechanism designed to grab and fold or cut the paper.

The glue presented a different hazard. The tapioca spoiled in the heat, which often exceeded one hundred degrees in the brick building. The glue was still sticky after it curdled, but sometimes food and drug inspectors showed up on those hot days and slapped an indelible "condemned" label on the barrels. Then we would wheel the barrels to the loading dock for disposal, but we couldn't afford to lose a whole barrel of glue. So when the inspector left, we would roll the barrel back inside and pour the glue into a fresh barrel, adding a flavoring to cover the spoilage. The mint-flavored envelope actually sold for a premium.

One of the best workers was a big, muscular black man, whose job included handing down supplies from the high shelves. One day he lost his footing and tumbled down, feet first, into an open glue barrel. We tried everything we could think of to get him out without wasting any glue. The man kept apologizing for spoiling the glue. Work in the factory came to a standstill as we puzzled through the predicament. We tried rolling him under a shelf so he could pull himself straight up with his arms. Several of us pulled downward on the barrel. It didn't work—too much suction. Finally, a decision was made to pour the precious glue out onto a tarp. However, it spread all over the floor and all over us, and then it spread to everything we touched. Some pulled on the man, some pulled on the barrel. Out he popped, along with a dead rat. Completely drenched in glue, he was given $20 and sent out to buy himself new clothes. He never returned. I was assigned to scrape the glue off the floor and put it back in the barrel for later use.

Needless to say, when I mail a letter, I never lick the envelope.

The business encountered a few other setbacks, too, such as the time it printed a big order of stationery—never delivered—for the doomed ocean liner *Andrea Doria*. But it was the day-to-day operations that were my mother's greatest challenge. She knew nothing about business when my father died. She couldn't reconcile invoices with payments or create monthly statements. She barely knew how to use an adding machine. At the end of her long work day, she would sit at the table with me or Amy, having us read lists of fifty or sixty figures from an adding machine tape to help her find errors. Amy made the beds and did the shopping. When I reached my teens, I began cooking dinner so we could have a hot meal with Mom when she got home from work, and I fixed things around our deteriorating house. We had housekeepers over the years, but none made an impression. Mostly they were babysitters. Money never was plentiful. Anything I wanted beyond the necessities of food and clothing I earned myself.

Our house stood in a row with nearly identical wooden houses on a street like the typical Queens neighborhood made famous by Archie Bunker's home in the TV program *All in the Family*. My school, PS 109, stood five stories, kindergarten through eighth grade in one building, with a chain-link enclosure on the roof. Juvenile crime was common. Gangs fought with fists, clubs, and zip guns. To become a police officer or fireman was the best hope most families had for their boys.

I spent my time in the streets with Irish kids—ours was one of few Jewish families—pulling pranks, playing stick-ball with parked cars as bases, and shooting baskets at Our Lady of Lourdes Catholic parish, where I attended mass for the sole purpose of getting into the gym. Most of my buddies attended parochial school, so I didn't see them until three o'clock, when we all converged on our few blocks of home turf. Mom didn't get home until 7 PM, so I had four hours of unsupervised time every day, plenty of time for mischief and minor scrapes with delinquency.

What saved me from serious trouble was the Police Athletic League. Cops volunteered to work with kids after school, essentially to wear us out so we wouldn't have energy to get into trouble. These were the few men in my childhood, and I still feel grateful for the time they gave me. I worked hard for the cheap little medals they awarded for our physical prowess, winning them for shooting baskets, jumping hurdles, and, most memorably, for rope climbing. The last one was memorable because when I got to the top of the rope, I froze in terror and refused to come down. The cop down below first tried reasoning: He said he'd never seen a skeleton on a gym rope. Then everyone in the gym got involved, pleading and coaxing until I started bawling. A young cop finally climbed up behind me and slowly worked me down with kindness, but by then my embarrassment was complete.

Of course, every kid has ample opportunities for embarrassment. Mine were no different except for the lack of adult guidance in my youth. A special third-grade teacher at PS 109, Miss Smith, befriended me the year my father died. Her class was fun. Living in the neighborhood, she looked out for us in the streets as well. The next year, my teacher wasn't aware of my circumstances when she called me forward to speak about favorite things I did with my father, bringing tears of embarrassment again.

For all of my mother's strength and the powerful values she instilled in us, she never once talked to me about sex, even to explain the physical changes of puberty. Except for what I picked up from my buddies in the streets, I had no inkling of what was happening to my body. In sixth grade, a willing girl allowed me to explore under her dress in a wardrobe at PS 109 and I allowed her to find out what was in my pants. When I asked her for a repeat session, however, she refused, saying she was having her *period*. I thought she meant something about English period. I had a lot to learn about girls.

I was smart enough, however, to realize that Amy's boyfriends wanted to get her alone, so I used that knowledge to extort from them thirty-five cents for a movie. All I had to do was be a pest. Amy did turn the tables on me once, when one of her rough and probably broke boyfriends refused to pay. He became so aggravated that he showed me a huge gun. I knew he wasn't going to shoot, so I kept up my routine, whereupon he and Amy lured me outside and locked me out of the house. I was outraged. When I had to use the bathroom, I did it in the flower garden. No harm done—until that night at dinner, when Mom asked about our day, and Amy reported, "David peed in your azaleas." All hell broke loose, and my bringing up the gun didn't help. My mother loved her garden. Amy had found the perfect revenge.

Whether my extortion of Amy's boyfriends showed an aptitude for business I'm not sure, but even as a boy I knew how to work the system. At school I became a student monitor, handing out penalties to my classmates for playground infractions. This meant I could be late for class. Stuffing envelopes at my aunt's print shop a few blocks from the envelope factory, I sustained high productivity to earn the impressive sum of $1 an hour. At the same time, closer to home in Queens, I had another job I enjoyed—loading and tallying deliveries of Wise potato chips and other snacks on a distributor's loading dock. Working with a couple of other guys, practicing quick draw with a hose to shoot the owl's eye on the company logo on the side of the trucks, I whiled away my afternoons after school and longer days in the summer through my teenage years. Although I had little time for friends—I was too shy to make new friends or meet girls anyway—I had money to do what I wanted and the opportunity to see the value of business skills such as accounting.

In retrospect, I don't think I was any more unhappy than most other teens. At least my mother had given me a wide enough view of life to know that I didn't want to stay in Queens forever or to become a police officer. I wanted to get out. At fourteen, I went to the Philmont Scout Ranch, a Boy Scout camp in New Mexico. Mom paid for my uniform, and I paid for whatever expenses were not subsidized by the Boy Scouts. The train carried me west from New York to the desert southwest, a region with an exotic terrain I had barely imagined. At Santa Fe I joined a troop for two weeks, climbing mountains, working with pack mules, making camp, and learning to be a member of a team. For the first time, I had to be self-sufficient and to share responsibilities with other boys and men. The landscape made an enormous impression on me. I had been to rural New York, but this was something completely new—big, grand, harsh, and a place you could survive only if you knew what you were doing. The parallel with Alaska was strong; I realized that when I headed north as a young adult. The relationship I had missed with my father may have played a part in my great satisfaction with this environment of male teamwork, although of course I never thought of this at the time, or later when I joined the military, which in some ways was similar to the Boy Scouts.

Back home, Jamaica High School was a lonely place for a shy, overweight kid like me. The student body of five thousand was broken into three shifts due to overcrowding, making almost everyone anonymous. Ethnic and class differences made the situation worse. Those of us from Queens Village ranked lower than kids from the more affluent Jamaica Estates, and most of my friends from Queens Village were Irish Catholics who attended Catholic school. The Italians ranked even lower. I would ride my bike home with Mal Goldberg, one of the few Jews in my neighborhood, but I could never break in with the cashmere crowd of Jamaica Estates, even though it was a largely Jewish neighborhood. Still, I had more ambition than my neighborhood friends. Being a Jew meant having to look out for yourself, and my mother's example influenced me as well. The injustice of being excluded because we lived on the wrong side of the figurative tracks stung me. Without ever giving it conscious thought, equal rights became a major theme in my life.

My first foray into activism came about because of exclusion by this "in" crowd. I wanted to join the Jamaica High Booster Club, wear a white sweater, and cheer through a cone-shaped megaphone. But when I asked about signing up, the head of the club, Gail Shannon, said the club was full. Upon checking, I discovered that every member came from Jamaica Estates. Gail's explanation was that poor kids from Queens Village couldn't afford fifty dollars for the uniform, so she was saving us the embarrassment by not asking us to join. I decided to protest even though the coach, who was also my gym teacher, was Gail's father. My indignation gave me courage and I knew Mom would back me up if I got into trouble pushing the issue. The coach said he would investigate, and a week later his investigation revealed that I should stop making trouble for his daughter. It was my fault for failing to seek out the sign-up list when she had circulated it. To my continued protests, he agreed to allow me to join the club, but none of the other excluded kids could join. I turned him down. The injustice stood, and I considered my protest to have been a failure. But I learned that I was capable of stepping forward when others would not.

I bought my first car in high school with Mom's help and my potato-chip earnings. This was crucial for attracting girls. I drove a yellow convertible for several years, into my college years. It had a hole in the floorboards that I stitched together with old license plates, which were perfect for this purpose because they had holes in the corners that could be tied together. The convertible top didn't fold all the way down because the boot was full of old newspapers. It was a classy car, I told girls: these were copies of the *New York Times*, not the *Daily News*. Once, when Amy borrowed the car with some friends in upstate New York, the brakes failed on a big hill. No one was hurt, but from that day on, she never drove again! This was my fault, of course.

By the time I graduated from high school, I was sure I wanted more from life than my neighborhood could offer. I applied to several Big Ten schools in the Midwest, hoping I could afford to attend by living with relatives and qualifying for resident tuition. I was accepted, but, as it turned out, the cost was still beyond what I could afford. The free, local choice was Queens College, but my grades were marginal for admission. Women needed average high-school scores of 88 and men needed an 85, a form of affirmative action in the 1950s, supposedly intended to balance women's earlier academic maturity. My high school score was 84.6, which the college rounded up to 85.

I've often wondered how differently my life might have turned out but for the two-tenths of a percent in my grades and a twenty-four-dollar registration fee that got me into college. It was at college, away from the old neighborhood, where I escaped from being the fat, shy kid from Vanderveer Street and began to develop the political and social skills that served me through my life.

CHAPTER 2
Education and escape

When I got to college, I was ready for some fun. My interests were my fraternity, girls, student government, and—if time allowed—academics. My yellow convertible served me well and I actually began dating. My fraternity, *Phi Epsilon Pi*, offered a group of friends, poker games, and parties with sorority girls at our frat house in Flushing. Running for office in the student government was exciting and created another new circle of friends. The student body of Queens College was smaller than that of Jamaica High, too, and that made it easier for everyone. For the first time, but not the last time in my life, I discovered the benefits of new surroundings where old rules and prejudices did not apply.

Academics came as an afterthought. I was a lazy student and tended to argue with my professors, playing devil's advocate or advancing my own pet theories in opposition to what they had to say. The result was predictable—poor grades. I tried parroting back what the instructor said, obtaining better results but learning less. The experience offered a valuable lesson about when and how to speak up—a requirement for survival in politics.

My first campaign, as a sophomore, had three elements for success—a good team, a good slogan, and a unique and effective way of reaching voters. A friend, Marty Wagner, and I ran together. We went from classroom to classroom writing our campaign message in colored chalk on the blackboards, along with the word *SAVE*. My slogan was "Fighting Dave," and that was how I became known. Fighting Dave was fighting for a fair shake for the students for... what? Better parking. It was a darned good school and there wasn't much to fight for, but I sure enjoyed being ready to fight. Marty came in first and I was second. He became president and I was treasurer and a member of the student senate.

My election put me into a role of helping arrange events, which led to a real fight. The student-led Marxist Study Group wanted to invite John Gates, editor of the *Daily Worker*, to speak during academic-freedom week. Their purpose, of course, was to stir up outrage, which they did. This was in the mid-1950s, not long after U.S. Senator Joseph McCarthy of Wisconsin had put the nation on edge with his theatrical hunt for Communists in the federal government. The student senate adopted a resolution supporting the Gates invitation. The American Legion announced it would picket the school if Gates came. Then the provost banned the event, whereupon members of the student senate staged their own protest, calling the TV stations first to make sure cameras would be on the scene. We took our signs to where the American Legion members were picketing—some of their signs had changed to say Thank you, Provost Garvey—and we joined the picket line with our contrary signs.

Garvey was not happy and called us into his office, demanding to know why we admired Gates. Our spokesman explained that the issue concerned academic freedom and the ability to learn from all points of view. I chimed in that Columbia University had invited Gates to speak. At Columbia, I told the provost, any speaker was welcome so long as speeches contained no obscene or indecent content. The provost suggested I go to Columbia, threatening to expel all of us so that we could do so. That ended the protest.

That night, I experienced an unforgettable rush when I saw our protest on the evening news. We weren't the lead story, but we did rate a minute and a half on all three network stations. The feeling was like taking a powerful drug for a kid in the ant hill society of New York City, who a little earlier had been an anonymous face in a huge high school in a second-rate neighborhood. The *New York Times* and *Daily Worker* editorialized in support of our protest while the *Daily News* called Queens College the "little red school house" and suggested it didn't deserve public funding. After a taste of the media drug I became an unabashed addict—a publicity hound—and I never turned back.

During my junior year I was delivering a news release to *The Crown,* one of our two student newspapers, when I met an extremely interesting woman stepping out of a broom closet. Frances Dushman was associate editor as well as chair of the student government's Academic Affairs Committee. On Wednesday nights until the wee hours, the staff would put together the newspaper and then carry the pages by subway to a printer in Hell's Kitchen, where it was set in hot type. This was a dirty job. That Wednesday, Fran had introduced Margaret Mead at a lecture. Upon returning from the lecture to the newspaper's grubby basement office, she had borrowed a tall, male student's sweat suit so she wouldn't mess up her best clothes. When I met her coming out of the broom closet she was wearing those baggy sweats, many sizes too large, but even so she was such a knockout that she stopped me in my tracks.

Although we both had attended Jamaica High and served in the Queens College student government, Fran and I had not met. But she had written a scathing editorial blasting me and the other protesters in the John Gates affair. Fran charged, accurately, that we were just flexing our muscles over an issue of no real importance. I was quite angry about it at the time—I thought everyone should support the student government, especially a newspaper editor writing about a free-speech issue.

At the time, Fran was a conservative and I was liberal. Yet the attraction between us was much stronger than any political differences; in fact, the differences enhanced the attraction. For my part, Fran was not only good-looking, she also was bright and had a powerful personality, always full of emotion, and held her own in any argument. She was smarter than me, and the fire of her convictions was just below the surface. Fran says my positive outlook on life balanced her natural pessimism. She says she was physically attracted to me just as I was to her, and she liked the fact that I was involved and active. I produced news releases at the slightest provocation. The one I was carrying when we met pushed an idea for a student health-insurance program. As we spent more time together, however, and certainly over our many years together, our mutual ability to hold opposing views and enjoy debating them has kept our relationship fresh, even as our political outlooks reversed—she became more liberal, and I eventually became a

Republican. After we established the Frances and David Rose Foundation years later, Fran and I disagreed every year on how to allocate our philanthropic donations, and we usually ended up splitting the amount fifty-fifty, with Fran sending her half to liberal causes such as Planned Parenthood and me sticking to middle-of-the-road charities such as the American Diabetes Association.

I asked Fran out on a date that first night we met. We saw a crazy comedian and the date went well. We made a date for New Year's Eve, but before that we got together at her family's apartment to babysit her younger brother, Barry, while her parents went to a holiday function for members of the electrical workers' union. Fran lived in Flushing and her family was not well off. In fact, she thought my family must be rich because we had our own house and owned a factory. Her parents returned from their party at 10 PM, and I took Fran for a drive to look at the dazzling Christmas lights put up by our Irish-Catholic neighbors.

The evening ended uneventfully. We learned only the next day that a woman had been knifed for her Christmas money at an intersection we had driven through at about the same time. Police cars with sirens blaring showed up at my house and I was taken to the precinct for questioning. It seems they had narrowed down the address of the killer to just a few blocks, which included our house. I wasn't unknown to the police; once I had been picked up for breaking curfew while studying for an exam. A sergeant questioned me. My alibi for the murder was babysitting for a thirteen-year-old, which seemed questionable to him. He wanted to call Fran's mother to check. I thought, There goes *that* girlfriend.

The sergeant allowed me to call the Dushman apartment before handing over the phone. Fran's mother confirmed my alibi. However, in truth, at the hour in question—after 10 PM—we had finished babysitting and were near the murder scene. In any event, a boy who lived across the street was arrested for the murder.

The incident didn't cause a problem with Fran's mother, but the New Year's Eve date seemed likely to be our last due to my own reservations. Fran got sloppy drunk and threw up all over the yellow convertible. I felt uncomfortable, in my innocence, with her comparative aggressiveness. She scared me off.

I was cautious to an extreme and personally conservative as a young person, still a virgin as a college junior. I intended to marry and have children as early as possible. I had been a fatherless boy, and I was determined that my own son would know his father. My career plans simply were to avoid the financial insecurity my mother had faced. That was why I majored in accounting at Queens College, despite having little interest and no great aptitude for the subject. My work experience had shown me that regardless of economic conditions, someone always would be needed to keep track of money, so I would always have job opportunities. Socially, I hadn't gotten over being from the wrong neighborhood, and I pursued girls from the cashmere crowd.

After breaking off with Fran, I got a taste for what success with that group was like. One girl, Harriet Pakula, was the prettiest at Queens College, and rich too. Everyone thought she was the perfect, unattainable woman. I happened to be talking to her casually one day and asked who she was seeing. Harriet said she hadn't had a date in weeks. Everyone thought she must be booked solid, so no one ever asked.

I said, "We can fix that. What are you doing on Saturday night?" We went to a movie and had fun.

Clearly I was outclassed by Harriet Pakula, but having dated her gave me new confidence. Neglecting all my other activities, especially classes, I began flirting as a full-time occupation. I kept track of my dates with the cashmere crowd—thirty dates with seventeen women over the course of that spring term. I had a lot of fun and took some of these girls into the private rooms at the frat house for necking, but mostly I was experimenting with a social group from which I had been excluded. I arranged a lot of double dates and other group situations. What I learned was that these girls were shallow compared to Fran. The grass wasn't really greener on the other side of the tracks. In April I asked Fran out again. We went bowling, the safest date possible. No one else had her special spark of intelligence and excitement.

I remember a friend asking me how I had spent the summer. Out of the blue I made up a lie: I said I had been to Alaska. The truth was too drab. I was stuck in New York City, still working on the potato-chip loading dock. As graduation neared, I realized my job prospects were not as good as I had hoped. A fellow student applied to one of the big eight accounting firms and learned that they would not hire Jews. A classmate confronted one of our professors with this information, asking why he hadn't told us earlier. The professor's weak explanation was that there were plenty of accounting jobs outside of the big eight. But the truth was that those eight major firms controlled the lucrative jobs that would make the long process of becoming a CPA worthwhile. Besides, I knew by then that I didn't enjoy accounting much. I'd studied it and earned a B average only for the economic security it promised. I decided to go for a law degree, thinking I could combine my financial skills with the law and become a tax attorney or go into some similar profession. I was accepted into night school at New York University to study law in the fall.

In the meantime, I answered an advertisement for a junior accounting job that would be on a track to getting a CPA. My new employer was Lazarow and Company. Mr. Lazarow's main clientele came from the entertainment industry. Musicians and comedians used his services to keep track of their money and calculate taxes, and some permitted him to keep them on a strict allowance to avoid blowing their good fortune all at once. One of the clients whose names I recognized was Archie Bleyer, Arthur Godfrey's musical accompanist, who had numerous ex-wives to support. I received his checks, disbursed his alimony payments, booked the transaction for taxes, and gave Archie his allowance out of what was left. Patti Page was our most successful client. She was a good businesswoman as well, investing earnings from her hit records in rental housing in Minneapolis through a company called Egap, which is Page spelled backward. Two clients I had never heard of were Conway Twitty and Johnny Carson. Carson's meager paychecks came from one-night stands out in the Midwest. Paul Anka's account was a big headache because his receipts would come in Japanese yen, or the currency of whatever country he was touring in, and had to be converted into U.S. dollars.

I made one dollar fifty cents an hour, barely more than I had earned loading potato chips, and it was a long commute from Queens. All I got out of it was a portion of the tuition at NYU and a few good anecdotes.

I was never star-struck working with celebrities. The best of the stories concerned Carol Burnett, the comedian. One day she came into the office out of a heavy rain with a pink-dyed poodle. The dye was starting to run. Burnett had blown her allowance for the month and wanted another fifty dollars. I firmly said, "No," following my standing instructions from Mr. Lazarow. Carol Burnett was furious and demanded to see the boss, who was then ensconced in his luxurious inner office with its two-inch-deep white shag carpeting. Lazarow was always "out" when the celebrities came in asking for more money, but Burnett flew through his door with her pink poodle dripping its dye on the rug. The boss needed only seconds to evaluate the situation and yell at me to give her anything she wanted—"Just get her and that dog out of here!"

After work I would fight rush-hour traffic to get from Lazarow's midtown office to NYU in Washington Square, and after class I would commute home to my mother's house, ninety minutes away by subway and bus. Then I would get together with Fran, when possible. I had little time left for study, and besides, I wasn't enjoying my law classes. When called on in class I was either too timid or simply unprepared. Nor did I enjoy working for Lazarow. To become a CPA, I would have to put in three years at low pay and take four exams. As my first year out of Queens College approached, I was still living with my mother at age twenty-two, unhappy with my job and my studies and feeling pressure from Fran. She was finishing her senior year and was ready for a commitment. I was happy with her, but I didn't like the thought of getting married then, given my circumstances and the track I was following. Besides, how could I know Fran was really the one? Maybe she just wanted to escape from her parents and their tiny apartment.

Without telling anyone, I took a drastic and unexpected step in April 1959. I contacted the Draft Board and asked to be drafted. I had a student deferment that was good as long as I remained in school, but I knew I would quit NYU—I didn't even take all my final exams—so I told the draft board officials I no longer met the criteria for 2S and I should be changed to a 1A.

The clerk said, "You'll be drafted immediately."

I told him to move me to the top of the list. He asked if I would like to see a recruiter.

I declined. That would mean a three- or four-year enlistment, while a draftee served only two. At that age, I had no respect for anyone who would choose a military career. I just wanted a short-term job and a ticket out of New York.

"But if you volunteer," he said, "you could choose the service."

Any service would be fine with me, I told him, except the Marines. At that time the Marines were in Lebanon. I asked if they were drafting for the Marines. The clerk smiled and looked me in the eye. He said they hadn't had a Marine call in a couple of months.

Fran was not happy when I told her, but she didn't seem mad. As she saw the situation, I was playing an angle. With my bad eyesight, surely I would be ruled ineligible for the draft—4F. That, in turn, would improve my chances for getting a better job because no one wanted to hire a young man who might be drafted. As it turned out, I received a telegram ordering me to report a few weeks later, but I wasn't given an eye exam until I was almost ready to be processed into the army. The doctor said my eyesight was deplorable and asked how I had gotten so far. With perfect military logic, however, he passed me anyway because my equipment had been issued and it would be too much trouble to put everything back.

I called Fran from Fort Dix and said, "I got the job." There was a long silence on the other end of the line.

My mother already had given me her opinion of the military. No Jewish boy would ever go in except as an officer destined for a brilliant career. In my entire generation in the family, on both sides, including the sons of all my mother's eleven brothers and sisters, no one had joined the military. All had found a way around the draft. But Mom didn't get angry, either. She punished me with guilt.

After a long silence, she asked, "Are you going to leave us all alone? Who is going to take care of the house? How often will you come home?"

Fort Dix, I assured her, was only a short bus ride away. Alaska hadn't even crossed my mind.

CHAPTER 3
The indirect route to Alaska

On my first day of basic training at Fort Dix, four men raced by me with a man on a stretcher. It was an alarming sight for a new draftee, but someone explained that the patient was the company clerk being rushed to the hospital with appendicitis. The unit would need a new clerk. One of the first lessons of army life is *never* volunteer for anything, but I could see advantages to having this job, so I stepped forward later when the commanding officer asked who knew how to type. My typing wasn't very good, but I was the only volunteer so I got the job.

The former clerk never came back. I spent basic training in the orderly room, filing and filling out daily reports listing the head count, keeping track of who was sick or absent. I was privy to whatever was happening and was excused from drill, classes, and training films, although I did have to take part in physical training—crawling under barbed wire, going over barricades, and of course climbing ropes, which I managed to do without panicking.

I was anxious to remain one of the guys in the barracks despite my special position among the career army men—or "lifers," as we draftees derisively called them. One day I got word that a sewage hauler had arrived to pump the tank at the barracks latrine. The worst detail in the camp was crawling under the building and attaching a hose to the sewage tank, then washing out the empty tank and adding chemicals. It was a nasty job. I scurried to the barracks and spread the word. Faster than I could have imagined possible, forty-four guys disappeared, leaving me alone in an empty room. When I heard the sergeant's footsteps coming down the hall, I scooted into the latrine and sat down on a toilet. Another man was in there, too—McGinnis, a huge Irish kid, who had chosen to hide in the shower, plastering himself against the wall behind a corner.

The duty sergeant, a lifer, was no dummy. When he found the empty barracks, he went into the latrine and called out, "Who's in here?"

I said, "I'm here."

"OK, Rose." I was off the hook for the moment. Then the sergeant heard a tinkling of dog tags in the shower and looked around the corner, finding this big kid from Brooklyn pressed against the wall.

He said, "What are you doing, McGinnis?"

McGinnis said, "I'm hiding, sir."

The game was up. McGinnis got latrine detail for hiding, and I got it for tipping off the men. But I was a hero to my buddies, who enjoyed the story immensely.

On another occasion, I paid the price for missing drills as company clerk. A training session came up that I could not avoid. We were practicing dismounted drill when the sergeant ordered, "Stack arms." This is a procedure where soldiers pass their rifles according to a pattern, with one man—who turned out to be me—receiving and stacking them. I had no idea what was going on. Suddenly, guys were handing me rifles and it was all I could do to keep them off the ground. At least I knew that a rifle could never touch the ground.

The drill sergeant blew his whistle and said, "Gentlemen, we're going to have to do this again for the benefit of Mr. Rose."

He thought having the other men angry with me would shape me up. So they did it again, and once again I juggled all the rifles without a clue what I was supposed to do with them.

The sergeant asked, "Is there a problem, Private Rose?"

Like an idiot, I said, "I'd be more than glad to do it, if you'll only tell me how."

With that, the sergeant said, "Give me twenty-five push-ups."

I took my time, knowing I couldn't do twenty-five push-ups. The guys stood around cheering me on. I reached nineteen and collapsed. The sergeant told everyone to wait while I tried again. But it was the wrong psychology because the guys were enjoying the break. By the time I finished, the drill session was over.

Later, I asked the guys, "Why didn't you just tell me what was going on?" They said it had been much more fun this way.

The worst part of basic training was a three-day camp on burning hot sand. I remember lying in a sweltering pup tent, covered in sand fleas, when I received a nicely scented letter from Fran. Pictures of china patterns fell out. She wanted my approval for the dishes she was picking out.

If my plan was to escape marriage by joining the army, I failed because Fran and I had become engaged before I left for basic training. My memory is that Fran suggested we get married, and I suggested we elope. I was in love, and we both were passionate: Sex was on our minds and the engagement made it acceptable. I suggested a trip to the courthouse, but Fran pointed out that a civil wedding would be reported in the newspaper, so we drove to New City, across the Hudson River in Rockland County. There, a court clerk told us of a three-day wait for a blood test. When we got back to Queens, we let it be known that we were thinking about marriage. Suddenly, Amy's wedding dress came out and discussion of rings and synagogues and every other detail of wedding planning took over. We were under the control of our two mothers from then on.

Our relationship became intense and heated. Leaving for the army only made me want Fran more. We set the wedding date for the few days of leave I would have after basic training, but one day at Fort Dix I got a frantic call from Fran saying the day we had chosen wouldn't work. She had been to see the rabbi and learned that a ceremony was strictly forbidden on or near the date we had chosen, a day of mourning called Tisha B'Av. I already had orders to go to Fort Benjamin Harrison in Indianapolis for more training in military accounting. The only solution was to use my position as company clerk to produce the paperwork saying I had failed basic training. That would keep me at Fort Dix for another eight weeks.

I presented the papers to my commanding officer, a 1st Lt. Pond, who didn't take the army much more seriously than I did. He thought the situation was marvelous.

"So, you scheduled a religious ceremony when your religion prohibits you from having it?" he asked. "Not very religious, are you?"

Lt. Pond wouldn't sign, however. He sent me back to redo the form to say I'd failed only marksmanship. Otherwise, I'd have to go through the entire program a second time. Meanwhile, my buddies all decamped and left me behind, waiting for my wedding and my supposed passing grade on the firing range. Lt. Pond transferred out, too, and his replacement, Capt. Torrez, a lifer, didn't have a sense of humor. He demanded to know what I was doing there, with new recruits not due for five days. I told him about my predicament, and he was shocked. "You lied to the United States Army?" he said in a thick Spanish accent.

Capt. Torrez marched me out to the rifle range. It was a new set-up where targets popped up as the trainee walked through a course. I missed them all and got killed fifteen times. I went back to being company clerk until Tisha B'Av was over, and then sent through the paperwork saying I had passed. The big mill of the army's bureaucracy turned slowly and once again I was ordered to report to Fort Benjamin Harrison.

Torrez was disgusted. He said, "You learned the system pretty good."

I said, "Yes, sir," and put a marksman badge on my uniform.

The wedding went off beautifully. Fran and I retreated to an air-conditioned room at a nice motel in Peekskill that we hardly left for the remaining three days of my leave. Then I departed for Indianapolis while Fran went to stay with my mother and numerous aunts at Rosebrook, where she received a thorough examination in domestic capabilities and hazing into the Nadelstein sisterhood.

The army had decided, according to regulations, that my low rank and pay status did not qualify me to have a married life in service—at least that was how I interpreted the news that my dependent wife would receive neither housing nor other support except for a paltry $52.80-a-month allowance. When I arrived at the accounting school in Indianapolis, the army tried to make me an officer, which surely would have improved my status, but I steadfastly refused because that would have meant another three years in the service. We were determined to be together, so I found an efficiency apartment in a shabby area for $80 a month. My pay was $78 a month, so Fran's allowance gave us

$50.80 a month to spend. That was good enough for us, and we drove out together.

Fran's mother, who was fairly high strung, was distressed that I was taking her daughter so far away. Indiana was the equivalent of the other side of the world. But we were delighted to be free and on our own, despite our poverty. Without knowing how long we would be staying—our time there would depend on my training—Fran couldn't get a good job using her history degree, but she did find work packing tricot panties into envelopes for a mail-order company—white, pink, or yellow, according to the order. The job paid $1 an hour, giving us another $160 a month. Fran's mother sent us many care packages, including sheets, towels, and anything else that might help us at the end of the earth. On one of her frequent letters, which we saved, she wrote "122nd day" at the top—her count of the time Fran had been away from New York.

My work was easy enough. The army was training me to be an accountant. Because I already had a four-year accounting degree, I got 100 percent on the introductory course. The rules said anyone who got a perfect score automatically moved on to the next level. I got the maximum score in the second course, too. Another draftee, Nobby Naborowski, was similarly overqualified for the instruction we were given. Together, we took class after class until we got to the most advanced accounting course offered. At that point, someone looked at the record and realized we had been in the army for eleven months and had spent the entire time training. We were halfway through our enlistment and hadn't done anything yet.

Everyone had assumed I was an officer. My uniform was devoid of any insignia. Finally, the captain reviewing my record realized my true, lowly status and again pressed me to take a commission. I stuck to the rules, requesting that I be allowed to take the final accounting course, whereupon he asked where in the world I wanted to go after training. I said I would go anywhere that I could take my unauthorized wife, which left plenty of opportunities. But when the course was over and orders were posted, they said I was going to Korea, one of the places where wives were not allowed to follow. I couldn't face breaking the news to her. The first thing I did was to make a call arranging to send her home to New York. The next was to stop for a five-cent ice cream cone on the way home—anything to delay her disappointment. She was as upset as I expected. We felt betrayed. Why had the army asked where I wanted to go and then chosen to send me one of the few places I wanted to avoid? Fran demanded I *do* something.

I knew that any order could be changed until it was typed on a mimeograph stencil. Under the army's procedures, no stencil could be wasted, so orders typed on one were as unchangeable as if chipped in stone. Fran frantically sent me back to the post to do anything I could before the stencil went into the typewriter.

Returning to the fort, I found Nobby Naborowski in a classroom with his head in his hands, teary-eyed. He had been assigned to Alaska and was devastated, imagining ice, snow, and endless cold. I talked up Korea—the girls came two to a sleeping bag, I told him—and suggested we trade. I took Nobby by the elbow and walked him to the personnel office and asked for a switch. They checked our records and found they were amazingly similar: We both had taken every available accounting course and had earned perfect scores. So the officer drew arrows switching our names and handed the orders to the secretary, who began typing them onto a stencil. We were locked in.

As I left, the captain asked how I felt about going to Korea. When I told him I was going to Alaska instead, he seemed disappointed. Apparently he had planned to give me a chance to get out of having to go to Korea by committing to be an administrative medical officer for three years.

Our families were shocked. Each of our mothers dealt with the news in her own way. My mother went to the library and checked out books on the subject, reporting that parts of Alaska were amazingly well developed, not simply snow and ice, as she had expected, and that Fran might get a job teaching. Fran's mother packed her a trunk full of woolen underwear and shipped it north by slow freight.

For Fran and me, Alaska was an adventure. We had no expectation of staying, certainly not for the rest of our lives, but at the time it was a perfect place to be—far from Queens and our mothers, starting a new life of our own.

I was going to be doing important work. Reportedly, Fort Richardson desperately needed four accountants. I was to lead the group because, after one year in the army, I was the most senior. The urgent need for accountants was so great that normal transportation by ship was out of the question. My crack team of bean-counters was sent to Oakland where we caught a flight north on Western Airlines.

My first command was not easy. The three accountants under me were reluctant draftees, unhappy to be in the army and even less happy being shipped express to Anchorage, Alaska. I took my responsibility as group leader seriously, chasing these drunken accountants from bar to bar at each airport on our way north. We arrived in Anchorage on February 15, 1960, my birthday, and I presented myself at Fort Richardson with the air of a well-trained military commander— Private Rose, group leader, reporting for duty with his men.

The guy behind the desk laughed. He said, "We don't need any finance guys." He couldn't figure out what we were doing there. In case of disaster, Fort Rich had four extra accountants. We were assigned to work lifting boxes on a loading dock, and my team slowly broke up. One became a cook, another went to finance. We weren't very good lifting the boxes, especially after we realized dropping them could get us reassigned more quickly. I was the last to go, assigned to edit proposed regulations. I was to edit the army field manual, transforming military bureaucratese into plain English that operations and intelligence personnel could understand. I enjoyed the work.

Despite having arrived in mid-winter early in 1960, right after Alaska became a state, I liked Anchorage from the start. The place couldn't have been more different from New York. Mountains, white with snow, rimmed one side of the town and the gray, glacial water of Cook Inlet lapped at the other. The community was small but growing fast. Newcomers outnumbered old-timers, and everyone could find a role, regardless of race, religion, or ethnicity. The military dominated the state, providing the economic impetus for growth and the mind and manpower to build the society. Friends were easy to make among the young people on the base and civilians in town. Frank and Maxine Reed, pillars of the community who were organizing the Anchorage Fur Rendezvous, the annual winter festival, quickly recruited and befriended us. My barber, Earl Rose, became an early friend. And Irv Bennett effusively invited me to join the Mountain View Lions Club, where I made many more friends.

Fran arrived on a magical night in mid-March, with the city asleep under a fresh blanket of snow and the northern lights dancing above in a crisp, black sky. We rode in my 1950 Plymouth to an apartment I had found in Mountain View, a low-rent area but also a strong community within Anchorage. Our place wasn't ready, so the landlord put us in a half-finished addition that didn't even have plumbing. Fran found a pitcher and a basin for washing. She was delighted. The beauty of the place, the feeling of openness and opportunity, and the friendliness of the people charmed her as quickly as it had me. We began hiking, camping, and cross-country skiing, exploring the state and experiencing the pleasure of being together in the wilderness. It was on one of those trips, camping in a tent between Glennallen and Anchorage, that we conceived our first son, Evan Denali. I had less than a year to go in the military and was determined to make good use of my health benefits by having a baby. I remained driven by the promise I had made to myself—and which Fran had agreed to—that we would have children while we were young so they would never be left behind by their father, as I had been.

Mostly, we remember the great joy of those days. Our friends were young couples like us, and we shared our lives together as surrogate family. Friends would knock on the door at 2 AM to share Chinese take-out or point out the northern lights. Over time, couples were reassigned or moved on to other phases of their lives and we lost track of them, but at the time we felt warmly encompassed by friends who were the closest we had ever known, even though we had just met them.

At work, the management tasks that crossed my desk kept me engaged intellectually and provided an outlet for my competitiveness. I was eager to do my work well and gain recognition and promotions in the military system. But I also enjoyed working with young men, most of whom took the army's absurdity no more seriously than I did.

Periodically, in those Cold War years, the brass would call an alert, which required that the functions of Fort Richardson had to be moved as if we were expecting a nuclear strike. In the middle of the night, we would relocate our headquarters down the Glenn Highway to Eklutna, a Native village that was expected to be outside the blast zone. The wives would get together for a 2 AM pajama party while we men were camping out at Eklutna. Our close friends, Tom and Peg Stockley, were always part of this midnight party. They remained our friends until their deaths in the Alaska Airlines flight that crashed into the ocean off Los Angeles in 2000. Tom served as assistant to the chaplain at Fort Rich, so the alert required him to relocate a trailer of sacramental wine and wafers to Eklutna. We weren't fond of the wafers, but sipping the wine was a highlight of our Eklutna campouts. As it turned out, Tom went on to become a noted wine critic, writing for the *Seattle Times* and other publications. I was there at the start of his brilliant career as a wine connoisseur!

My job at Eklutna was to help produce operations orders, including situation reports, called SITREPS, and orders of battle. In fact, I prepared them in advance, knowing an alert would come along eventually. All I had to do when the time came was date the documents and have them signed and reproduced. My superiors thought I was a wizard for producing the orders so quickly, and I had plenty of free time to hang out with Tom and my other buddies.

We occasionally had to stand guard duty at Eklutna. Each soldier received ammunition that our superiors counted and repeatedly checked and rechecked. One day we were standing this tedious guard duty in the winter darkness when someone saw a moose and, out of boredom, shot it with a single round. We panicked. A dead moose lying across the wire from us was sure trouble. We began running through the village banging on doors, waking people up, trying to find anyone who wanted a moose. Finally a group gathered to drag it off. I remember a woman walking backwards sweeping the snow with a broom to cover their tracks—a ridiculous precaution, as anyone could see the signs of a large crowd of people and a huge, bloody, hairy animal.

With the moose disposed of, we still had a problem: One round of ammunition was missing. The guys decided I should cover up the shortage because my shift had ended and I was supposed to be off duty. I resisted briefly, because I hadn't shot the moose and I wasn't interested in being court-martialed, but the guys promised to cover for me. I took a single round from the front of my bandolier to make up for the missing bullet, then, when the sergeant arrived, I lay down on top of the bandolier and pretended to sleep. The sergeant noted that the log was empty. "Nope," one of the guys said, "Nothing happened here at all."

The sergeant started to count the ammo. Upon coming to me, he said, "What about that guy?" I snored a little for realism.

My friends explained that I couldn't possibly have used any ammo. "He's as blind as a bat," one of them said.

The sergeant said they had better wake me up anyway.

"We can wake him," was the response, "but he's not going to like it. He just got off shift. And he's an irascible guy."

I was having trouble not laughing at this point. My body started to quiver.

"Look, is he all right?" the sergeant asked.

"Oh yeah," one of the guys said, "Rose has a bit of palsy. He shakes. You know, he just does paperwork, so he is still fit for duty."

Finally, the sergeant relented. A blind, ill-tempered man with palsy did not need to be disturbed. Nor would such a soldier likely be shooting off ammunition. So, with that, we escaped detection. Back at the base, we dispatched someone to town to buy a round for an M-1 rifle at the Army-Navy Surplus Store, replaced the missing bullet, and never got caught.

This became a standing joke, trying to get our friends to crack up by telling wild lies about them to their superiors. I recall one conversation that went something like this: "Sir, didn't you know that Fred's father won the Medal of Honor in Korea? Yes, he's really famous. Tell the major about your father, Fred."

I've never been a great athlete, but at Fort Rich I got to be the hero of the headquarters company football team in our championship game against the artillery battalion. I was matched up against the other team's best player, a star on offense and defense who had the potential of single-handedly embarrassing our headquarters company team. He was huge, fast, and talented. I was none of those things, but I did get angry when he twice kicked me in the groin. I knocked off his helmet and punched him in the nose, knowing that both teams would join the melee, saving me from certain death at the hands of this gorilla. It took four guys to hold him back, and we both were kicked out of the game for fighting. With the artillery battalion's star player sidelined, the headquarters company went on to win the championship. I was the unofficial MVP.

By the time my military obligation was fulfilled, after two years of resisting extension of my service, I decided I liked my job, our friends, and the community too much to leave. So I applied to do the same job as a civil servant. After shedding my uniform, I took an overnight leap in the civil service and earned a much bigger paycheck too. Including an allowance for Alaska's higher cost of living, I would make the impressive sum of $6,900 a year.

I took off my uniform and returned to my desk at Fort Rich. When my superior came in to speak to me, I didn't bother to salute. We still promised our families we would move back to New York, and we did go back and look for work. But nothing I could get there came close to my pay in Alaska.

The truth was, Fran and I loved Alaska. We had found the place we belonged, where we wanted to raise our family and spend our lives.

CHAPTER 4
The 1964 earthquake

March 27, 1964, 5:36 PM In our little, square house in Anchorage's south Mountain View neighborhood, I was waiting in my best clothes for Fran to come home with the babysitter. That night we were hosting a Passover seder for our tiny congregation and guests, about sixty people, in the basement of All Saints Episcopal Church in downtown Anchorage. In those days, there was no synagogue. The food had been prepared, the tables set up, and all was ready. As soon as the babysitter arrived to watch our two boys, three-year-old Evan and the baby, Mitchell, we would drive downtown to take our place as congregation leaders on this big night in our young marriage.

Then the house started shaking.

I was standing near a cabinet of Fran's curios and dishes. I grabbed it and held on with all my strength as it swayed, keeping it upright waiting for the tremor to pass. But it didn't pass. Instead, the earthquake grew stronger and continued on and on. Some survivors began to wonder if the world was ending, having no idea that any earthquake could shake so violently or so long. I don't remember those thoughts, nor did I even register how much the floor was moving. I ran for the bedroom to grab Evan. The cabinet crashed down and everything smashed. I bolted out the front door with my son and planted him in a snow bank, telling him not to move and running back into the house to pluck Mitch from his crib.

A neighbor couple drove up, and the husband jumped out of the car to look at his tires, at first believing he had a flat. Meanwhile, water was spilling all over the house. The water heater had smashed through a wall and broken its refill pipe, which was spraying water. I took off my best suit to crawl under the house and shut off the main valve, but by then the pressure from the city water system was gone. There was no water for me to stop.

Returning to the neighbor's house, I found a different kind of chaos. They were avid collectors of tropical fish. Their aquariums had burst, spewing water and spreading brightly colored fish flapping all over the floor. An Easter display of colored eggs and jelly beans had been flung in all directions. As we tried to pick up the slippery fish, we kept sliding on the jelly beans and smashed eggs. Mitch and Evan giggled with amusement. Once the fish were corralled, wriggling around in a saucepan, our friends remained desperate to save them, but no water would come from the tap. I suggested the toilet tank. Placing their precious collection in the toilet went against the grain, but they had no choice. The fish survived.

Fran took a long time to make it home and I was worried sick by the time she finally arrived with the babysitter. She had taken the time to help clean up the mess from a toppled pot of spaghetti sauce at the babysitter's house. Only on the drive home did she realize that the damage to Anchorage was much worse than spilled dinners. When we tuned in the radio, we heard a Civil Defense emergency broadcast on KFQD, which was airing continuous announcements about the enormous disaster. Calmly, with professionalism and authority, announcers passed on messages, calling for doctors and pilots and heavy-equipment operators. They requested help finding missing people and volunteers for shelters. At that point in the disaster, entire towns were unaccounted for. For a time, the outside world believed briefly that Anchorage had been destroyed. Communications were down. Roads had been destroyed over the entire region. Quickly, it became clear we were in the midst of a calamity of historic proportions. The earthquake turned out to be the largest ever recorded in North America, and the second largest in world history.[1] Its power was almost inconceivable: land was permanently displaced as much as sixty feet horizontally and thirty feet vertically; a tsunami wave in Valdez Arm reached two-hundred twenty feet high; deaths were recorded in Crescent City, California, and fishing boats sank in Louisiana due to water sloshing in enclosed waters. The Civil Defense broadcast began to report the death toll.

Our low-income area of town survived the quake with relatively little damage, thanks to our firm gravel soils, but devastation swept the downtown area and the west side of town, especially the upper-income Turnagain area. There, the soils were underlain with clay that liquefied during the shaking. Turnagain's bluffs collapsed into Cook Inlet, opening enormous cracks and carrying homes downhill with them. Geysers of mud shot twenty feet into the air as homes were churned into a cauldron of liquid earth. One Turnagain mother, Marie Doyle, described standing in her front yard with her children and watching houses, trees, and roads disappearing around her. Homes sank out of sight one after another as the cataclysm came ever closer during four minutes of shaking. Only after the street in front of her and the houses of her close neighbors had vanished into the earth—and she accepted imminent death—did the quake miraculously end.

Wilda Marston, a woman known for her strength, saved eight children that day, leading them out of her collapsing house, where they had been watching the "Rocky and Bullwinkle Show" on TV, to a surviving remnant of yard just large enough to spread a blanket. There, by whatever divine intervention, the yard had remained upright and unbroken as it slid down the bluff, even though everything around it had turned upside down. During an aftershock, a huge crack opened briefly in the Marston driveway, and Wilda's Plymouth fell in. The crack closed as quickly as it had opened, and the car was crushed. Wilda told the children, "I never liked that car." After she and the children spent hours in the cold, a man lowered from a helicopter helped the survivors cross a chaos of chasms and cliffs to find solid ground. Julie Person, one of the children, remembers how an aftershock opened a crevasse, swallowing her sister. Just in time, the rescuer pulled the girl up as the crack quickly closed. The earth snapped shut on the girl's bunny slipper and held it too tightly for a grown man to pull loose.[2]

What little we knew of the terror gripping the west side of Anchorage came from the radio. I had turned off the gas in our house, leaving us without heat. Neighbors whose names we didn't even know invited us into their home, warmed by a fireplace. It was there that we heard the Civil Defense radio urgently call for everyone to get to higher ground: A tsunami was coming. By then, Valdez, Seward, Whittier, and Kodiak had been devastated by seismic waves. Native villages had been washed away, including Chenega in Prince William Sound and Afognak, Kaguyak, Old Harbor, Womens Bay, and Ouzinkie in the Kodiak Archipelago. In Mountain View, we thought we would be safe and, besides, we had nowhere to go. In west Anchorage, where shell-shocked residents were taking shelter in what buildings remained, a panicked evacuation ensued along Northern Lights Boulevard, the only major route out of the area. Cars choked the roadway while other survivors fled on foot, some beating on the windows of slow-moving cars. No wave came. The next morning, we woke to the noise of Evan and our neighbors' children playing a new favorite game—earthquake. After shaking wildly, they ran for higher ground. They played that game for weeks.

We moved back into our house that day, and I fixed the water heater. The town started pulling together magnificently. On the radio, among the death announcements and other disaster news, families and business people were offering places to stay to anyone needing one. Each family's name, address, and phone number would be announced, then how many beds they could offer and whether they had food, power, and heat. We took in our good friends and bridge partners, Art and Lillian Fried, and their children. Their home had fallen into a hole and was uninhabitable.

Art and I worked together at Fort Rich. At one time or another I had held positions subordinate and superior to him. I was a take-no-prisoners competitor at work, but Art, older and perhaps wiser, had a more relaxed perspective on life. He was a sweet, quiet guy and not easily perturbed, but this situation would test anyone. With another friend, Art and I went to the crevasse where the Fried home had stood to see what we could recover. Art and Lillian had lived in Turnagain. Down the street, the Salvation Army was handing out sandwiches and coffee. We climbed down on a rope (rope climbing no longer bothered me) into the hole that had swallowed Art's house while he remained up top ready to pull up anything of value we might find.

The house was a wreck. As it sank, it had rocked back and forth and ended up tilted almost perpendicular to the ground. Walls had become floors, complete with rugs that had fallen against them. The fireplace had crashed through the side of the building, leaving a huge hole. The furniture had been smashed to pieces. Art was particularly concerned about a chest freezer that had contained five hundred pounds of meat. We couldn't find it anywhere. Apparently it and part of the house had disappeared into the murky waters of Knik Arm. Later, we rented a metal detector to look for it, without success. All we found of value that first day was clothing from a smashed dresser, which we bagged and sent up on a rope to Art. Of course, he was upset by the loss. But he kept a good outlook, as he demonstrated when we found the liquor cabinet. By some weird chance, this cabinet, which was on wheels, had rolled around the room and stayed upright as the house went topsy-turvy. The glasses and bottles were unbroken. Art hoisted it all up with the rope. By the time we climbed out to street level, Art had set it up as a free bar at curbside, handing out cocktails to neighbors and strangers alike. The line at the Salvation Army cart up the street quickly disappeared as everyone moved over to Art's line for an impromptu party.

The Salvation Army may not have appreciated Art's generosity, but it was a perfect example of how Alaskans responded to the earthquake. Even having lost all their possessions, as had the Frieds, survivors pitched in to help others who were worse off, and kept alive a positive, optimistic spirit and the will to rebuild as soon as possible. The military threw itself into the disaster response. Air Force Lt. Gen. R. J. "Bucky" Reeves sent troops and equipment across the region. The missions included rescuing, sheltering, feeding, and inoculating people; gathering intelligence on the condition of the damaged roads, railroad, and remote towns and villages; making temporary road repairs; communicating with the outside world; patrolling the streets to prevent looting; and transporting emergency equipment and supplies. Emergency mobilization occurred almost instantaneously and the results were immediate. Businesses in Alaska and around the country donated supplies for rebuilding, and towns gave land. Banks made loans with little security and did not require earthquake insurance. Although official government disaster assistance often was slow and bureaucratic, Alaskans accepted their situation with a can-do attitude and self-reliant skills, and began rebuilding right away without waiting for federal handouts.

The Lions Club was offered cash and materials from clubs all over the world. I had become the secretary, handling public relations for the organization's 49th District, which included Alaska and parts of western Canada. We believed spending donated resources on our own communities would be self-serving. District Governor Ross Wood met with Alaska Governor Bill Egan and other officials to find out where we could do the most good. We decided to help one of the Native villages that had been destroyed. Two weeks after the quake, about twenty of us, including several journalists, flew in a donated aircraft to Kodiak, where we boarded an old shrimp boat for a ride to the island village of Afognak. Because of changes in the ocean depth and the loss of navigational markers, the vessel had to creep along at three knots, taking an entire day to cover thirty miles. We came ashore in a snowstorm on the far side of the island, two miles from the village. We set off on foot and motorcycle, not knowing what we would find in Afognak.

When the quake hit, villagers saw the water drain from their beach and leave the sea floor exposed for two miles offshore. John Larson, working on a seiner off shore, was heard to exclaim over the radio, "I see something coming... something big. Boy, this is a BIG one!" He was never heard from again. Villagers knew to head for high ground. Mothers dressed their children in their warmest clothes and filled boxes with food while men threw valued possessions into the back of pickup trucks. They took refuge in the mountainous forest behind the village as the first of the waves came in with three-foot breakers, covering the village six feet deep. The next wave brought nine feet of water, the third twelve feet. As each wave receded, it took everything with it. The villagers huddled on the snowy mountainside for three days, afraid that even bigger waves might be coming. They learned from the radio that boats in the Kodiak harbor had smashed through the downtown on tidal waves as almost every building was leveled. Yet all but one Afognak resident survived, and only eight died in Kodiak. The quake claimed 131 lives.

We found a strange scene on our arrival. Most of the village's great trees still stood, but instead of a village, we found wide pathways through the woods. Those had been the roads. Most signs of human habitation—buildings, vehicles, equipment—were gone. Some houses had washed away, moving as far as two miles from their foundations, while other buildings, including the community hall, disappeared completely. Here and there only front steps remained, leading nowhere. Twenty-three of the thirty-eight homes were destroyed. The wisest course would be to rebuild the entire village on a new, safer site. But the Bureau of Indian Affairs would replace only houses that had been destroyed and would not relocate those whose homes remained intact.

We met with the entire village and presented our proposal: The Lions Club would rebuild Afognak at a new location, including forty houses, a community center, school, sewer and water systems, a post office, dock, and an airstrip. We presented brochures of houses and maps of possible sites. The villagers listened solemnly. The decision was not an easy one, especially for the elders, who would be leaving behind lifetimes of memories and a cemetery where they had laid their family and ancestors to rest. Finally the chairman of the village council, Oscar Ellison, asked us to step outside while the villagers discussed the offer. When we were invited back in, we saw many tearful eyes in the room. The village accepted our offer and had decided to name the new village Port Lions.

We were all deeply moved. Villager Harry Knagin later described his emotions this way: "After the Lions left, my wife and I walked back to our temporary quarters. We just stood there. I saw her not too clearly. I was having trouble with my eyes. Then it occurred to both of us at the same moment. We lighted new candles in front of our family icon of the Virgin Mother and Child hanging on the wall. We crossed ourselves three times. Then, somehow, we felt better. Our voices came back to us. We were very thankful for the good people God had put into this world."

Over the summer of 1964, building Port Lions became a full-time volunteer job for many of us. The magnitude of the task was extraordinary. We received a donation of lumber sufficient to build forty houses, each nine hundred sixty square feet in size. The material list compiled by the skilled craftsmen in our club put the size of what we were attempting in perspective. I sent our request out to the world:

Kitchen and bathroom sinks, 40 each;
Bathtubs and toilets, 40 each;
Three-hundred-gallon oil tanks, furnaces, and water heaters, 40 each;
Bathroom and living-room light fixtures;
Copper pipe, total length exceeding one mile;
Cement, 1,240 sacks;
Cement blocks, 18,000;
Asphalt tile, 45,000 square feet;
Power plants, two;
Heavy equipment, miscellaneous;
Diesel fuel, 6,000 gallons;
Gasoline, 2,000 gallons.

And so on. With the permission of the army, I took on the task of managing logistics from my desk at Fort Rich. The donated goods and materials flooded in.

Certainly, others did more than I. Ross Wood essentially lived at Port Lions for the duration of the project. The BIA provided construction supervisors and paid for the new school. Villagers worked on construction, accepting modest wages. My contribution was the knowledge of how to organize large projects and aggressiveness in dealing with the military and other bureaucratic organizations. I called corporations for donations, including water-purification chemicals from Clorox and heavy equipment from John Deere. I managed the money, too, paying our expenses and growing payroll; the army paid my paycheck and phone bill.

Working the system was what I knew how to do. With the Mountain View Lions I had helped build a public park using military land. Applying the philosophy that it never hurts to ask, I approached the air force for a long-term lease on ten acres on the edge of Mountain View. I sold the idea based on the concept that a park would make a buffer between the base and the town. Then I asked the army reserves for heavy equipment and operators to clear and excavate the park. We raised money for the project, about $100,000, with a dinner dance and other fund-raisers. The finished Lions Park had two ball fields, a hockey rink, basketball, volleyball and badminton courts, and playground equipment. I came away with the belief that I could accomplish much more than I ever realized. The Port Lions project would test my conviction.

One summer day, when Ross and I arrived at Port Lions, the place looked deserted. The men were gone, work had stopped, and the only residents to be seen were a few old women, a lot of children, and some loose dogs. Because the village's annual cash income came from fishing, the men left to make their money for the year when the salmon runs began. Ross asked me to contact the Mennonite Disaster Service, a religious group of Canadian and American volunteers who traveled internationally to help in times of crisis. Within two weeks a crew of nine arrived from Canada, Iowa, and Ohio. We scurried for equipment to set up a camp to house them and food to feed them. The Mission Pasta company in San Francisco sent tons of spaghetti, macaroni, bow-tie pasta, and every other conceivable shape of noodle. That summer we used fish, meat, tomatoes, and even berries for sauce to put on the pasta, feeding some eighty-five Mennonite workers who cycled through. The volunteers worked hard, but I doubt they lost any weight, given all the pasta they consumed.

The new village rose along roughly plowed roads that were quickly surveyed and named. One afternoon, Mennonite farmers and businessmen pulled block and tackle rigging to raise large beams for the new village store; young workers drove nails into plywood on the side of a house; others organized the start of another house by laying beams across foundation piles; elsewhere, carpenters assembled roof trusses to be dragged on a sled behind a tractor to the next structure. The pace redoubled in the fall, when the village men returned from fishing.

When the building season ended, the new village of Port Lions stood above its black pebble beach, as it still does, with Mennonite Creek running through the middle of town. Other villages destroyed in the quake waited as long as twenty-five years to be rebuilt. As much as the Afognak villagers benefited from the Lions, those of us who worked on the project were beneficiaries as well. I acquired a broader sense of what was possible. The right leadership could bring people together to accomplish the impossible. The earthquake also opened doors for Fran and me socially. From that point on, our perspective turned from the military community to the civilian life of Alaska.

Part of becoming an Alaskan, in those days, meant learning to build things for yourself. In 1962 we had bought our little square cottage in Mountain View, newly built by Marston Real Estate, for $20,625 with a loan we barely qualified for. Later we decided to add a daylight basement. Fran expressed skepticism about my carpentry skills, but I decided to go ahead with help from neighbors. I hired a house-mover to jack up the house, and then we worked overnight to build a four-foot-high pony wall. The house-mover returned the next day and lowered the house onto the new walls. The sewer pipe didn't connect— it was four feet too short—so, on the advice of plumbing expert Tom Faccio, I found an inner tube, cut it, clamped the two ends onto the two ends of the metal sewer pipe, and called it good. The project took two more years to complete because we were paying cash from my paycheck as we went along. The front door remained four feet above ground for a long time, accessed with a ladder. In those days of miniskirts, Fran always had ample assistance from male neighbors who bolted for her like racehorses out of the gate when she began to climb the ladder. When I realized how eager they were, I got right to work building a proper entryway.

The summer of the earthquake, I took on the job of helping build Anchorage's first synagogue, Temple Beth Sholom. Few Jews lived in Alaska then. The names and addresses of our entire congregation fit on a single sheet of paper. When Evan was born, a shortage of Jews made the bris circumcision ceremony a challenge at the Elmendorf Air Force Base 5040th Hospital. There was no mohel in Anchorage, but we did find a Jewish doctor to perform the circumcision. However, we weren't sure we could find a minyan of ten Jewish men to observe the rite. We gathered as many as we could find, but still came up short. Just as we were getting ready to start, a hospital orderly wheeled a patient into the room, bandaged from head to toe, and said he was our tenth Jew. The moment the ceremony was complete, the bandaged patient was wheeled out again. To this day, I don't know if the tenth man was Jewish or whether he was even conscious. In light of the size of our Jewish community, building the temple would be difficult. I could not contribute financially—we could barely afford dues—so I pitched in with my hands.

I asked Art Kutcher, who had built our house, to be our contractor. He was a good carpenter, but I wondered how Art, a devout Christian, would feel about building a Jewish temple. I need not have worried. Anchorage still had a frontier attitude of tolerance and shared purpose. Religious and other differences among Alaskans didn't matter as much as they did elsewhere. Later, the biggest political fight of my life came over the defense of that spirit of equality when political forces saw a benefit in dividing Alaskans. The 1960s were a kinder, more innocent time. Our town was still relatively small and we all were building it together. Art was a special person as well and became our congregation's rock-solid friend as he constructed the shell of our modest religious school and place of worship.

The excavation began with a borrowed D8 Caterpillar driven by Burton Goldberg, a member of the congregation and a union organizer for federal employees. He drove with gusto into the wet peat with the objective of digging down to a hard surface upon which to place the foundation. Burton had a booming voice and supreme confidence, so I watched quietly as he maneuvered the huge machine into the muck and held my tongue as I saw the treads dig their way into the swamp. What did I know, maybe that was how it was done? As the minutes passed, Burton moved back and forth, and the D8 sank ever deeper. By the time I yelled, "You're sinking," it was too late. The mud was over the treads. Burton decided to gun it, which proved an effective way of digging out the mud from under the treads and sinking the machine even farther. When the mud was up to the seat he turned off the key, stepped out, and, with confidence unaffected, said it was time to rent a D9 Cat to pull out the D8. In fact, removing the bulldozer from the mud hole required two forty-nine-ton D9 Cats. To my enduring pride, I was allowed to drive one of them, engine roaring, as we finally extricated the D8. Later, when the building was up, a master electrician named Carter Sherman volunteered to wire the new synagogue. Carter was not Jewish, but his wife was a member of the congregation. I worked as his assistant, learning to bend conduit and pull wire.

We remained seriously involved in the temple for years—Evan and Mitch each had a bar mitzvah there—and we lived in our house in Mountain View for almost twenty years until after we paid off the mortgage. Forty years after the earthquake I learned what happened to that big Passover dinner that Fran and I had been all dressed up to host on that evening in March 1964. I had gotten the impression that the chicken soup, the matzo, and the rest of the feast had been fed to quake victims and aid workers. But when I ran into Father Norm Elliot, who had been the priest at All Saints Episcopal Church at that time, he corrected my story. The shaking, he said, threw every plate, bowl, and serving tray across the floor, making an enormous, rotting mess in the church basement that he cleaned up himself. The fact that Norm chose not to mention this to me for four decades goes to show something special about him, and about the spirit of those times—the spirit of unity and sharing, and the spirit of equality and respect among people of different faiths and backgrounds.

Later, when I entered politics, I fought to keep that spirit alive.

---

[1]U.S. Geological Survey, *Largest Earthquakes in the World Since 1900,* http://earthquake.usgs.gov/regional/world/10_largest_world.php (accessed 2007).

[2]These memories and others are contained in Joy Griffin, ed., *Where Were You? Alaska 64 Earthquake* (Homer, AK: Homer Public Library, 1996).

CHAPTER 5
Launching into politics

Honestly, I don't remember my first run for public office, so I can't say why I ran or what I hoped to accomplish. Reading through old files, we found a sample ballot and election results from the fall of 1969 when I threw my hat into the ring for Anchorage City Council, receiving 951 votes, finishing last in a field of six. A carbon of a letter I sent to the League of Women Voters thanks them for a two-minute spot on a televised candidate forum, noting ruefully that it was the only exposure I received during the three-week campaign. And so closed the file on that great moment in American political history, forgotten even by the heroic figure who lived through it.

In 1970 I ran again. I remember that election. It was fun. Working in the garage, my buddies Bill Liston and Don Irish helped me silk-screen some of the best-looking yard signs Anchorage had ever seen, each decorated with a red rose. A page of notes records my campaign committee's list of possible slogans:

> *People on their toes vote for Rose!*
>
> *Don't doze, vote for Rose!*
>
> *Among the usual garden variety of candidates there is one Rose!*
>
> *Put a Rose in your city council!*
>
> *He may not be an American Beauty, but he's still a Rose!*

I raised a few hundred dollars, which, with $1,000 of my own, paid for all my campaign materials, six TV spots, and forty radio ads. My platform emphasized my qualifications. Unfortunately, two other candidates also were qualified, and they were incumbents. I came in third, just out of the money.

Obviously I needed something more than a snappy slogan and pretty yard signs. I needed an issue. Over the next year, I found a powerful one—sewers. I led a ratepayer's revolt against the Greater Anchorage Area Borough. We went before the Alaska Public Utilities Commission to challenge the sewer utility's questionable accounting practices and a rate increase to pay for expanding the system. We refused to pay our sewer bills. I was in the news regularly as spokesman for one of the biggest local political issues of the day. My name became synonymous with sewers. When we won the issue and I finally paid my sewer bill, the event warranted headlines and a photo of me in both newspapers handing over my check to the clerk.

Sewers may seem a parochial issue, and certainly my effort was somewhat self-serving. My motivation wasn't *really* outrage over a $5 surcharge on my sewer bill. But it happened that my choice of causes, and the timing, put me in the middle of a critical issue at a critical moment in the history of Anchorage. As a result, I helped lead the city during its most important formative period.

Anchorage began as a tent camp of railroad workers on the banks of Ship Creek in 1914 and was incorporated in 1920, but the tiny town that existed prior to World War II bore little similarity to the city of today. Military construction and an associated economic boom began with the war and accelerated during the Cold War. The population exploded as Anchorage transformed from a dusty little railroad town into Alaska's largest city. Development ran far beyond the old city boundaries. The inadequacy of those boundaries marked a clear path to years of conflict.

The area outside the city lacked local government, was not taxed locally, and had few services. As urbanization spread, neighborhoods contracted with the city to provide police protection or created their own districts for water and sewer, but no rational system or equitable way existed to pay for government. In 1964, five years after statehood, the state legislature forced the area beyond the city to form the Greater Anchorage Area Borough, known as the GAAB, a county-level government that extended across the Anchorage bowl, down Turnagain Arm to Girdwood, and up Knik Arm to Eklutna. Under the local-government system created by the Alaska Constitution, the GAAB could, as a second-class borough, take over many of the powers of the city of Anchorage if voters approved. The city came to see the borough as a threat to its existence, while the borough saw the city as a barrier to progress. Each government became the other's nemesis.

I got involved in local government in 1966. Impressed by my work organizing the Lions Club to build Lions Park in Mountain View, city Mayor Elmer Rasmuson appointed me to the Anchorage Parks and Recreation Commission. It was a rare moment when ordinary people could help decide how a city would be built. An economic boom had followed the 1964 earthquake, as cleanup and rebuilding work brought new money and a wave of new people. That fast growth made it obvious where Anchorage was going, but so far the entire borough, including the city, had barely 100,000 residents and most of its land was undeveloped with no development plan. If acreage were to be preserved for public use, this would be the time to do it. Our commission wrote the city's first five-year parks plan, starting a tradition of protecting land in the city for green space and recreation that continued through the explosive growth of the next two decades. Thanks in part to our work, Anchorage today has an unequaled system of greenbelts and trails from sea to mountains, large parks that bring wilderness into the city, greenhouses that make Anchorage a city of flowers, and excellent recreation facilities.

The names of some of the people involved in this effort are well known, if not their specific accomplishments, because eventually those names were attached to parks and facilities we planned—a softball complex named for Pat Cartee, a baseball complex named for Bernie Kosinski, and the Chester Creek Trail named for Lanie Fleischer, the mother of the Anchorage bike-trail system. Many others worked hard but were not honored—Tay Thomas, Irma Besser, Judge James Fitzgerald, Jim Parsons, Betsy Tower, and Frank Nosek, among others. Besides planning for parks, we also set a pattern of protecting park land in its natural state. For example, when a group wanted to build a zoo in Russian Jack Springs Park, we pushed for a public vote that kept that remarkable land from being taken over for a single purpose. Today, Anchorage has 120 parks covering 10,800 acres, where hikers, bikers, and cross-country skiers often encounter moose and even an occasional bear on one of the world's best urban trail networks.

The sheer pleasure of this work and its satisfying impact gave me a taste for further service in local government. Besides, my chairmanship and accomplishments on the commission provided some of the bullet points for campaign brochures when I bragged of my qualifications for office.

Local politics was a natural extension of my ambition and competitive spirit at work at Fort Richardson, where I made a practice of anticipating what my superiors needed and trying to deliver it before they asked. I always kept an eye on my next promotion. The work was exciting and I moved up fast. I dug deep into army operations to produce management analyses and recommendations for improved efficiency. I participated in setting up the first computer for handling army finances in Alaska. I investigated problems. I had setbacks, too, such as when my audit of the officers club—dangerous ground, indeed—failed to detect that stacks of liquor cases in the warehouse had been hollowed out to disguise the fact that boxes in the center of the stack were missing. I listed all cases as present and accounted for, forgetting one of the basics in accounting school—never allow goods to be stacked in cubes with unseen units in the middle.

My patriotism pushed me as did my ambition. Part of maturing in the job was learning to take our work seriously, especially the contributions of those I once had derisively called "lifers," the career military men. Many were bright and dedicated. I learned a lot from them about leadership, management, and commitment to the mission. These were the Vietnam years. Some of my colleagues in uniform deployed to the war zone and never returned. Regardless of whether the war made sense politically, their sacrifices added to everyone's will to contribute to our team. We perceived ourselves as nothing less than defenders of America's homeland and way of life. Part of my job involved handling classified intelligence, some of it extremely sensitive. Alaska was the front line in the Cold War, primed with nuclear weapons and engaged in a cat-and-mouse game of testing Soviet air defenses and reacting when they tested ours. With a world conflagration potentially in the balance, our work couldn't have been more serious. Naturally, I came to identify with the team I was part of and to adopt its conservative outlook.

Many mentors, too many to name, helped me climb through the ranks of the Civil Service at Fort Richardson. One of our commanding generals, Maj. Gen. J. T. Folda, helped me get into a program that Secretary of Defense Robert McNamara created to increase professional management skills in the army. I was selected from U.S. Army Alaska to attend Syracuse University, expenses and salary paid, to earn a master's degree in business administration. In 1967 Fran and I packed up the family, rented out our home, and headed to Syracuse, New York, for a fourteen-month stay. The program was rewarding and the intelligence and drive of the other students made it challenging. My classmates were among the most promising and competitive career officers the army could produce. Fran and I enjoyed the time, socializing with the other young families in the program while making little contact with the social world of the rest of the campus, which was then dominated by a hippie culture divorced from our tight military group.

My training in management and accounting prepared me to analyze the Anchorage sewer system, and what I found was a mess. I began looking at the financial records and utilities commission filings after losing my run for city council in 1970. City officials and rate-payers already were upset about proposed borough rate increases, and we had no difficulty attracting donations in support of our Study Committee on Sewers. News reporters and property owners suspected problems in the sewer program, but without the inclination or expertise to dig through complex documents and regulations, they couldn't make a case before the Alaska Public Utilities Commission. I was willing and able. I took on the chairmanship of the study committee and started studying the documents and issuing news releases. I had help from S. B. Mitford, an Englishman with a strong accent and a formal manner who represented property owners, and City Attorney John Spencer. My report detailed how the borough had allocated costs unfairly, mixed funds that legally were required to be segregated, incurred excessive expenses, wrongly subsidized projects benefiting private property owners, and, in essence, exploited those who already had paid for their sewers to fund expansion. Calling the sewer system a flimsy house of cards, the *Anchorage Times* said, "Other people have objected and complained about the sewer system finances before. But until Mr. Rose began digging into things, nobody else was ever able to make any sense of them."

The issues were complex, and the conflict lasted many years. But we won more fights than we lost, and the local media consistently portrayed me as a crusader for the common rate-payer. I enjoyed the role and probably carried it too far. For example, I became convinced, in my overzealous frame of mind, that various borough assembly members were receiving personal financial gain from the sewer program as contractors and consultants. When I approached my friend Judge Jim Fitzgerald with my evidence and desire to see the assembly members indicted by a grand jury, he wisely counseled, "You're running for office. Forget about indictments." Fortunately, I followed his advice and dropped that tack. Some of the people I had planned to accuse later became my colleagues and good friends and made enormous contributions to Anchorage.

When I ran for city council in 1971, the headline on my brochure read, "You, Your Sewer, and a Candidate." Sixteen candidates were running for three seats. I was the top vote-getter. At the same time, a $4 million sewer bond issue was defeated. I had become so closely associated with the sewer issue that the borough was able to pass a bond only after I declared myself satisfied. In the end, our work probably helped the sewer-expansion project, which was critical for Anchorage's growth, because we forced the utility to adopt equitable and legally defensible methods of paying for its projects and a rational, transparent way of accounting for them.

My time on the city council was among the most rewarding of my life. I didn't mind working hard; in fact, I looked for more work. At home I installed one of the first telephone-answering machines, called a Code-a-Phone, and promoted it as the Dave Rose Hotline. Newspaper ads publicized the number. As calls came in, I would troubleshoot the concerns right away—a missing street light or a snow-plowing problem, for example—and then respond with a letter within seventy-two hours. This succeeded beyond my best expectations, bringing positive media attention and many happy constituents. My fellow city councilman and friend Jim Campbell took me aside and asked me to back off because my hotline was making Mayor George Sullivan look bad. Then I knew I was on the right track.

On one occasion, an elderly woman called from Government Hill to ask that the fire department get her cat out of a tree. I called the battalion chief on duty, but he wasn't interested in helping. He said he'd never seen a dead cat in a tree. I kept pushing, but he made no promises. He called back later, though, having had time to remember that the city council approved the fire department budget. The chief apologized and said he was rolling a ladder truck to rescue the cat. A firefighter went up the ladder, got the cat down, and then the crew lowered the ladder, got on board the fire truck, and drove over the cat. The woman called me in a fury. "You killed my cat!" Of course, I offered to bury the cat, take her to the pound for another cat, anything—all to no avail.

Actually, I don't remember if that's what really happened because after I told the cat story to fellow council members, it kept getting better in the retelling over the years. It became our inside joke about the difficulty of pleasing constituents. On those occasions when our attempts to help went wrong, we'd say, "I ran over the cat."

Our odd local government system allowed the city council to designate five of its members to serve on the eleven-member borough assembly. One of those seats was mine for the asking and I took it, because I had a big appetite for the work and because membership on the assembly came with a stipend. The ghost of my father still pushed me. Rather than being motivated by pure ambition, I was driven by my need for financial security. I thought of the city council and borough assembly work as moonlighting. My mother, still living in Queens, didn't particularly like my political involvement—she thought of local politicians as crooks—but she needed my financial support. The envelope factory suffered from increased competition, a weak economy, and the shortcomings of its two elderly partners—my mother and the then very ill Ernest Harper. In one of her letters Mom said, "Things are really bad—poor business. A curtailment of credit on purchases has us in a down spiral. Frankly, David, I don't see how we continue at all, and can't see how we can go on much longer." I was able to send her money and Harper's sons also pitched in to help the factory.

We kept the wolf from her door and slowly helped Mom recover from debts she had accumulated over the years. However, I never lost the fear of what would happen to Fran, Evan, and Mitch if I died, like my father. Even while serving as chief of management for U.S. Army Alaska and as a member of the city council and borough assembly, I prepared tax returns on the side and invested in real estate. My one regret is that I didn't leave enough time for Evan and Mitch, who went through puberty and their teen years while I was in office. In avoiding one of my father's mistakes, I made another. Fortunately, my relationship with my sons blossomed later as they became successful men in their own right.

The assembly met Monday nights in a flimsy modular building housing the borough on Tudor Road. The city council met Tuesday nights in the basement of the Loussac Library downtown. The five of us who were members of both bodies would vote on resolutions castigating the city on Monday night and then on Tuesday night vote on resolutions directing criticism back at the assembly. Naturally, those representing the city usually voted in a bloc on the assembly. Those representing the area outside the city generally voted together, too. The weekly face-off between the two legislative bodies made assembly meetings bitter and full of intrigue. Only one vote had to switch to reverse many issues, so some members felt constant temptation to make deals or to give in to inappropriate pressure. The acrimony and interminable debate commonly extended meetings past three o'clock in the morning when sheer fatigue would cause the discourse to degenerate into verbal brawling.

Conflict was built into a system in which the elected bodies of two overlapping governments competed for powers. The city was a compact, urban area with professional management and many years of experience. By the time I joined the council, the city had done most of its growing. We were paving the last of our gravel roads. Houses downtown were giving way to glass office buildings. We wanted to continue doing a good job without interference. The borough, on the other hand, contained the city; urban streets that had spilled beyond the city's limits; large suburban areas; and even larger areas where residents lived a rural lifestyle on large tracts or even butted up against wilderness. The borough's history of just eleven years was one of rapid growth in population and in government. New borough staff and services were cobbled onto ad hoc service units that had been formed during earlier, simpler times. The result was a confused and dysfunctional organization. Population and community development raced onward while the borough's planning and zoning powers remained largely dormant through its first nine years, without a comprehensive plan and largely without zoning designations. Anchorage still suffers today from illogical and conflicting land uses that resulted from unplanned development then. Borough Chairman John Asplund's easy-going style compounded these problems. He concentrated almost exclusively on expanding the sewer system, giving broad authority to construction personnel to run the borough. Asplund didn't set up a disciplined management system. The borough was unable to produce a timely budget, document its procedures, or account for its funds.

My background in management analysis made these faults immediately evident to me, and I moved to the forefront in the city's conflict with the borough. Egged on by my council colleagues, Mayor Sullivan, and the *Anchorage Times,* I may have gone too far at times. In a 1972 speech to professional managers, I declared, "To say that our borough is mismanaged would be an overstatement. The fact of the matter is, our borough is unmanaged. The organization is running out of control and, unless swift and significant action is taken, we face the possibility of a complete breakdown of that government." Of course, there are two sides to every story. Asplund faced a nearly impossible job. Besides trying to build a metropolitan government during a time of extreme growth, he had to deal with the downtown business crowd that fought his every move. Often he could act only with the support of every member of his out-of-city assembly voting bloc, effectively giving each member a veto power and complicating even simple actions.

Asplund did not run for reelection in 1972. He was replaced by Jack Roderick, an intelligent, affable but politically inexperienced attorney. Roderick may have been the first Anchorage politician who could credit TV commercials for his election. The ads were produced by Tim McGinnis, the same consultant who two years later started Jay Hammond on the way to the governorship with his famous wood-splitting ads. A cameraman was trying to run out a reel of film when he happened to catch the Roderick family dog swiveling its neck back and forth watching a badminton birdie fly over the net in their back yard. It was eye-catching and cute. Besides winning Roderick strong support from the dog lovers, it distinguished him from the ten other candidates.

As Jack later admitted, he had no idea what he was getting into when he walked into his first rancorous assembly meeting, or when he tried to get a handle on the borough's chaotic finances and sewer program. Asplund hadn't briefed him on the problems. Although later we became friends and under normal circumstances would have been allies—we both strongly supported parks and trails, which became Jack's great legacy—Roderick and I were fierce adversaries then.

"I kind of got blindsided," Roderick said later. "I had to rely on my financial people at the borough, who had been apparently fighting that fight before I got into office, so when we would get lambasted—primarily by Dave, with his figures—I would have to turn to my people and say, 'Is he right?'

"I always had the impression that Dave had the better figures, had more experience, and had done the research."

In 1973, while researching park and recreation bond funds, I went through a printout of all the borough's accounts. The bond money was missing. As I searched further, I discovered what appeared to be a $17 million gap in the borough's financial records. Roderick likes to tell the story of what happened next. The Anchorage Times trumpeted the discovery in a banner headline—"$17 million deficit." The borough's financial people went over my work and found most of the money, at the same time exposing an enormous flaw in their data-processing system, which had failed to show the funds in its printout. Roderick then went to meet with Times publisher Robert Atwood and editor Bill

Tobin to explain that the deficit was not $17 million, it was less than $2 million. Roderick ruefully remembers the next day's headline: "Mayor Admits Deficit."

Roderick became so disgusted with the assembly, especially with the vote-trading and attempts to manipulate him by some of his own out-of-city members, that he announced he would stop attending the meetings—a move the media interpreted as a boycott. The newspapers kept up a running story for weeks about the mayor and assembly refusing to speak to each other. The conflict had reached a point of absurdity and could be resolved only by dissolving both governments and creating a new local government unifying the Anchorage area.

The unification idea had been discussed as early as 1966, less than two years after the borough formed. In 1970 a hotel fire on Northern Lights Boulevard, the road which served as the city-borough boundary, demonstrated the consequences of the bickering between the local governments. The ninety-nine-room Gold Rush Motor Lodge had been built only four years earlier. Due to the borough's complete lack of building codes, the wooden structure was a fire trap with no alarm system. When the fire started in extreme cold at 2:30 AM on January 13, it raced through hidden voids that carried flames the length of the hotel. Borough firefighters arrived within two minutes of the call and found the building half engulfed in flames, guests screaming for help from their windows. The borough firefighters immediately called for assistance from the city fire department, whose jurisdiction ended on the opposite side of the road. A city ladder truck arrived quickly and personnel helped rescue some guests, but when the borough commander on scene asked the city truck to set up an aerial water spray, city firefighters refused. Five guests died in the fire. The next morning, each side blamed the other for errors and confusion in fighting the fire. The story created a public uproar. A legislative investigation documented that the city-borough conflict had been a factor in fighting the fire, but discounted that it had cost any lives. No one could have stopped a fire in that building.

A commission elected the year before to draft a charter for a unified government was holding public meetings. Most community leaders recognized the need for unification and saw the fire as a tragic example of the problem that would persuade voters to unify. City voters did approve the charter that fall, but voters outside the city turned it down. Residents in rural areas liked living with minimal government and didn't want to pay more taxes. Therein lay a large part of the problem. Those of us living within the city limits paid taxes to both the city and the borough while those outside paid only borough taxes. The borough provided services with limited benefit to city residents, while drawing on the city tax base. Moreover, borough residents used city services such as urban roads, libraries, the museum, and other downtown amenities that were supported solely by city taxes. This arrangement gave borough residents a financial disincentive when voting on a new government that would make everyone pay and receive services equally.

After the first defeat, the charter commission revised the proposed charter and brought it back for another vote in 1971. The results were the same. In that fall's city election—the same one in which I won my seat on the council for the first time—residents were asked in an advisory question whether they wanted to secede from the borough if unification should fail. They overwhelmingly said yes. In 1972 mayors Sullivan and Asplund offered a compromise solution to unify most of Anchorage. The assembly rejected it. Next, the city tried to get out of the borough by forming its own independent borough, to be called the Cook Inlet Borough, which then could annex areas of the existing borough as a back-door way of unifying (or the city taking control of the borough, depending on your point of view.)

I spoke to the state's Local Boundary Commission in January 1973 as it considered the city's petition. I told the commission, "The self-determination of a people is never detrimental in a free and democratic society. If there is detriment at all, it will occur in the rural areas, which will now be faced with the burden of bearing their own fair share in the cost of government. They will no longer be able to have somebody else pay their bills. They will have to carry their own load rather than ride on the backs of city residents. Is this unfair? Is this odious? I submit that it is an honest and straight-forward approach and in accord with state and federal law and the principles upon which this nation was founded."

The commission turned us down a few hours later.

The next fall, I co-sponsored a resolution at the assembly with fellow city council members Wilda Hudson and Peg Benkert calling for a new charter commission. Again I attempted to inspire with oratory: "What we have today is two huge bureaucracies. Each is trying to perpetuate itself. Each is trying to increase its power. Each is attempting to grow. In all cases, each is trying to do so at the expense of the other. As long as the two exist, the fighting will continue and the interests of the people will not be best served. ... The bickering and squabbling must come to an end. Not only is it costly in terms of resources used by both governments involved in the infighting, but it is costly in terms of the people's loss of confidence in their governments and in our loss of credibility as effective elected representatives. ... We are wandering aimlessly from issue to issue continually voicing narrow and parochial views rather than taking a broad view toward solving common problems. The time has come for all of us to take the high road, to behave as statesmen rather than simply as politicians."

The resolution failed. Out-of-city assembly member Jessie Dodson, a unification supporter, said we had not been statesmanlike enough in presenting it because we didn't have an out-of-city cosponsor. Wilda Hudson vowed to bring up the resolution every two weeks until it was approved. Peg Benkert resigned.

Meanwhile, new battles in what had become the city-borough war highlighted the no-win position of taxpayers who funded both sides. In 1974, with the region facing a fast-growing crime problem, the borough called a special election to establish area-wide police powers. The Anchorage Police Department protected the city, but the borough's coverage came mainly from the thinly spread Alaska State Troopers, even in urban areas just outside the city. Those nearby areas demanded help. Roderick's plan, as he saw it, would spread police protection throughout the borough. As the city saw it, however, the intention of the borough campaign was to take over APD, which would, in fact, be the practical effect of approval. We feared that our taxes would go up and our police service would go down. The city funded a campaign to defeat the proposal. City-sponsored newspaper advertising accused the borough of mismanagement and misrepresentation of costs and said the plan would leave residents vulnerable to crime. "If they administer the police like they administered the sewers, we'll all go down the drain," one city ad claimed. The borough ran its own ad campaign, starting with a positive pitch and then charging the city with not telling the truth in its advertising. The taxpayers paid for both campaigns.

Taxpayers had other reasons to be frustrated. Soon after the area-wide police proposal was defeated, the borough and city began fighting over $2.6 million in emergency funds granted by the state and federal governments to help the Anchorage area with a population boom caused by construction of the trans-Alaska oil pipeline. The assembly allocated only $200,000 of the funds to area-wide services, spending the rest of the grant money to lower property taxes in service areas outside the city. I complained to Governor Bill Egan, who agreed the money was being misused. On the council, I supported suing the borough for its "gross misrepresentation and a callous and morally corrupt action." Once again, taxpayers footed the bill for both sides of the suit.

Late in 1974, the assembly finally created another charter commission. The commission was elected the following February, to be chaired by my first friend in Anchorage, Frank Reed. A remarkable group of civic leaders filled out the group. Wisely, the commission concentrated on writing a charter that would be acceptable to voters in all parts of Anchorage. Rural areas could keep a lower level of service and lower taxes. Another smart move: Election of officials to run the newly unified government would take place at the same time as the vote on the new charter itself. Candidates for the unified offices and their supporters could be expected to campaign for the charter.

The election for mayor of the unified city and borough pitted two incumbents against each other—City Mayor George Sullivan and Borough Mayor Jack Roderick. To most observers, it appeared to be a mismatch. Sullivan, a life-long Alaskan from a political family, had been mayor since 1968, had been elected to the council in 1965, and previously had served in the legislature and on the Fairbanks City Council. The city had been run smoothly by a professional manager, and little bad publicity had come George's way in his largely ceremonial job of mayor. Roderick, a relative newcomer to politics, was finishing his first three years as borough mayor—years consumed by constant, bitter controversy. He had taken over a chaotic bureaucracy in the midst of explosive growth while facing the implacable opposition of the city and the *Anchorage Times*. Bad press dogged him at every step. Even Jack knew George was the favorite.

Regardless of the probabilities, George Sullivan was a bare-knuckles campaigner who left nothing to doubt. The campaign degenerated into personal attacks and charges of campaign-finance law violations on both sides. The *Times* lamented that it was the ugliest election ever seen locally. As a member of the city team, I pitched in to help Sullivan and carry his negative message about Roderick. I was a valuable ally. In the previous year's council election, I had far outpolled all other candidates and then won election to the assembly in my own right early in 1975. A court ruling had ended the practice of appointing assembly members from the city council. The *Anchorage Daily News* backed me to become assembly president while the *Times* praised me for doing "yeoman work in a distinguished manner," speculating why I had not run for mayor myself. Both cited my reputation as a reformer and detail-oriented advocate of good government. This reputation may have made my attacks on Roderick particularly damaging.

In hindsight, and having developed a friendship with Jack, I recognize that once again I went too far, becoming caught up in the heat and excitement of my role as Sullivan's ally. I allowed my picture to appear in large newspaper ads alleging a litany of Roderick's faults. One, under the headline "Roderick Shirks His Office & Duty," charged that his boycott of assembly meetings was a childish attempt to "crawl into a shell and hide from the public." In letters and public appearances, I went even further, leveling charges of "breach of the public trust" and declaring in one speech, "Jack says he should be elected because he is doing the job now. I submit that he has been doing a terrible job and that absolute chaos will result if he continues in office."

On September 9, 1975, the charter was approved, George Sullivan became the unified government's first mayor, and I was elected to the Anchorage Municipal Assembly—my third election in a year. The

City of Anchorage and the Greater Anchorage Area Borough ceased to exist six days later. Voters had not approved a name for the new government, but had turned down calling it a "city," surely due to the bitter aftertaste of years of conflict. Staffers didn't know how to answer the phone—they couldn't just say "Anchorage." Over drinks one evening, we settled on calling it the Municipality of Anchorage, which is the name that sticks to this day, or "Muni" for short.

Unification immediately changed assembly politics. Before, we had split on lines of city versus borough. Now we split as liberal versus conservative. Five members stood on either side of that divide, and I was the moderate in the middle. On one hand, my fiscal and managerial caution put me with the conservative camp; on the other hand, my support for parks and planning aligned me more with the liberals. I also supported freedom and civil rights, issues that straddled political boundaries.

Being conservative also meant defending freedom, not just strict morality. When the Alaska Legislature decriminalized marijuana in 1975, both liberal Democrats and libertarian Republicans cited the right to privacy in explaining their votes. I had faced a vote on an anti-pornography ordinance early in my political career, amid much impassioned public testimony. I said local government should not attempt to legislate morality. That might make me conservative, in that I wanted to limit government, or it might make me liberal, because I wanted to permit personal expression.

On the unified assembly, my independence put me in the driver's seat. I could organize as chairman by joining either side. I had wanted to move into the assembly chairman's position for some time, and this was the opportunity. I invited the entire assembly to dinner one night. Assembly member Lidia Selkregg invited me to her house to meet with the liberal wing. With a few agreements on priorities, I won majority support to be the chairman of the new assembly. Within the month, I also was elected president of the Alaska Municipal League, representing local governments before the legislature. The league had a critical mission that year. The coming of Big Oil meant the state government would be flush with money, but local governments were straining under the load of providing services during the oil boom and needed aid from the state.

My work chairing the assembly for the next year was extraordinarily challenging. Two governments had become one, but only in name. We still had two sets of laws, two organizations in two headquarters, and two sets of employees with two sets of job classifications, pay rates, labor agreements, and unions. At first, we had chaos. Municipal workers didn't know who their bosses were, where their jurisdiction lay, or what ordinances and regulations they were supposed to apply. Employee morale crashed as the assembly and mayor churned through the work of establishing a functioning system. But while we worked, there was no rest from the external pressures and needs of citizens. Indeed, demands on the Municipality reached a feverish height as Anchorage lurched through an unprecedented growth shock brought on by construction of the trans-Alaska pipeline.

The pipeline project, said to be the largest private construction job in human history, paid astronomical wages to armies of outside workers. The local economy superheated in gold-rush fashion, with insane prices and wild behavior similar to that of the Klondike seventy-five years earlier. Prostitutes and construction workers cruised the streets with huge wads of money in their pockets. Crime rates soared. Organized crime moved in. We lacked housing, our roads were clogged and disintegrating, and over-extended utilities could not afford construction materials due to soaring prices. The very nature of the community changed with an influx of hardhats from the Bible Belt.

I was proud of how the assembly responded. In the first year of unification, we rewrote the dictionary-sized Anchorage Municipal Code, approving 2,640 separate legislative items. Assembly meetings occurred, on average, every two and a half days, and that doesn't count informal work sessions. We saw each other more than we did our families. We took an active, independent approach. The assembly dug into issues and grappled with details to reach its own conclusions. Although evenly divided philosophically, we made a strong working group when faced with the daunting task facing us, and we performed well.

The assembly's activism surprised and antagonized Mayor Sullivan. Our mutual congratulations after the election soon gave way to sharp-elbowed jockeying for position as we defined the balance of powers in the new governmental structure. Being on the opposite side of the table from Sullivan rather than working at his side made me realize how brutal a fight with him for power could be. After I helped him get elected, he seemed to expect me to support him unconditionally. As Suzan Nightingale put it in a column in the *Anchorage Daily News* a few years later, "Sullivan, who had expected Rose's help, was learning that when basic philosophical differences arose, help was not the same thing as cooperation. When irreconcilable differences of opinion arose, Rose led the Assembly in publicly passing ordinances that Sullivan had already promised to veto." The fatigue of endless eighteen-hour days for both of us probably fed the conflict, as well.

Sullivan seized control of the assembly agenda and set up the municipal attorney's office under executive rules, meaning that its staff would serve at the mayor's pleasure. Both moves stripped the assembly of the autonomy we needed to work independently, giving us neither the ability to manage our workload nor to obtain unbiased legal advice. I fought back. In a series of votes, I changed or reversed Sullivan's agenda plans and finally won control of the agenda for the assembly chair. Nor would I back down from policy disagreements, going against Sullivan's wishes on various ordinances—taxicab regulation, the airport budget, and powers of the ombudsman. Sullivan wanted a toothless ombudsman, a position reporting to the assembly with the power to investigate the administration. When we overrode his veto, Sullivan refused to recognize the override. He even vetoed our rules of procedure.

The breakdown in our relationship happened fast, like a lot of things in those frantic years. Unification occurred in September 1975. By February 1976, I publicly declared dissatisfaction with Sullivan's performance and proposed amending our new charter to bring in a city manager who would assume many of the mayor's executive duties. Although Sullivan had supported the manager form of government prior to unification, he shot back that my proposal amounted to sour grapes over policy differences. Yet even he was aware of the problems. The administration bogged down in litigation and other setbacks on labor relations, a utilities crisis, borough finances that wouldn't balance, and public dissatisfaction with our inability to cope with sudden changes in the community. After barely nine months in office, rumors made the newspapers that Sullivan was so unhappy he would quit before his term was up. Instead, he announced that he definitely would not run for reelection, although that race was more than two years away. I suspected that he had a run for governor in mind. He charged that I was fighting him to set up my own run for mayor.

Thankfully, those conflicts have faded over the years. Indeed, most of these events slipped from my memory until, while writing this memoir, we reopened my old files. Recently, when the municipality celebrated its thirtieth year, George graciously recognized my contribution to Anchorage as it exists today. Our relationship is cordial. The organization we built together through the tension of divided government is a singular success with a proud history. The signs of our work are all over town.

Unfortunately, however, the events of the unification years also planted seeds of conflict—based on religious intolerance—that grew to deform much of Alaska's civic debate in later years, as we will see in the next chapter.

CHAPTER 6
Fighting for equal rights

Unifying the city and borough required the assembly to pass forty major ordinances comprising a new law book for Anchorage. Thirty-nine ordinances went through smoothly. One brought about the end of my career in elected office and set the stage for the religious right to transform Alaska politics. The fight for that ordinance, which would have assured equal rights for everyone in Anchorage, mobilized reactionary forces that continued to distort our civic debate three decades later.

My defeat stands out as a point of pride for me. As with so much in my life, I share the credit with Fran. She played a pivotal role in the battle for equality for gays and lesbians. When the issue erupted around me, I was caught ignorant and unprepared, but Fran had thought hard about it and spoke up eloquently at a crucial moment. To trace how this all came about, and how Fran developed her sensitivity about the rights of homosexuals, it's worth going back a bit in our story.

In college, Fran was the better student. While I got by in my accounting classes, she eagerly devoured her chosen subject—history. When we became engaged she already had been accepted into a graduate program in history at New York University. Her ambition was to become a museum curator at a major institution. Instead, my haphazard military career took us to Anchorage, a town with neither professional opportunities for a historian nor much history of its own. The Anchorage museum consisted of a room of keepsakes and bric-a-brac in the basement of city hall. Before leaving New York, Fran had applied for her dream job at the Smithsonian Institution in Washington, D.C. Because those civil service jobs were apportioned by state, it was a tremendous honor when she beat out all other New York competitors and was offered a position. I recall with pain and gratitude her decision to give up that opportunity—her only chance to pursue her career interest—so that we could continue our life in Alaska.

Her second-best option was to teach history in the Anchorage schools. Fran took education courses to get her teaching credentials, but her student teaching experience convinced her that she had no interest in managing unruly and unmotivated teenagers. On the first morning of class, one student tried to hit another and struck the wall instead, breaking his hand. Instead of conveying her excitement about history, Fran spent her first day filling out paperwork about the accident and maintaining order among kids who were throwing things at each other in her classes.

Then Fran worked at Fort Rich and on Elmendorf Air Force Base, doing such jobs as operating the old-fashioned telephone switchboard and editing the fort's telephone directory. For a year she taught high-school equivalency classes to GIs. The students were mature and appreciative, so the work was somewhat rewarding. After our sojourn to Syracuse University for my MBA, Fran began looking for a more serious job. A friend suggested she apply to a program offering adult basic education, one of the many new poverty programs started in the late 1960s. Fran was intrigued, and that was how she met Wayne Hussey.

Wayne was a brilliant, dynamic leader, and a charming man. He ran the grant-funded adult basic education program through Anchorage Community College, operating out of a run-down store-front office in a gritty part of downtown. Wayne also was the self-proclaimed "Empress of Alaska," all three-hundred pounds of him, with his strawberry blond hair and beard and the light blue gown he liked to wear. He called himself Margaret in his alter ego, and his favorite garment resembled something Martha Washington might have worn—a shimmering, billowy dress with puff sleeves and lace at the neck and cuffs. Along with his work in education, he founded the Imperial Court in Anchorage, which organized a huge gay ball each year at a downtown hotel, attended by a flamboyant collection of drag queens.

The late 1960s and early 1970s was a time of openness and experimentation, words that described Fran's approach to life. She thrived on her work and her unusual students and coworkers. The adult-education program made a difference in many lives—teaching adults to read, teaching English as a second language, training women in work skills, preparing and testing students for the General Equivalency Diploma (GED), preparing trade apprentices for their math tests, and offering other vocational training. Fran taught classes at night in the city jail. Wayne Hussey became her good friend. She enjoyed his overwhelming presence and overflowing ideas. At Wayne's insistence, she joined the crowd after work at the Mermaid Room and sometimes at gay bars, listening to his views on equality and justice. She met many other gay friends and came to believe strongly that discrimination against them should end.

In learning to administer new programs for which grants were available, Wayne led a group to Los Angeles for a workshop. The group consisted of Fran and Wayne, Wayne's lover, an ex-con armed robber who was the audio-visual technician, and another female teacher. The Alaskans arrived in LA's warm weather in their winter parkas, utterly out of place, and went to Watts for immersion in an all-minority world they had only imagined. At a sensitivity training session, they endured shouting, confrontation, and insults. They were indoctrinated into the radical politics of the day. They drank in wild gay bars, where Wayne would get crazy and mean when he became intoxicated. The other female teacher, a devout Catholic, prayed for deliverance. At the climax of the trip, Wayne jumped out of a car and broke his knee. After a time languishing in eloquent misery in a friend's apartment, Wayne had to be moved. The group finally contrived to ship his huge bulk back to Alaska, stewed on alcohol and pain killers and wailing in full voice.

I had nothing to do with this side of Fran's life. Aside from a plaid jacket and sideburns, I remained as personally conservative as my military career and political work suggested. Yet, at heart, Fran and I shared common values. Within months of the unification, a citizens committee appointed by Mayor Sullivan brought forward an ordinance to create the Municipality's equal-rights law and commission, as required in our charter.[1] At the last meeting of the year on December 30, 1975, the ordinance came to the assembly. The draft was identical to what the committee had created, with one change: Sullivan had deleted the words "sexual preference" from the definitions of illegal reasons to discriminate, which included race, color, religion, national origin, age, sex, marital status or physical handicap. The committee, whose members were neither radicals nor gay-rights activists, simply had decided that the new government should be founded on equal rights for all. When the ordinance arrived at the assembly, Sullivan wasn't there to explain his editing, having departed for Hawaii on a holiday vacation. Although Sullivan is a Catholic, his written message raised no moral objection to equal rights for homosexuals; instead, he suggested that the issue required more study.

A parade of equal-rights supporters came forward during the public hearing, including minorities and members of the committee, but the strongest testimony came from homosexual men who talked about discrimination they faced, their value to society as human beings, and their fear of being identified and punished for speaking out. One was afraid to give his name. The rules would not permit him to speak anonymously, but I told him he had made his point. Another gay man asked assembly member Fred Chiei, his former boss, to vouch for him. Fred, as irascible and extreme a conservative as ever sat on the assembly, assented—he said the man had been an outstanding employee. No one spoke against restoring protection for gays to the ordinance.

When the testimony was complete, assembly member Lidia Selkregg moved to restore the words "sexual orientation" to the definitions. Her motion passed unanimously, as did the ordinance, bringing a standing ovation in the assembly chambers.[2]

I thought the issue was settled. So did everyone else. New Year's Eve passed with assembly members receiving congratulations from friends and constituents. The following Sunday, the conservative *Anchorage Times* ran an article noting that the equal-rights ordinance had not aroused community opposition, and quoted the most conservative assembly members, including Don Smith and Jim Campbell, who proudly noted that almost no one had opposed the ordinance. Fred Chiei, the most reactionary of all, said, "The general vibes I've gotten since could be summed up that most people felt that if we're talking equal rights for everybody, while they may not condone the practice, equal rights should apply."

In the Alaska of 1976, we shared a culture of live and let live—individualism that dated from the gold rush. Mention of the "Alaska spirit" brought images of the eccentric, bearded prospector or homesteader doing his own thing on his own land, likely quite conservative in politics but having a heart of gold and an iron-clad respect for privacy and independence. If a line could be drawn between that traditional Alaska tolerance and the rise of the religious right, it would have to be drawn on Sunday, January 4, 1976. At 9:30 that evening, the day the *Anchorage Times* article appeared, assembly members' phones began ringing continuously with angry, hateful phone calls from Christian fundamentalists opposing the ordinance. What had changed? Rev. Jerry Prevo had spoken at his evening service.

Prevo had taken over the Anchorage Baptist Temple in 1971. As newcomers from the Bible Belt states flooded into Anchorage for oil pipeline construction, his congregation became the largest in Alaska, occupying a huge campus on twenty acres in east Anchorage. Prevo's clean-cut appearance and stiff smile fit the stereotype of the intolerant Southern Baptist TV evangelist, and he successfully used all the new tools of mass religion to gather money, power, and followers. Until he mobilized his congregation that Sunday, Prevo may not have recognized his own political strength.

The calls were ugly. Lidia Selkregg, an Italian immigrant who had fought the Nazis in the underground during World War II, was abused and harassed and told to go back where she came from. Fran and I received vicious, anti-Semitic calls. The phone never stopped ringing, creating a sense among assembly members that we were under siege.

Sullivan's original opposition to the sexual-orientation clause had been soft. Given seven days to veto the ordinance, he had hesitated. As a social conservative, Sullivan says today he knew he would veto the ordinance as soon as it passed. But publicly, he was undecided. No mayor wants to veto a unanimous vote and then be overturned by a two-thirds majority of the assembly. Until Prevo's move, it appeared we had the community on our side. Sullivan says he was as surprised as the rest of us how the issue suddenly blew up.

The *Times* used Sullivan's supposed indecision to help Prevo rally his side. On Monday and Tuesday, it published stories reporting that

Sullivan was undecided about a veto while reporting that Prevo planned to flood our Tuesday night meeting with followers. Sullivan's veto message arrived on our desks that night containing, in subtle form, many of the scare tactics and distortions that would cloud the debate for years to come. It said that "sexual preference" would apply to "any type of sexual deviation." This point was used to suggest that landlords would be forced to rent to animals because bestiality was a sexual preference. The message asserted that mothers would be unable to discriminate in hiring domestic help, causing concern that mothers might be forced to hire pedophiles as babysitters.

Nearly one thousand people turned out on Tuesday night, overflowing the assembly chambers—the largest crowd we had ever seen at a local government meeting. Prevo led a demonstration outside. Each of the three conservative assembly members who had spoken proudly of supporting the ordinance two days earlier—Chiei, Campbell, and Smith—flipped and now supported the veto. We still had the eight we needed to override the veto, but one of our eight—Tony Knowles— was out of town. Jim Campbell, taking the mayor's side, made a motion to override the veto, hoping to use Tony's absence to defeat it, but we tabled that motion, giving us three weeks to take it up. That also meant we would twist three weeks in the storm of community debate. Prevo marched his people out of the meeting after we voted to table, but supporters of the ordinance stayed. At the end of the meeting, when the agenda allowed audience participation, gays, supporters of equal rights, and supporters of separation of church and state gave more stirring testimony in support of the ordinance of the kind we had heard the week before.

I had asked Fran to stay cool and not go "crazy liberal" on me. I knew she was upset and was liable to speak from the heart, as she always did. As the testimony neared an end, she got up from her chair. I thought she was headed for the restroom, but instead she walked to the lectern. And then she brought the house down.

"Between Tuesday and Sunday we didn't receive one call against this vote," she said. "The telephone started ringing at 9:30 last Sunday night, and it has not ceased since. At 9:30 Sunday night, things started to happen. What happened was that someone started such hate in this community that even Dr. Selkregg got abused. Someone got a congregation together last Sunday night and incited them to hate. In the name of God, they should go out and hate people. All were members of Rev. Prevo's church.

"We're not dealing with homosexuality. We've dealing with the issue of can people do this sort of thing and go against anybody they want. This won't just stop with one Sunday. It's possible that every Sunday from now on someone else can get a congregation together and incite them to hate. Last Sunday, it was homosexuals. Next Sunday, it could be blacks, the Sunday after that Catholics and the Sunday after that Jews.

"It scares me that this sort of thing could happen and that the mayor—who was not here last Tuesday and is not here now—knuckled under to the pressure."

The audience exploded into applause. In the next day's *Anchorage Daily News*, reporter Suzan Nightingale quoted Fran at length, writing, "Although many homosexuals testified in favor of the ordinance, one of its most eloquent supporters was Fran Rose, wife of assembly President Dave Rose." I had rarely been more proud than I was that night after hearing Fran. I also began to realize that this radioactive issue, which I'd never before given serious thought, would become closely associated with my name.

Early in my adult life, a wise, older man gave me a piece of advice that I have repeated many times and always tried to live up to: "Always adhere to the harder right rather than giving in to the easier wrong." In politics, however, that rule has exceptions because survival requires compromise. To accumulate political power, which gives those who have it the ability to make a difference, sometimes you have to dance around the fringes of issues, shade the truth a little, and even sacrifice a minor principle now and then. Anyone unwilling to dirty his or her hands a little shouldn't run for office in the first place because rigid or naive moralists don't last long and thus do little to further their causes. On the other hand, a politician must have a foundation. You have to know whom you ultimately serve and why. The difference among public servants comes in the purpose of their compromises. Do compromises have no goal other than having personal power, or are they a means to an end, with the goal being to remain alive on the political battlefield when the time comes for the real fight? Equal rights represent an acid test that exposes those who serve with purpose and those who serve themselves. When I heard Fran's stirring speech in the assembly chamber, I knew that moment had arrived for me.

By the time we voted on the veto on January 20, five assembly members had collapsed under the pressure of phone calls that came day and night along with a deluge of thousands of letters and telegrams from both sides of the issue.[3] We could afford only three "no" votes. Many of the letters we received were polite and well-reasoned. Some were photocopies that individuals had signed. A few were hateful. In my files is a lovely, flowered envelope and letterhead from a woman containing the scrawled words, "Equal Rights for Homos? NO WAY! How about giving them a one-way ticket to S.F. instead!" Amid the ugly emotions were legitimate arguments made against the ordinance? Yes, it did have flaws, but those could have been fixed easily without throwing out the basic document. The core of the opposition was simple: Many people wanted to discriminate against homosexuals. The *Anchorage Times* bluntly added its voice to this chorus of hate. In an editorial, it said, "Extending the normal rules of non-discrimination to cover those whom society still regards as sexual deviates is carrying things too far."

Despite the predetermined outcome, the assembly was at its most eloquent before a huge audience when we took up the issue again. Emotions were high. Opponents shouted out their objections and insults. Reasonable people on both sides were embarrassed by the hotheads. assembly members gave lengthy explanations for their votes.

Tony Knowles said those supporting the veto in effect were asking that the government turn away from an injustice, thus becoming a silent partner in one group of citizens' attempt to force its will on another. "I will take no part in this complicity," he said. "In the words of Jose Marti, the famous Cuban liberator, 'To witness a crime in silence is to commit it.'" Lidia Selkregg said those who opposed the equal-rights ordinance had a different concept of democracy than she did, one that excluded people unlike themselves. "This is democracy for many people in this room," she said. "For myself, it is different. It is different for this reason: I came to this country about thirty years ago and I was in Italy in 1941 and 1942, when using the same Book that is used now to condemn the sexual preference, those students at the University of Florence were recruited to go fight with the Germans against the Jews.... I joined a group of partisans which assisted and helped the American troops in occupied Italy, and I prayed and thanked when the American plane bombed my city because with that bomb, I saw democracy, freedom, equality for everybody."

When it was my turn, I noted how extreme the debate had become, and how this level of anger and fear was a new phenomenon in our community. "We as Alaskans have never really debated and fully explored individual rights issues," I said. "Perhaps we have never really gotten involved because we, as Alaskans, have always had a strong, independent streak, a *laissez faire* attitude, an attitude of live and let live, a desire to settle on this frontier feeling free to think, act and believe in our respective private ways.

"I believe deeply in the Constitution and feel strongly about its guarantees of individual rights and freedoms. The Fourteenth Amendment to the Constitution guarantees equal rights to all under the law. In guaranteeing these rights, it does not take away freedoms of others, except perhaps the license to be a bigot, or the license to make laws that apply to some segments of our population rather than all of our citizens. The ordinance at hand not only fulfills the mandate of the new municipal charter, but, in prohibiting discrimination, it meets the word and spirit of the Constitution."

Unfortunately, the predetermined failure of our veto override did not end the issue that night. assembly members introduced four more ordinances with various different approaches to solve the equal rights conflict. Three weeks later, I convened a special meeting at the performing arts center at the University of Alaska Anchorage. In the meantime, the debate degenerated further. Prevo bought TV commercials. Gay bars were hit with rocks, eggs, and a smoke bomb. Gays and lesbians lived in fear. Petitions were filed to recall Selkregg, Dick Hart, and Ernie Brannon. Although Alaska law allows recall only for misconduct, no reason was given other than the assembly members' votes on equal rights.

On February 10, most of the 910 seats in the performing arts center were filled. Testimony started at 7:30 and ended only with the mandatory adjournment at midnight. The crowd was as raucous as a lynch mob, deaf to my repeated attempts to settle them down. Anti-gay voices shouted catcalls at pro-rights speakers. One yelled, "You're a liar," to a critic of Prevo, and many called "Amen" to statements they agreed with. A woman who admitted that she "didn't understand about homosexuals" added that, "If I were a homosexual, I would fear for my life in this crowd tonight." Yet gay speakers continued to get up and testify bravely in the face of open hatred. Leroy Williams, speaking for the Alaska Black Caucus, said that he suddenly understood why no public hearing had been held on the Emancipation Proclamation. Yet the vicious hostility made the case more strongly than ever—homosexuals needed protection.

We did pass another ordinance. Sullivan vetoed it. We failed again to override the veto. Finally the issue was laid to rest, I thought for good, on March 23—three months after it had arisen. Like so many other assembly wars I lived through, the equal-rights fight quickly faded in the face of the next issue.

With the exception of the equal-rights crisis, the assembly worked remarkably well as a team for the year after unification. We had to, or we wouldn't have gotten through our immense work load. That pressure may be what held us together. Yet relations with Mayor Sullivan continued to deteriorate. I challenged his right to collect an incremental increase in his paycheck normally given to municipal employees for longevity. The charter stated that salaries of elected officials were set by an independent commission, and the commission hadn't awarded longevity pay to the mayor. Sullivan viewed the issue as an attack on his integrity and allowed it to drag out by refusing to ask the commission for the money. He viewed me as a threat to run for mayor in 1978. Meanwhile, I saw him as a candidate for governor in 1978.

As the unification workload eased, political wrangling among assembly members increased. In November 1976, I was elected to a second year as assembly chairman with the same six-to-five bare majority of the previous year, despite a conservative insurrection led by Fred Chiei. The core of their opposition concerned my conflicts with Sullivan and the prospect of the upcoming mayoral race. By the following spring, they had found their sixth vote in the unlikely person of Lidia Selkregg. Deeply liberal and no friend of Sullivan's, Lidia had been offended when I cut her off during a meeting—she tended to be long winded. I didn't speak at the meeting when Don Smith made the motion to remove me from the chair, but Arliss Sturgulewski and Tony Knowles spoke up for me. After the motion was approved, Tony led a round of applause thanking me for my service. Still I said nothing. I was seething. Before the meeting ended, I invited the media to meet me at 10 AM the next day for a statement.

Everyone knows it's not a good idea to send a letter when you're angry. Holding a news conference under those circumstances is even worse. I compared Sullivan to Richard Nixon. In a prepared statement, I said, "The plot to replace me was conceived in a local bar a week ago and finalized in the mayor's smoke-filled office yesterday afternoon. The action was clearly political in nature, executed by the mayor's five puppets and a sixth dissident assembly member bidding for personal attention and revenge."

Today, Sullivan says he had nothing to do with the ouster. I admit that at the time I was thinking more about hampering his run for governor than anything else. Besides that, I was venting my anger. Of the five who had brought Lidia to their side, I said, "They seem to occupy public office for only two purposes—first, to satisfy their own quest for ego and power and, secondly, to support an administration that is slowly strangling in the morass of its own ineptitude. The needs of our people and the community seem to take third place. I perceive that these people are concerned that they not do anything to offend the mayor, lest he succeed to the governorship and thus be in a position to dispense favors, position, or prestige."

Making this statement was not smart, and not true, either, as I have a lot of respect for some of my opponents. The media portrayed me as a red-faced sore loser. Sullivan became a more committed adversary and later used my own words to portray me as a hothead once we did get into a head-to-head race. Antagonizing Sullivan wouldn't help me. My hope of running for mayor depended in part on his running for governor in 1978. Before the blowup, I had met with him to discuss that possibility and suggest a truce that could have made it easier for both of us. Meanwhile, I had no difficulty winning reelection to the assembly in 1977, while thinking about the mayor's election scheduled a year later.

With Sullivan having said he would not run again for mayor, I had a better shot to win than anyone else. After I got my campaign started, however, Sullivan began playing the game of feeding speculation that he "might" run for mayor again. After saying he definitely wouldn't run, he then said he was "99 percent sure" he wouldn't run. Next he said, "The door is still a little bit cracked." Meanwhile, supposedly he was flooded with calls asking him to run. He suggested to some businessmen that if they wanted him to run, they should start a petition drive. That group, which the *Anchorage Daily News* said included Jerry Prevo as one of its organizers, presented the mayor with a big pile of "We Want George" petitions.

Of course, Sullivan still had to "think" about it, producing more headlines. Finally, in May 1978, Sullivan gave in and agreed to run. It was great political theater, but what I think really happened was that the Republican primary field for governor already contained candidates that Sullivan couldn't beat—the incumbent, Jay Hammond, and former governor Walter Hickel. So why not run for mayor instead? The next term was sure to be an exciting time in Anchorage with growing oil tax revenues beginning to flow to the state. Another term as mayor might position Sullivan to run for governor in 1982.

The third major candidate for mayor was Dick Fischer, a former charter commissioner who outspent his opponents by pumping his own money into the race. All the candidates attacked Sullivan— standard strategy in a race with a clear front-runner. Sullivan lashed out bitterly in response a few weeks before the election in an address to the Bartlett Democratic Club. What he had to say about me was a bad omen. Sullivan said my "greatest claim to fame" was "staunch support for the gays and the Gay Coalition, and evidently that continues on because I understand he and his wife attended their annual ball of the Gay Coalition a couple of weeks ago."

Fran and I had attended the ball just before Labor Day, the same event Wayne Hussey had organized. We were invited by Guy Bassett and Jim Williams. For years, Guy had been manager of the Downtown Deli, which we co-owned with Tony and Susan Knowles.

Also in the audience was assembly member Jim Campbell, who was sent to represent Sullivan and to report back that I was present. Should I have avoided the ball to keep from giving the opposition a weapon against me? Probably, but I naively assumed that attendance at one event would never overshadow more than a decade of successful public service.

On election day, October 3, I did much better than I expected. Sullivan got 35 percent to my 32 percent. Fisher and the four other candidates did poorly. The charter required a 40 percent plurality to win the election, so a three-week runoff campaign began with Sullivan and me running head to head.

At first glance, the vote totals in the primary election appeared promising, but closer analysis suggested that I faced a nearly insurmountable challenge. Thanks to the support of the business establishment, Sullivan would be able to outspend me heavily. The dominant *Anchorage Times* supported him. And his long tenure in office added to his incumbent's edge. Taking no chances, however, Sullivan was true to his habit of scorched-earth campaigning and came out swinging at our first forum together, calling me temperamentally unfit to lead. The nastiest election campaign in Anchorage history had begun.

With less than two weeks to go, Jerry Prevo formed a group called "Concerned Citizens Against Dave Rose," saying I was committed to promoting homosexuality in Anchorage, asserting that the main issue in the election was "whether our municipality is going to continue to be a decent place to live." His charges were similar to Sullivan's attack on gay rights at the Bartlett Club, again focusing on my attendance at the gay ball. I was shocked that George Sullivan would want to reignite the fires of hatred that had seared the community three years earlier, and I hoped it would backfire on his campaign. But Sullivan hid behind Prevo. While admitting that they had met in the mayor's office, Sullivan claimed he had not encouraged Prevo's plan to exploit the equal-rights issue. Sullivan maintains to this day that he did not know his campaign was in touch with Prevo's group and paying for some of their ads. Reports filed with the Alaska Public Offices Commission show that Sullivan's campaign gave Prevo's committee pre-paid advertising space, with the cost to be reimbursed after the election. This was important because Prevo's group had trouble raising money, falling short of their goal and relying on Prevo's personal cash to get started. One of their typical newspaper ads—perhaps the one funded by the Sullivan campaign—said a vote for me would be a vote for a mayor "...that supports homosexual causes...that is supported by homosexuals...that attends homosexual balls." Television commercials aired on the same nasty theme.

The hysteria of the equal-rights debate had flared up again with the same intensity as if no time had passed. The main difference was that I was the only recipient of their message of hate. The phone calls started again, many of them anti-Semitic. We couldn't eat dinner without interruption by these unsettling calls. Our family felt demoralized as the focus of so much bigotry. Our mood swung from disbelief to outrage to despair. One anonymous caller to our home said he wished the Nazis had made a lampshade of my grandfather.

I was knocked on my heels. Responding was difficult. My initial comments, assisted by my able campaign spokesman, Pete Carran, took the right tack. In a statement I said, "I am not concerned about what this issue will do to Dave Rose. I am concerned about what it will do to our community. ...One cannot be against discrimination and then state, 'but I'll discriminate a little against this group or that group.' If you take that approach, you are not truly opposed to discrimination." But as the attack grew more frenzied, I saw the mayor's office slipping away and I tried to soften my position, promising that I would not personally advance an equal-rights ordinance as mayor, although I couldn't honestly say I would oppose one sponsored by someone else. This path of appeasement was dangerous, and shortly before the election, I stumbled. During a public TV debate, Sullivan asked directly if I would hire homosexuals as police officers. I said I would not. This was a stupid mistake. My impulsive answer, given without thought, wasn't consistent with my own views. And I paid for this—soon I began taking hits from the left as well as the right.

I did have defenders. A group of nineteen ministers came together to denounce Prevo's scare tactics. Prevo responded that the ministers were really attacking the Baptist faith. Reporter Don Hunter declared in a front-page story in the *Anchorage Times* that "Tuesday's mayoral runoff has escalated from a political contest to a holy war." A group of residents, some of them local celebrities, counter-punched with humor, running an ad with a picture of a jug. It said, "We the undersigned heterosexuals have not yet decided whether Dr. Jerry Prevo's recent political statements or this ceramic jug is the bigger crock!" Under signatures of various people, some of them well-known locally, was the disclaimer, "This ad paid for by the Committee to Lock Dr. Jerry Prevo in a Closet With Truman Capote."

My campaign advisers recommended we run ads showing Fran, Evan, and Mitch. This would counter the charge that I didn't care about family decency and the impression that I was gay—as the opposition implied by harping on my presence at the gay ball. I decided against the strategy. I couldn't bring myself to use my boys, then teenagers, or my wife, as a shield to deflect the hatred inspired by Prevo and Sullivan. Politics was my job, not theirs. What little money I had for a response I spent on newspaper ads linking Sullivan to Prevo's bigotry. The *Anchorage Times*, which had run all of Prevo's ads, refused to print mine. Campaign supporters stepped in and forced the issue, getting the ad into the paper the weekend before the election. But I knew I was on the ropes and needed much more than a newspaper ad to win.

The day before the election I appeared with Sullivan at an Anchorage Chamber of Commerce luncheon. I told the business audience that Sullivan was using "bigotry and the stimulation of hatred to divide this community, in the end deciding that getting elected is worth tearing apart the fiber of the community." The moderator put me up first, and I kept to the allotted time. When Sullivan spoke, he went well over the time limit while attacking me and denying the truth of my ads connecting him to Prevo. The moderator stood by, allowing the mayor to talk on as long as he wished. At that moment, I realized it was over. The sense of unfairness and indignity I felt symbolized my hopeless campaign. I never went back to another Anchorage chamber meeting.

Sullivan won 54 percent of the vote to my 45 percent. On election night, he called his re-election a vote of confidence, but everyone else focused on the gay-rights issue. Bitterly, I told reporters, "I hope and pray for George Sullivan's sake that he has not unleashed forces in this community which even he cannot control."

That remark turned out to be a prescient comment. Prevo began building on his success. In 1979 he formed Alaska's chapter of the Jerry Falwell Moral Majority, whose goals included outlawing abortions, opposing equal rights for gays and women, and ending sex education and gambling. Prevo hired a permanent staff and began a voter-registration drive in churches throughout Alaska, rallying support by claiming that religion was under attack. When presidential precinct caucuses were held in 1980, Prevo was ready to flood them with supporters. Under party rules, any Republican who shows up at the caucuses can vote for district delegates, and in turn the delegates elect officers who control the party. Old-line Republicans were openly fearful of a take-over, but it was too late to do anything about it. Prevo's troops overwhelmed traditional party members in enough precincts to put him in complete control. He drew up a list of candidates for party offices and his followers voted in lock-step. The Alaska Republican Party passed into control of one man with an extreme viewpoint. Moderate Republicans never again had an effective voice in their party in Alaska.

Just as the 1978 mayoral election signaled the beginning of Jerry Prevo's political career, it marked the end of George Sullivan's. After finishing his term in 1981, and unable under the municipal charter to run again, Sullivan began a campaign for governor in 1982, but later dropped out citing heart problems. Instead, the Republicans nominated hard-right conservative Tom Fink, who was defeated by Democrat Bill Sheffield in the general election. The Republicans, their party taken over by right-wing social conservatives, failed to win the governorship for another twenty-two years.

I finished my last term on the assembly in 1980 and decided not to run again. I realized I was done one evening at home when the phone rang with a constituent concern. I asked Fran to tell the caller I wasn't available. The energy that had driven me to establish the Dave Rose

Hotline in 1971 was gone. I had moved on to other interests. In retrospect, I did not regret losing the 1978 mayoral election because my new work proved to be unique, rewarding, and important on a world scale.

In my announcement, I said, "A person needs the stimulation of engaging in a truly difficult pursuit; of treading new ground; of fashioning and transforming ideas, goals and aspirations into realities. Quite frankly, I found that I am involved in several endeavors that offer far more challenge than that of filling the position of assemblyman."

In the end, I was glad that the issue that ended my rise in Anchorage politics was one of principle.

"I make no apologies for my position on equal rights," I said. "I have never deserted a minority of any type for political expediency. Politicians make many compromises, but they must have the courage never to compromise on the questions of individual human freedom. I never have and never will."

---

[1]Anchorage Municipal Charter, section 17.01, Equal rights: "The assembly shall enact ordinances against invidious discrimination in housing, public accommodations, employment, education, and financing practices on the basis of race, religion, age, sex, color, national origin, marital status, or physical disability"; section 17.02, Equal rights commission: "The assembly by ordinance shall establish an equal rights commission and prescribe its duties."

[2]The first municipal assembly included Tony Knowles, Ernie Brannon, Bill Besser, Jim Campbell, George Dickson, Ben Marsh, Dick Hart, Lidia Selkregg, Don Smith, Fred Chiei, and me.

[3]January 20, 1976, vote on the veto override had Selkregg, Brannon, Dickson, Hart, Knowles, and me in favor; and Chiei, Marsh, Besser, and Smith opposed. Campbell was absent.

CHAPTER 7
Riches on the horizon

I n the 1970s the oil industry and oil-funded state government grew like twin giants to dominate Alaska. The building of the trans-Alaska pipeline brought people with a different cultural and political outlook to the state. The economic changes were huge and far-reaching. The immense wealth found under the North Slope of Alaska boggled the mind. Thus far, the state government has collected more than $100 billion in oil revenue, more than $150,000 per resident.[1] That state revenue, far more than expenditures of the oil companies, controlled our economy. Whether people prospered in the private sector or lost their shirts depended heavily on the state's decisions about when to spend or save, invest or waste, and at what pace.

Since World War II, the military had supplied the largest share of paychecks in Anchorage and imported much of the city's population. With construction of the pipeline from 1974 to 1977, oil became the primary economic force and attracted people to Alaska. But the decline of the military's influence wasn't only a matter of money: Civic affairs and attitudes changed as well, leaving the army and air force behind. These changes were wider than our town. The armed forces lost its central place in American life during the 1970s as the draft ended, the war in Vietnam wound down, and the urgency of our conflict with the Soviet Union relaxed under diplomatic détente. At Fort Rich, I saw our sharp sense of mission relax. At the same time, the quality of the brass declined as well. Gone were generals such as "Bucky" Reeves, who had led us through the earthquake; and J. T. Folda, who had mentored me and others before rising himself to the Pentagon; or Norman Schwartzkopf, whom I knew as a colonel before he led the victorious forces in the first Gulf War. During my last years at Fort Rich, we were commanded by several lackluster leaders who neared the end of their careers.

As comptroller, I was a member of the general staff and the top civilian at U.S. Army Alaska. It fell to me to try to keep the post on track financially and in a management sense, and also to try to redirect ill-conceived or foolish orders from the managing officers. Senior officers feared offending their direct superior, but they might back me, a civilian, if I took the lead. At one point, a particularly uninspiring general announced his idea to improve the soldiers' morale in our harsh northern climate. We would repaint all the fort's buildings, replacing the drab military green and gray with bright pastel pink, orange, red, or yellow. The officers were afraid to disagree, but one or two did call me the night before a staff meeting. When the meeting turned to the general's plan the next day, I mentioned that although this was a wonderful idea, we hadn't budgeted money necessary to repaint the entire fort. I asked for guidance on what to cut to cover the new cost. That emboldened the others. One officer, our G-4 (logistics), mentioned that we didn't have any pastel paint in stock, and it would be difficult to requisition before winter. Another, the G-1 (personnel), pointed out that we would have to hire painters because our soldiers weren't trained to build scaffold or work on high ladders. Another officer, the G-3 (operations), suggested we review the field manual on cover and concealment because yellow and orange might not blend in with our surroundings. The bright-color plan went to the resting place for dumb ideas. I was pleased to play the role of the ignorant civilian, asking simple questions, and the principal staff never deserted me, always answering with the information the leadership needed. As the generals cycled through, some needed more care and feeding than others, but we usually kept things running smoothly with our team and focused chiefs of staff, including Bill Coghill and Bruce Staser.

By the mid-1970s, I had moved up to a rating of GS-15, the highest level in the competitive civil service in Alaska, earning $40,000 a year. As comptroller, I handled management and finances and was responsible for two hundred employees and a $300 million budget. I had two years in uniform and fourteen years in the civil service toward a federal retirement. By all the measures I had set for myself, I had made it: at thirty-eight, I was at the top of the ladder. But when I looked around, I didn't feel what I had expected to feel. A stellar civilian career in the military had left me with a folder full of promotions and positive work reviews, documented management savings of $18 million, and even the military's second highest civilian honor. But those were just pieces of paper. Now that I had received them, they seemed less valuable than when I was competing for them. Whatever it was that I had expected for my years of striving, it wasn't there when I arrived at the top of my field.

Despite my dissatisfaction, however, anxiety about financial security remained in the lingering shadow of my father's early death. That uneasiness might have tied me to Fort Rich if not for the ROSE project—no relation!—that stood for Restructuring of Overseas Elements. Army installations in Alaska enjoyed a privileged status as an overseas posting, with foreign duty pay for soldiers and a 25 percent cost-of-living allowance for civilians. We had our own polar bear insignia and independent command structure. The ROSE project was a massive management review—with the outcome probably predetermined by the Pentagon—seeking more efficient management with a different arrangement of players. I worked on this project for two years. When we finished in 1975, the brass concluded that the army could operate better with its Alaska assets commanded from outside the state. In addition to a reduction of personnel, the polar bear would be retired. I served on a team to recommend which jobs to eliminate or transfer. We identified 3,500 positions, and one of them was my own. Alaska no longer needed a civil service worker at my level; instead, some responsibilities could be transferred and the rest given to a colonel at Fort Rich. By applying the analytic skills the army had given me, I worked myself out of a job.

No other GS-15 civil service position was available in Alaska, yet it made no sense to leave Alaska. We loved the place and at that time I had a promising political career. That left two options, each appealing to a different part of my personality. I could drop down to my previous job as chief of management analysis and deputy comptroller, taking a reduction from a GS-14 to a GS-13. That option would feed my hunger for security, but it would be a discouraging reversal of my career. Or I could leave the military and look for a new career. That option would feed my ambition and competitiveness. In November 1975, unification of the city and borough had been approved and I was chairman of the Anchorage Assembly and president of the Alaska Municipal League. Moving backward seemed unreasonable. Still, I was nervous about throwing myself into the private sector and squandering the seniority, employment record, and job skills I had established in the military.

Fran made the difference—as she did when we decided to marry, when we chose to live in Alaska, and when she gave up an opportunity to work at the Smithsonian. Fran told me not to worry. Wayne Hussey had left the continuing-education program when his hard living had caught up with him and Fran had become director, responsible for bringing in the money that kept the program alive through grants from and contracts with the departments of labor, education and health and social services, the Alaska Psychiatric Institute, and the jails. Fran and her program were thriving. She said I should not act hastily. She would support the family for a year while I took all the time I needed to find a great job that would lead to a new career. I accepted her advice and offer, which I believe changed the course of our lives.

My break was much shorter than a year. When a newspaper article revealed that I had analyzed myself out of a job, the phone began ringing with job offers. One came from Norm Levesque, who had been both the city and borough finance director during my time in office, and who had been appointed to the board of directors of the Alaska Municipal Bond Bank Authority. I had helped lobby the legislature earlier that year for the creation of the bond bank—an entity that would help small local governments obtain funding for capital improvements. Eric Wohlforth, Alaska's leading bond attorney, had initiated the idea, traveling in 1974 with Levesque to Maine and Vermont, two states that had bond banks, to find out how one could be started in Alaska. Legislation creating Alaska's bond bank passed in 1975. The bank was given a board, but had no employees, no office, no accounts, no files, and no assets. It was a blank slate. The opportunity to be the bank's first executive director, to create the organization from scratch, was tremendously appealing. My unemployment lasted two days.

The bond bank would help local governments borrow money on the bond markets. A bond issue is a large loan borrowed from many investors rather than from a single creditor. When an investor buys a bond, he or she is lending the bond's face value to the issuer in exchange for the issuer's promise to repay at a set rate of interest. Bond investors rely on private firms called rating agencies to study bond issues and determine the ability of the borrower to repay the loan. The three rating agencies—Standard & Poors, Moody's, and Fitch—evaluate the financial solvency of the borrower, how the bond issue is structured, and all the details that help predict the quality of the debt. Based on that information, each bond is given a grade. A better grade means a lower interest rate is established by the market, as investors are willing to accept a lower rate of return if they know their money is safe.

Chief financial officers of towns around Alaska—organized by the Alaska Municipal League—had a particular need for the bond bank. Their local governments had the wherewithal to borrow and repay loans for schools, roads, and other public facilities, but they couldn't sell bonds because their communities were small, their finances were unsophisticated, or they had no credit history. Some of the proposed bond issues were too small and needed to be consolidated with other borrowing to make sense. Juneau had lost its good credit due to the many years of discussion of moving the state capital, a move that had the potential to devastate the city's economy and bankrupt its government. Other communities were unattractive to rating agencies because they were remote and obscure, their books might not be professionally kept or audited, or they didn't have enough cash in reserve. Typically, bond-rating agencies required the borrower to keep a reserve account equal to a year's worth of debt payments to assure that payments would always be made on time.

The great idea behind the bond bank was to use a little of the state's wealth and solidity to bolster the credit ratings of local governments. We sold bonds on the public markets and then used those proceeds to buy bonds issued by the cities and towns. The legislature provided a few million dollars as start-up cash to use as reserves. The reserve would never be spent, but would spin off enough interest to cover our expenses, thus making our agency self-supporting. To assure that local governments would repay their debts, the bond bank received a pledge of "full faith and credit"—meaning local taxes would be levied if necessary to make the loan payments and the bond bank had the authority to seize a municipality's state revenue-sharing payments. The statute also allowed the bank to ask the state government for help to reconstitute the reserves if a local government ran out of money, could not repay a debt, and forced use of the reserve account to make the payments. This so-called "moral-obligation pledge" of the state was the brain child of New York attorney John Mitchell, who later became President Richard Nixon's attorney general and a central figure in the Watergate scandal. The bond bank established the financial controls, stability, and reputation to make rating agencies happy.

I set up shop on a shoestring in a tiny office. The room was part of a real-estate office where the secretary would answer the phone differently depending on which line rang—either "Globe Real Estate" or "Alaska Municipal Bond Bank Authority." Yet, from this modest base we soon helped finance hospitals in Sitka, Ketchikan, and the Kenai Peninsula, roads in Sitka, electric lines in Seward, and many other projects. Making deals happen often took creativity and a willingness to work the system. Government grants and loan guarantees were used in combination with our bond sales to bring in more money or lower interest rates. Federal and state bureaucrats responsible for these programs were only too glad to give their money away because successful projects bolstered their reason to exist. For example, the Aleutian community of Unalaska wanted to add four classrooms and a swimming pool to a school. The town had the borrowing capacity for the classrooms, but not for the pool. However, grant funds were available for firefighting facilities, so we designed the project to use the pool as a reservoir for the fire department's pumper trucks. The town got all the money it needed. Nome wanted a library and a firehouse. We borrowed money by combining the two on different floors of the same building. The librarian covered the fire house in emergencies. Meanwhile, Bethel couldn't afford a new city hall. But we made it possible by financing a building that would house a state courthouse. Lease payments from the state covered the debt payments, and the community installed its new city hall—without cost—in space remaining in the building.

My job was to bridge two worlds—the gravel streets of remote small towns in Alaska and the concrete canyons of Wall Street. I enjoyed visiting friendly little communities around Alaska and traveling to financial capitals such as New York and San Francisco, where we closed our bond sales. Local elected officials were ordinary people volunteering to serve their communities. They needed to learn the basics of the bond world to get comfortable with technical, fifty-page city council resolutions and, at closings, walking around a table signing as many as twenty-five different legal documents in quick succession. For each side in these transactions, the most important asset the bond bank brought to the table was trust.

The idea worked. To this day, the bank has remained a solid institution without a single default. Within two years of its founding, the bank started paying dividends back to the state. No more state appropriations supporting the bank were needed after 1987. By 2005 the bond bank had paid back to the state $26.2 million in dividends, surpassing state appropriations totaling $18.6 million—a profit of $7.6 million. The bank remained healthy and self-sustaining with $50 million in reserves, an active program of new borrowing, and more than $350 million in bonds outstanding.

The job built my confidence as well as my experience. Being the sole employee of the bond bank meant I could arrange my hours as I saw fit. That flexibility let me manage my busy life. The first year there coincided with my service as chairman of the assembly, president of the Alaska Municipal League, a leader of my religious congregation, and my heavy involvement in securities and real-estate investments.

Fran was busy, too. She had been active in Democratic politics since working on Governor Egan's successful 1970 campaign. Egan appointed her to the Advisory Council on Career and Vocational Education, where she served for ten years, part of that time as chair. The council drafted a statewide vocational education plan. Besides running the adult-education program in Anchorage, Fran traveled to small communities to train other teachers to deliver adult education. She made many friends and learned a lot about Alaska, later building a career as a city manager for rural Alaska villages.

In 1976, in the midst of her work and the equal-rights debate in Anchorage, Fran decided to run for the State House on a frankly liberal, slow-growth platform. She refused my help, but found she didn't enjoy campaigning herself. The district included the conservative and rural Eagle River area, where door knocking turned into long-distance hiking. Fran credited the experience with losing fifteen pounds. It also revealed the natural talent of our younger son, Mitch, who was then ten. Mitch, too young to leave at home, knocked on doors at Fran's side, and often his charm upstaged the candidate, his mother. After a visit, walking to the next house, Mitch would critique Fran's performance. Fran lost the primary by twelve votes to another Democrat, who then lost to the Republican candidate in the general election. Mitch, however, went on to build a great career from his personality and political skills. While still in school, he was a state debate champion. As an adult, he served as chief of staff to U.S. Senator Ted Stevens, and also served as an aide to Senators Robert Dole and Frank Murkowski and to Representative Don Young. He worked as a lobbyist for the Walt Disney Company and started his own lobbying firm in Washington, D.C., in 2006.

In addition to everything else, Fran and I had started a business in 1976. One Saturday night we were sitting in front of the fireplace at Tony and Susan Knowles' log house near downtown when Tony asked me, "What do you want to do when you grow up?" We didn't socialize much with other politicians, but Tony and Susan were different—smart and well educated, attractive, young, fun, and obviously going somewhere. Tony and I often disagreed as members of the assembly. He tended to be well to my left. When I voted against an ordinance he sponsored to require small parks be included with every new subdivision—I believed the idea was impractical—Tony felt betrayed and angry. For my part, I didn't believe Tony was sufficiently committed to the political work of finding compromises needed to keep the body moving forward—he was too willing to just show up and vote. Yet, as friends, we agreed to set politics aside.

When Tony asked what I really wanted to do, I immediately answered that I wanted to run a real, New York-style kosher delicatessen. Fran's eyes lit up as she described a perfect deli, what kind of food you would sell, and how you would prepare and serve it. Susan became excited, too, amplifying what Fran had said. Tony loved the idea, although he knew how hard it was to be successful in the restaurant business. He owned a couple of burger joints called Grizzly Burger (the name always made me think of gristle, unfortunately). Tony talked about the profit margins and turnover we would need to make money. We all added details to the dream.

In March 1976, I noticed that a sporting goods shop on Fourth Avenue was going out of business. I struck a deal with the landlord of Two-Wheel Taxi and Ski to lease the space. The location was perfect, across from city hall in the heart of downtown. I lined up financing and we began planning the menu and hiring contractors to remodel the space. Tony and I put paper on the floor to represent tables and booths while Fran and Susan walked around with trays pretending to be waitresses. Tony and I flew to San Francisco to get first-hand advice from the owners of several famous delis. Anchorage dining at that time was basic—small-town diners, hamburger stands, steak houses, Italian family restaurants, or the better restaurants inside the hotels. Our deli would be something new.

My mother was highly skeptical of our idea. "A kosher deli in Alaska?" she wrote, pointing out that ever fewer delis were left, even in New York. "That doesn't mean that Anchorage couldn't become famous for its kosher delicatessen, but how many Jews are there?" Once we got started and she saw the menu, her reaction was shock. "I have shown the deli menu to everyone who asks about you," she wrote. "All express the same surprise at the prices and the items offered. After all, even at the crazy prices here, ninety cents for a bagel is pretty fancy."

We did adjust the menu, but not because of the prices. Anchorage residents didn't know what to make of kosher food. We offered more choices, leaner food, and even ham. Our restaurant, The Downtown Deli, became the "in" gathering place for politically active people. Tony and I didn't encourage a political atmosphere, it just happened. People were hungry for an intellectual scene. We sold the Sunday *New York Times*—Mom helped line that up—for $5 a copy. On days when the paper didn't miss the plane or end up in the wrong city, customers spent Sunday afternoon reading it and asking one another for help with the crossword puzzle. Each week, when the assembly agenda came out in the Anchorage newspapers, people would gather at the deli to talk about what was coming. The day after the assembly meetings, they came to kibitz about our decisions. We ran an ad campaign using local celebrities. One with a picture of the irascible newsman Herb Shandlin said, "You don't have to be a nice guy to enjoy the Downtown Deli." One with Mayor Sullivan showed George hiding from the camera with the collar of his coat turned up under the headline, "You don't have to love both owners to enjoy the Downtown Deli."

We made a practice of hiring street people, alcoholics, drug addicts, starving artists, and gays. Our staff became a family—employees looking out for one another and fighting addictions together. They also performed as a team that gave great service. One of the best rewards of our twenty-eight years of owning the restaurant was seeing many of the people whom we gave a chance becoming successful on their own. We got a nice tax deduction for hiring them, too.

Those were wild years in Anchorage. The pipeline was under construction. The city was bursting with high-paid and uninhibited construction workers. Numerous strip joints materialized in downtown Anchorage. Reporter Don Hunter remembers attending a candidate forum for an assembly election in a gay bar that was downstairs from a topless club, listening to conservative incumbent Fred Chiei wisecracking through the evening with off-color jokes. Don, just arrived from North Carolina, could only wonder what alternate universe he had stepped into.

The freewheeling real-estate market put me in the position to buy an apartment building that turned out to have a certain clientele without my finding out in advance. I made the deal over dinner one evening at Bob Gillam's house. Bob was my stock broker, and later became owner of his own investment company. Previously we had formed a real-estate partnership in which we sold a choice commercial lot to the city's most notorious operator, Pete Zamarello, and were paid in cash. At Bob's dinner party, Vern Padgett was pushing to sell an apartment building with nine three-bedroom units in the low-rent Fairview neighborhood. Vern said the owner, a well-known gambler, was highly motivated to sell because his legs were going to be broken in twenty-four hours if he didn't come up with $10,000. I drove by the place. It looked all right to me, so I put down $10,000 and Vern financed the rest. In addition to being a real-estate agent, he was also an officer at Home Federal Savings and Loan (one of the many Alaska banks and S&Ls to go under in the real-estate crash of the 1980s). When I visited the manager of my new building, a guy named Sam, I found his office full of children. Who were they? With a wink, Sam replied that the kids' mothers were "tenants," and that they were all busy "working." I didn't get it. Sam winked again and bragged about all the money we were making on the coin-operated laundry in the basement, where the working ladies constantly washed their linens. I finally got it. As an elected official, I didn't want to spend any more time there than I had to, so I sent my son Evan to check up on the place and collect the rents (which never added up) or my campaign spokesman, Pete Carran, or a friend of Pete's. Fran didn't like the arrangement, and I managed to sell the place for a good profit.

My former whorehouse makes for a good after-dinner story, one told many times, because it perfectly illustrates the social and economic tenor of those times. Alaska had a booming economy in the late 1970s and early 1980s, especially in Anchorage, with money flowing more easily than anyone ever imagined possible, financial institutions acting as crazy as college students on spring break, and few sober citizens giving serious thought to the hangover that inevitably would follow such a wild party. The pipeline was finished in 1977. Thanks to OPEC, the Organization of Petroleum Exporting Countries, oil prices had more than quadrupled in inflation-adjusted dollars since the project was conceived. A year later, when Iran deposed its Shah and students took hostages at the U.S. embassy in Tehran, prices doubled again, eventually reaching a high that equates to $86 a barrel in 2005 dollars, ten times higher than expected following discovery of oil on the North Slope. Money gushed into the state treasury at an inconceivable rate, and everyone with a cockeyed dream scrambled to get a piece of the action. Many did, often with disastrous results.

Alaska wasn't the first government to face the challenge of sudden oil wealth. The question we faced was whether we would be the first to survive the challenge with a significant portion of our wealth intact.

---

[1]Scott Goldsmith, personal communication; Institute of Social and Economic Research, University of Alaska Anchorage, *UA Policy Brief: The Natural Gas Pipeline—What's It All About?* November 2005, http://www.iser.uaa.alaska.edu/ Publications/revisedgaspipeline.pdf.

Edward Rose, shown here in 1938 with Dave and Dave's sister, Amy, was a successful printer, owning a small envelope factory at the time of death in 1946.

Dave with the family dog, MacTwiggle.

Dave's sister, Amy, mother Marion, and Dave at the family's summer home, which they called Rosebrook, near the upstate New York community of Lanesville in 1948.

In 1967, the army sent Dave to get a Master of Business degree at Syracuse University. Fran, Evan, and Mitch joined Dave for his fourteen months in Syracuse.

Weary of mowing their four-acre lawn at Rosebrook, a two-day task with a push mower, Dave negotiated a deal with his mom that earned him a power mower.

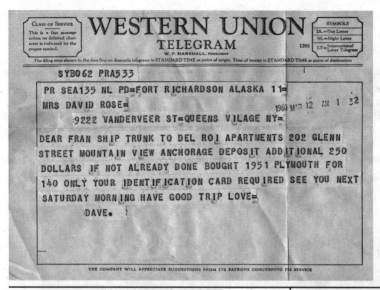

The army sent
Dave to Fort
Richardson in
1960. Dave
liked it, and
asked Fran to
follow. She did
and fell in love
with Alaska, too.

Dave served on the Anchorage City Council
from 1970 until 1975, when the city and
borough unified.

Dave Rose, 1970
*Anchorage Times/ Copyright
©1970 Anchorage Daily News
archive*

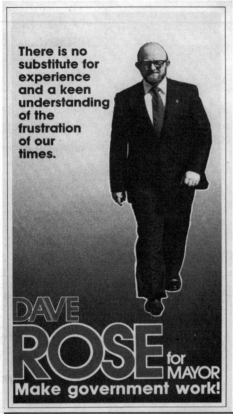

There is no substitute for experience and a keen understanding of the frustration of our times.

DAVE ROSE for MAYOR
Make government work!

Dave placed a close second in the 1978 Anchorage mayoral election, forcing a runoff with incumbent George Sullivan, who was re-elected.

The *Alaska Advocate* shot this playful photo of Dave for a profile during the 1978 mayoral campaign.
Ken Roberts/Alaska Advocate

On the Anchorage Assembly, Dave often found himself a deal-maker between political opposites such as conservative Fred Chei and liberal Lidia Selkregg.
Copyright ©1980 Marc Olson /Anchorage Daily News

In this scene from his TV commercial, Dave had fun spoofing another candidate's commercial in his final run for office, an unsuccessful bid for lieutenant governor in 1982.

Mitch, Fran, Dave, and Evan Rose on a family vacation. Mitch owns a lobbying firm in Washington, D.C. specializing in telecommunications issues. Evan is CEO of Alaska Permanent Capital Management.

Dave dressed as Ben Franklin and Fran as Betsy Ross for Juneau's Independence Day celebration in 1986.

In the Permanent Fund's early years, the public paid close attention to market value fluctuations. *Anchorage Times* cartoonist Jerry Flu personified the issue with these scenes of Dave going up and down an elevator. *Copyright ©1984 and 1985 Anchorage Daily News*

As Alaska Permanent Fund director, Dave urged caution in the debate whether the state should bail out real-estate investors hurt in the economic crash of the late 1980s. *Erik Hill/Copyright ©1987 Anchorage Daily News*

Susan Knowles, Dave and Fran Rose, and Tony Knowles in the late 1980s. The two families started the Downtown Deli in 1976 when Dave and Tony were serving together on the Anchorage Assembly.

For several years after opening the Downtown Deli, the owners occasionally worked in the kitchen, as Dave is seen doing here in 1980. *Copyright ©1980 Anchorage Daily News.*

Dave and Fran at Governor Tony Knowles' inauguration in 1994. Dave served as Knowles' transition chief.

Fran and Dave dressed for a St. Patrick's Day fundraiser for the American Diabetes Association in 2003.
Doug Ogden/ AutoGraphs Photography

Jay Hammond, left, governor from 1974 to 1982, and Clark Gruening, a member of the state house of representatives from 1974 to 1978, were key figures in the successful effort to enshrine the Alaska Permanent Fund in the state's constitution in 1976.

In 1996, the founders, former trustees, staff, and investment advisors of the Alaska Permanent Fund gathered to share memories of the institution that had, by then, become a fixture of Alaska life. From left are Bill Price, Charlie Parr, Dave Rose, Jay Hammond, and Byron Mallott.

Kidney failure required Dave to undergo lengthy dialysis sessions three times a week. For Easter 1998, Dave lightened the grim mood at the dialysis center in Anchorage by showing up dressed as a bunny rabbit.

Dave received an honorary doctorate at the University of Alaska Anchorage in 1999. Regent Chancy Croft, left, and Chancellor Lee Gorsuch conferred the honor.
University of Alaska

PART II

THE ALASKA PERMANENT FUND

INTRODUCTION
The problem of wealth

H ow does a democracy save for the future? When democracy works, citizens speak for themselves, joining together voluntarily for community benefits they cannot achieve on their own. We hire police and build roads through government because we must band together to do so, but voters who approve those actions do so for their own good, not primarily to benefit others. A potential flaw in the system is that no one speaks for those who follow. Citizens may consider their own offspring in their decisions, but the community of the future has no voice. This includes many people who will move into the state. Borrowing in the name of the unborn is easy, but it would seem counterintuitive for people in possession of large collective resources to save their money for undetermined future purposes by unknown future people. Theory would suggest instead that, in a democracy, everyone would want a full share of the wealth right away, through collective possession of goods or just by dividing up the surplus.

Yet this is not what happened in Alaska when the bonanza of North Slope oil began to flow into the state's treasury. Instead, the multigenerational Alaska Permanent Fund gathered a significant portion of the wealth into investment accounts whose principal can never be spent. At this writing, those investments and their reinvested earnings represented an impressive one-third of all the money Alaska has received from oil and gas in the state's nearly fifty years of existence. Per capita, these savings amount to double the annual income of Alaska's residents.[1]

We were not the first to achieve such savings, but we were the first democracy to do so. Regimes controlled by a single person or a clique had succeeded in setting aside, at least for a time, large resource windfalls, just as a family is able to save for its own future needs. In Alaska, however, the body politic as a whole made the decision to transfer current receipts to future citizens. It's a decision that deserves examination, both to understand how it happened and to find out how it could be made to happen again.

Today, many Alaska leaders claim parentage of the permanent Ffund, and there is plenty of credit to go around. The truth is that no single person conceived the combination of institutions, laws, and policies that made possible creation and growth of the fund. A series of fortuitous events set the stage. A number of leaders took the time to learn about the opportunities of saving and the pitfalls of spending. New agencies took on the burden of meeting contemporary needs so citizens would be willing to allocate resources to future, unknown needs. At critical moments, people of principle stood firm against short-term greed. After the fund was created, its policies and success built trust and respect that helped keep it safe, as did the annual dividend paid to Alaskans from the fund's earnings, which was intended in part to build a public constituency for the fund. In the minds of many Alaskans, the dividend became what mattered and the much more important long-term savings in the principle of the fund was of little interest.

As the first executive director of the Alaska Permanent Fund Corporation, a position I held for a decade, I often have been asked to advise foreign governments how to use our model. In hindsight, it's not difficult to profile the policy structure that made the permanent fund successful, even to suggest how to make it better. The Alaska Permanent Fund is ready to be copied by other governments with large natural-resource incomes. It's important to remember, however, that the fund was created without any such model. Time, luck, and the contributions of many people built the fund before it became an institution that could survive independently. No one envisioned the final product until it was nearly complete. I think of the fund both as a money machine for preserving resources and as a historical lesson about political progress, each instructive in its own way.

Rather than pretend we knew what we were doing from the start, I have chosen to tell the story of the fund in parts. Chapter 8 covers the history of the fund's creation from Alaska Statehood to the 1976 passage of an amendment to the Alaska Constitution establishing its name and flow of dedicated revenue. Chapter 9 covers the critical period 1976-1980 when the state determined the long-term nature and makeup of the Fund. Chapter 10 covers the permanent fund dividend and legislation that put the fund in its final form, from 1980 to 1982. Chapters 11 and 12 discuss my primary role as executive director from 1982 to 1992 when the fund reached maturity as an institution. Chapter 13 discusses the lessons of Alaska's fund from an analytical perspective. Leaving aside how the fund came into existence, the chapter covers the qualities that made it a success to be emulated. Chapter 14 contains my conclusions and thoughts for the future.

---

[1]Scott Goldsmith, personal communications. Per capita income, $24,830; permanent fund per capita, $50,221 (based on $32,916,500,000 in the fund and population of 655,435).

CHAPTER 8
The will to save, 1959-1976

After Russian fur traders arrived in the middle of the eighteenth century, Alaska's primary basic industry became the export of natural resources—furs, fish, timber, minerals, oil. The population remained sparse and the economy small. In the fight for statehood in the 1940s and 1950s, proponents struggled to overcome the reasonable belief that Alaska lacked the economic resources to support its own government. Taxes on its residents weren't sufficient to finance far-flung services, infrastructure, and social development.

The potential solution arrived in 1957, with the discovery of oil on federal land on the Kenai Peninsula and the promise of the revenue oil could produce for a new state government. The Alaska Statehood Act, which became effective in January 1959, provided transitional funds to support the new state and granted it the right to select 103 million acres of land. Up to that point, the federal government owned virtually the entire 365 million acres of the former territory. The young state's land selections would become its endowment for fiscal survival.

The early years were tough for the new government, and for a time it appeared the statehood experiment might fail as transitional funds were spent and new revenues were slow to materialize. Governor Bill Egan kept the lights on with small oil-lease sales while at the same time working aggressively to build the state.[1] He launched the Alaska Marine Highway System ferries in 1963 by selling bonds that barely rated investment grade. The influx of reconstruction money after the 1964 Earthquake saved the day financially, but the state still lacked a clear fiscal path for the future.[2]

That same year, Alaska's first commissioner of natural resources, Phil Holdsworth, persuaded Egan to make the single most important decision in the state's history—to select 1.6 million acres near Prudhoe Bay as part of its land endowment from the federal government. Oil men long had expected a large discovery of oil to take place on the plain extending from the Brooks Range to the Arctic Ocean—a region known as the North Slope. They were keenly focused on the acreage Holdsworth claimed, bidding around $10 million for leases from the state.[3]

Oil producers paid the state of Alaska several ways. Companies competed for state oil leases by trying to offer the largest "bonus bids" in a sealed-bid auction. The winning bidder also made regular lease payments and, if the company found oil, delivered a portion of it to the state as a royalty, which the state then sold. In addition, the state levied various taxes: severance tax for removing the oil, property tax, and income tax.

In 1967 an exploratory well at Prudhoe Bay struck the biggest oil reservoir ever found in North America. In 1969 the state sold additional oil leases in the area. The state, estimating it would take in $11 million from the sale,[4] instead took in a staggering $900 million in bonus payments. Due to the high cost of losing even a single day's interest on the money, a jet was chartered at the end of the day to fly the checks south for deposit into the Bank of America.

In 1969, $900 million appeared to be a nearly infinite amount of money. The state's entire annual budget for fiscal year 1968 was a little more than $100 million. Investment advisors and other consultants rushed to the state with self-serving suggestions how to handle the money. For example, Lehman Brothers submitted a position paper recommending the entire $900 million be deposited into a capital-improvement fund invested in high-grade securities as backing for bond issues to finance public works. Debate began immediately about how to spend the windfall, or whether to save it and spend only the interest. Many of the assumptions used in those discussions turned out to be drastically inaccurate: In those years of oil selling for less than $2 a barrel, the state expected its annual petroleum revenues to peak at $234 million when oil started flowing from the North Slope. In fact, however, oil prices rose twenty-fold over the coming years, allowing the state in

1982 alone to spend more than $6.4 billion. But if the numbers were off, the concepts were right. Alaskans knew their state was changing, and their attitudes on how to handle the new riches depended in large part on whether they welcomed change and how they wished to direct it.

Representative Gene Guess, an Anchorage Democrat and chairman of the legislative council, hired the Brookings Institution to lead a one hundred-member Conference on the Future of Alaska in Anchorage in December 1969. The document they produced is a fascinating window on what Alaskans were thinking on the threshold of the era of Big Oil. Their fear balanced their optimism. Many Alaskans were apprehensive about change, including the loss of the frontier way of life. Yet their optimism aroused hope that oil money could help solve long-standing, previously intractable problems. At the Brookings conference, the optimists prevailed. Participants considered but discarded the concept of saving the initial $900 million in lease bonus payments. The state's needs were urgent—extreme rural poverty, inadequate or nonexistent schools and public facilities, and a lack of basic services. Discussions centered on how to invest in education, protect the environment, improve public health, and build the economy. One discussion group reported, "It is premature to set up trusts to handle state monies. Such trusts are probably not needed. Whether or not a trust (or trusts) is established for the control of the bonus monies, we must recognize that this generation is the present trustee for the future of Alaska."[5] Education seemed to be regarded as the best use of the new money, benefiting both the present and future.

A contrary trend in political thinking focused on apprehension about the money's impact on government. Representative Tom Fink, a Republican insurance agent from Anchorage, consistently opposed either saving the oil windfall or spending it on services. His priority was to prevent government growth. He saw the oil money as a problem as much as an opportunity. In 1969 Fink preferred paying off the state's debts and using the balance of the $900 million for infrastructure, capital projects in local communities, and economic-development loans. Above all, he wanted to keep the one-time windfall out of the state's operating budget, even while conceding that state government was so poor in the 1960s that it could not meet some legitimate needs. Philosophically,

Fink opposed any government investment account or even use of state assets to leverage debt for capital improvements.

"Government is not supposed to make money," Fink said. "Government is only supposed to do things that need to be done." He believed that surpluses inevitably would lead to wasteful spending—to this day, he still predicts that the Alaska Permanent Fund ultimately will meet that fate, warning, "If you have a big surplus, it's just an attractive nuisance like gambling or prostitution."[6]

Republican legislators such as Representative Clem Tillion and Senator Jay Hammond and Representative Earl Hillstrand, a Democrat, exemplified a different kind of conservatism. All three served long careers in the Capitol: Tillion from the seaside village of Halibut Cove, which he founded; Hillstrand from Anchorage, which he had represented in the territorial Legislature; and Hammond representing the rural Bristol Bay fishing region, and then serving as governor from 1974 to 1982. They considered Alaska's new oil income to be a resource to be conserved. Hammond liked to dabble in political philosophy and always was willing to advocate creative, unorthodox, and often complicated policy ideas. In the 1950s Hammond and Tillion had opposed statehood, Hammond preferring commonwealth status like Puerto Rico and Tillion favoring independence.

Tillion and Hillstrand predicted that spending oil money for large increases in government employment would bring salary and pension costs that could not be sustained in the long term. They regarded spending the windfall on unneeded capital projects as another form of waste. This conservationist form of conservatism, which extended to the development-versus-environment debate as well, led both Tillion and Hammond to a controlled-growth philosophy quite different from that of most conservatives. Spending the money, whether for operations or capital projects, could accelerate unwanted growth. Tillion recalls, "As Hammond used to say, to err on the side of conservation is easily corrected at a later date."[7]

Tillion remembers each of his late friends making his own contribution to the fund concept. He credited Hammond with conceiving of the dividend—a direct payment of fund income to residents—but says Hillstrand was the first one to advocate an investment trust to "soak up" oil dollars so they could not be appropriated rashly by the legislature. A Tillion-sponsored bill that passed the 1970 legislature included Hammond's and Hillstrand's ideas. It created a trust fund of $100 million whose earnings would be used to make direct payments to elderly Alaskans who had lived in Alaska at least twenty-five years. The concept bore several resemblances to the Permanent Fund and dividend program enacted into law a decade later, including the set-aside of oil income, the long-term endowment approach of the investments, and payments to Alaskans based on length of residency rather than need. The concept served Tillion, Hammond, and Hillstrand's goals by reducing wasteful growth as well as rewarding old-timers who remained in the state and alleviating the poverty of elderly Alaska Natives.

Hammond's first attempt to give resource money directly to residents had come years before when he was mayor of the Bristol Bay Borough. He had pushed an idea, shot down twice by voters, to issue all residents shares of stock in an entity called Bristol Bay Inc. The stock would pay as dividends the proceeds from a new tax on the bay's lucrative fishing industry. One of Hammond's favorite features of the plan was that the longer residents lived in the borough, the more stock and dividends they would receive. It may seem strange today, but the concept of giving greater benefits for longer residency was popular and ingrained in the Alaska of the 1960s and 1970s. The population had grown rapidly and lifestyles had modernized. Many believed that those who had come to Alaska and toughed out the early pioneer years deserved more from government than recent migrants who had contributed little to the state. Rapid social change, much of it negative in the eyes of long-time residents, probably added to the acceptance of a magnified entitlement for sourdoughs.

The preference for long-term residents reflected the fundamental philosophy behind the direct payments advocated by Hammond, Tillion, and Hillstrand. They believed Alaska's citizens deserved the money because, in effect, they owned the state's resources. Those who lived in the state longer had acquired a greater share of ownership. Freely distributing resource money also meant limiting government. Once resource money had been handed out to residents, the state would have to impose taxes to generate revenues, and the resistance of the taxpayers to the taxes would have the effect of checking the size of government.

Other leaders, especially statehood advocates such as Governor Walter Hickel, adamantly disagreed. Hickel believed Alaska's 103-million-acre land endowment belonged to the people only collectively through their government, not personally. He charged that direct payments were socialistic and corroded the community and the Alaskan spirit.[8] Hickel preferred, like Fink, to spend the money on capital projects or loans. It was no coincidence that this approach was strongly pro-development. Hammond and his allies countered that loan and construction programs were less fair and less efficient ways of distributing the wealth. As Hillstrand quipped, "Let's not feed the sparrows by feeding the horses first."[9]

Tillion maintains the direct-distribution concept was the true conservative path. "Tom Fink and some of those others were liberals because they'd spend the money recklessly on government, on support for cities, and stuff like that. They just wouldn't spend it on little old ladies. A true conservative wouldn't spend it on either. It's a very simple system, if you believe in it: The government shouldn't be bigger than the public is willing to pay for. And therefore give the money to the people and then you take back what they'll let you have (in taxes)."

I discussed this point at length with Hammond over the years, but we never agreed. The hidden problem with the Hammond-Tillion idea of imposing income taxes while continuing to pay the dividend, I believe, was that the state would put itself in the business of redistributing wealth. Today's dividend is a flat annual payment to everyone, regardless of income, but a fair system of taxation is progressive, taking a larger percentage of income from those with higher earnings. Suppose the state were to give a flat dividend while simultaneously taking residents' income with a progressive tax. Residents in higher income brackets likely would pay more tax than they received in dividends, while dividends paid to middle-and low-income Alaskans would exceed the amount of taxes they were paying. The result would be to take income from wealthier people and give it away to anyone who made less money, even if they did not need it.

Only a small percentage of dividends go to poor families. I don't object to paying taxes for needs-based programs that are designed carefully to alleviate poverty. I *do* object to paying taxes simply to spread my money around to anyone who wants some.

In 1970 these thoughts were far in the future, but the seeds of the debate had been planted. As it happened, however, little was saved at first. Governor Keith Miller vetoed Tillion's longevity bonus bill on the grounds that its twenty-five-year residency requirement was unconstitutional, as courts later found extraordinary residency requirements to be.[10] Miller introduced his own bill for a "resource permanent fund" to set aside about half of the $900 million bonus money and invest it safely in financial institutions outside the state. The bill passed the state Senate but was defeated in the House.[11] The reasons given for its defeat vary. Miller maintained House members opposed the bill because they wanted the money to be invested in Alaska banks, even though the banks said they couldn't handle so much cash at once.[12] Others blame the bill's failure on Miller's lack of political skill or the unwillingness of legislators to set aside the money before considering all options.[13] Some opinion polls said the public supported creating a savings account,[14] but in fact opinions were mixed and contradictory. The Anchorage Chamber of Commerce ran newspaper ads urging the Legislature to save the money while at the same time sending a representative to Juneau to ask for millions of dollars in new projects. [15]

In the end, the point of view that prevailed was that of the attendees of the Brookings Conference on the Future of Alaska. They believed that a poor state should invest in education and other public needs rather than in securities, and that is essentially what happened. The state increased its annual spending. Although the increases were not sustainable, the money was used on real needs identified at the time. About 65 percent of the windfall went into education.[16] Even Tom Fink admits the $900 million wasn't wasted. "Probably two-thirds of it was used well," he said. "That's probably as good as you can expect government to do."

In 1970 the Legislature increased the state budget from $168 million to more than $300 million. Investment earnings covered almost one-fourth of the total, and about $85 million of the 1969 bonus money was used for the rest.[17] With withdrawals at that rate, the state had a rational strategy to make the funds last. Construction of the trans-Alaska oil pipeline appeared to be just around the corner. The oil companies had bought the pipe and had started design work. Leaders expected the line to begin operating by 1973, pumping enough annual oil revenues into the treasury to sustain budget increases and to replace the $900 million.[18] The one-time lease bonus money had front-loaded new programs, but the budget would become sustainable when the oil began flowing.

State officials' belief that the $900 million was in some sense a permanent surplus is underlined by how they invested the money. The treasury bought $102 million in certificates of deposit from Alaska banks for terms of up to fourteen years. The goal of the program was to provide funds to loosen credit in Alaska, thus boosting the economy. The CDs carried an interest rate of 6.25 percent, compared to a 7.5 percent return the state was earning with its liquid investments, which were handled by the Bank of America.[19] However, when Alaska banks received the deposits, they didn't make more in-state loans. Instead, the banks sought the best investments available to them, which in many cases were the same high-grade securities the state otherwise would have bought itself. An analysis of the program later found no discernable impact on credit, lending, or economic activity in the state.[20] At the same time, the state loaned tens of millions of dollars directly to Alaskans, businesses, and local governments, and bought Alaska-based loans from lenders. Like the bank deposits, these subsidized loans blended socio-economic goals with the expectation of repayment and income to sustain the surplus for the long term.[21]

However, in 1971, just two years after the Prudhoe Bay lease sale, Commissioner of Revenue Eric Wohlforth and others recognized that the state was on a trajectory to run out of money. By the middle of the decade, the $900 million would be gone and a deficit yawning in its place. The state's reversal of fortune came simply because the pipeline was delayed. Rather than being operational in 1973, the most optimistic projection called for completion in 1975, and in fact the first oil did not flow until the summer of 1977. When industry executives had made their original predictions of a quick project, they had spoken from extraordinary naiveté about the pipeline's huge challenges related to engineering, environmental policy, and land ownership.[22] The revenue department's projections now showed that the state budget, rising with inflationary and salary increases, would require ever-larger withdrawals from the general fund surplus; those withdrawals, in turn, would diminish investment income, requiring an even larger withdrawal the following year. The spiral would dry up the remainder of the $900 million at an accelerating rate. These projections proved accurate. By fiscal year 1975, the state was drawing more than $200 million a year from its 1969 windfall to cover 40 percent of the budget. With the short-term investments depleted, the treasury started liquidating long-term assets such as its loans to Alaskans and extended certificates of deposit in Alaskan banks. The revenue department expected to run out of money within a year or two.[23]

How could seemingly infinite riches be gone in so short a time? The public believed the money had been squandered by crazy spending and mismanagement. Attention focused on issues such as a $6 million loss the state posted on stock market investments, even though the entire stock investment—mostly intact—had comprised just 3 percent of the original $900 million.[24] The *Anchorage Times* blamed legislators for giving themselves pensions and pay raises. "They ignored the fact that income would be inadequate to cover the expenditures, and made it inevitable that the $900 million nest egg would be dissipated by state programs that could be called 'high living,'" the *Times* editorialized.[25] Politicians joined in, denouncing the wasteful spending. Even knowledgeable leaders got on the bandwagon, including Governor Jay Hammond and House Finance Committee Chairman Hugh Malone. In 1976 Malone said, "What happened to the $900 million has given people a lot of food for thought. It's hard for people to point to worthwhile improvements in the state as a result of the expenditure of that money."[26]

Two decades later, Malone admitted that the legislature, in fact, had done a good job investing and spending the $900 million and that the perception that it was wasted resulted from exaggerated expectations.[27] But Malone's statements to the contrary served a purpose. The loss of the $900 million represented the most powerful exhibit in the case for creating a permanent fund.

Malone led a crop of bright, young Democratic legislators who took over state government in the early 1970s and who, over the next decade, guided the Permanent Fund from idea to institution. Malone himself was elected to represent the oil town of Kenai in 1972, the same year 22-year-old Terry Gardiner was elected to the House from the southeastern fishing town of Ketchikan. In 1974 a backlash against the Watergate scandal brought the rest of the Democratic advocates of a permanent fund into office, with Republicans elected to only nine seats in the forty-member House. Among the powerful and ambitious young Democrats were two attorneys, Clark Gruening (grandson of the late territorial governor and U.S. senator, Ernest Gruening) from Anchorage and Steve Cowper from Fairbanks. In that same election, Hammond, perceived as an outsider, had defeated the incumbent Egan to become governor. At least two gifted staffers added to the brain trust that worked on the Fund: Jim Rhode and Gregg Erickson.

Although politically similar, these leaders' personas ranged widely. Malone projected icy brilliance while Hammond dripped honey-thick folksiness. Gruening crisply articulated complex ideas while Cowper spoke in a country-western drawl to match his long sideburns. Rhode talked people's ears off with detailed policy considerations while Erickson effortlessly commanded the facts of the state budget and oil and gas revenues. But despite the differences, all shared qualities that allowed them to work together to bring a big idea to life. They breathed the idealism and indignant public spirit of the time. They possessed intellects capable of handling unconventional thinking, complex issues, and legislative politics. And they respected analysis and education and enjoyed philosophical policy debate.

Hammond was older and more seasoned in office than the House Democrats, but he shared their enthusiasm for public policy and thoughtful debate. Young Fran Ulmer directed Hammond's Division of Policy Development and Planning with a substantial staff dedicated exclusively to figuring out the right thing to do. They held meetings all over Alaska with the governor and his commissioners to hear ordinary citizens' views on creation of a permanent fund and other issues. Ulmer presented Hammond with detailed position papers with pro and con arguments. After reading these papers, the governor often called together experts, stakeholders, and administration officials with differing views. "Sometimes we would have this wonderful debate in the governor's office," Ulmer said. "Jay really enjoyed having the wide variety of opinions expressed in his administration and in his presence."

The Alaska Permanent Fund largely owes its existence and success to the care and wisdom of these leaders, who made a series of remarkably farsighted decisions. Unfortunately, such care in crafting public policy is far out of fashion in Juneau today, where majority legislators hold their substantive discussions in closed caucuses and deep study of issues is for wonks or do-gooders. At the birth of the permanent fund, the wonks had the power. "It's a different world in some ways," Ulmer said. "At one level, it's hard to believe the political world has changed as much as it has."

Hammond came into office in 1974 with his idea still foremost in mind to create a fund that would distribute income to the public as if residents were stockholders, which he now called Alaska Inc. rather than Bristol Bay Inc. After the public meetings around the state he introduced a bill to start the program. Half of all natural-resource income would go into the fund, with the income distributed to resident stockholders. Each year of residency would entitle Alaskans to an additional share, giving long-time residents more dividends. All stock would be forfeited if a resident moved out of Alaska. The idea was politically and legally complex and hardly seemed urgent to legislators. Hammond, new in office, may have lacked the political know-how to force his bill through. Alaska Inc. died a quick death of multiple committee referrals.[28]

Yet, while the idea of giving away money to the public didn't have much support, the political momentum to address the "waste" of the $900 million remained a potent force. As the new Legislature arrived in Juneau in January 1975, the pipeline was under construction, the Arab Oil Embargo had created gas-station lines around the country, and the price of oil had risen above $12 a barrel. As Hammond later wrote, "The scent of anticipated oil revenues hung like musk in the halls of the Legislature."

Some projections of the amount of future annual oil revenues far exceeded even the extravagant levels they actually achieved. (Projections of Alaska's future wealth have consistently missed the mark over the years, mostly because they tended to rely on the false assumption that current trends in oil prices and state spending would continue indefinitely.) As much as legislators may have salivated for the revenue that would arrive in a few years, however, in 1975 the treasury was nearly empty, silencing the constituency for spending that might otherwise have opposed creating a savings account. Legislators would pay little politically for setting aside revenue that didn't yet exist, while they could gain points for being fiscal conservatives by voting to create a permanent fund and "restoring" the wasted $900 million.[29] This unusual situation created a unique historical moment in which the Legislature in 1975 easily passed a bill to set aside 50 percent of mineral lease bonus bids—but not lease payments, royalties, or taxes—in an investment fund. Besides drastically reducing the amount set aside from Hammond's proposal, the bill did not provide for a dividend to residents.[30]

Hammond vetoed the bill. His stated reason at the time was an attorney general's opinion that the program would constitute an unconstitutional dedication of funds.[31] The authors of the Alaska Constitution had thought carefully before prohibiting dedicated funds. Their consultants said that revenue channeled to the priorities of past legislatures could eliminate the flexibility of contemporary leaders to deal with more urgent problems.[32] In truth, however, Hammond's veto rested on the opposite logic: He did not believe the bill passed by the Legislature would dedicate sufficient funds to prevent future raids. It was only a statute, and a future legislature could always change it.[33] For legislators such as Clark Gruening, on the other hand, that flexibility was a good thing. If the fund were to serve as a rainy-day account, providing revenue after the oil boom ended, the Legislature might need to be able to dip into its principal.[34]

Another feature of the 1975 legislation that was not controversial at the time may have been even more critical to whether the fund lasted, and was lost with the Hammond veto. The vetoed original version would have mandated the fund to invest in Alaska development projects and make loans to residents. The purpose section directed that the fund "be used for investment capital by Alaska residents." Gruening and Malone, who later became the staunchest champions of making the permanent fund a trust, invested safely for maximum return, at that time envisioned it as a vehicle to provide low-income mortgages, fund hydroelectric projects, boost agriculture and fishing projects, build capital projects, and "prime the economy." Gruening pointed to the state's subsidized mortgage loans to veterans as one of the best investments it had made after receiving the 1969 lease sale bonus money.[35] As we will see in the next chapter, such soft, in-state investments likely would have squandered the coming oil revenue far more egregiously than any "loss" of the $900 million.

In 1976 the Legislature and governor compromised to put a simple constitutional amendment before voters, which read in full:

> *ALASKA PERMANENT FUND. At least 25 percent of all mineral lease rentals, royalties, royalty sale proceeds, federal mineral revenue sharing payments and bonuses received by the state shall be placed in a permanent fund, the principal of which shall be used only for those income producing investments specifically designated by law as eligible for permanent fund investments. All income from the permanent fund shall be deposited in the general fund unless otherwise provided by law.*

The simplicity and vagueness of the amendment were intentional. Hammond didn't get his dividend, but he could fight for that later because the amendment said nothing about how the fund's income would be used. The amendment didn't promise the fund as much money as the governor and House wanted, as it excluded oil taxes. But at the insistence of the House, where Malone chaired the Finance Committee, it did include the words "at least" before the 25 percent allocation, setting the stage later for large additional deposits.[36] (Because the Senate excluded taxes from the fund's automatic allocation, the minimum contribution amounted to 10 or 11 percent of all state oil revenue.)[37]

The nature of the "income-producing investments" might be anything the Legislature would later designate, leaving open the possibility that the fund's principal could be used for any kind of loan, toll bridge or highway, energy project, or economy-boosting industrial scheme concocted by business and political insiders. Some also saw the fund's "investments" as a means of providing money for health, education, and social needs, including such things as day-care centers.[38] Others imagined the fund's being used as a tool to shorten swings in the economy or to function as a state version of the Federal Reserve for Alaska, smoothing the business cycle by manipulating interest rates.[39]

Malone, Gruening, and Hammond encouraged extravagant and sometimes conflicting expectations about what the Fund could do.[40] In order to be added to the constitution, the amendment needed a two-thirds majority in the Legislature and voter approval in the 1976 general election. With the strategy of leaving so much about the fund open-ended, sponsors were able to gather support from all parts of the political spectrum. They deferred the hardest decisions and encouraged everyone to vote for the fund of his or her own dreams—even if the dreams were contradictory.[41]

The public debate, however, focused mainly on the savings aspect of the fund. Tom Fink wrote an opinion column and the official voter pamphlet essay in opposition, largely using the same argument he had put forward in 1970—the government should never keep money it doesn't need. He preferred to pay off debts, repeal taxes, and spend on capital projects, including paying cash to build a new capital city away from Juneau.[42] In the Legislature, Senator John Rader was a lonely voice in opposition. An Anchorage Democrat who had served either as a legislator or as attorney general since statehood, Rader's arguments recalled the reasoning of the drafters of the constitution. Rather than opposing savings as such, he objected to creating a savings entity separate from the workings of the democratic system of government. Rader told a reporter, "Most public policy positions have two sides, but this idea has no redeeming merit. Every state that has ever done it has ended up regretting it....How can we know what percentage of income should go into savings if we don't know what other state needs there will be in the future? ... Everyone says the Legislature is spendthrift, so this idea of a permanent fund looks attractive. But they must elect another Legislature if they want to solve the problem of overspending."[43]

In the days leading up to the election, the *Anchorage Times* also raised concerns but not outright opposition. An editorial cited fears the fund would absorb money that publisher Bob Atwood preferred to spend on two mega projects—building a new capital city and bridging Knik Arm from Anchorage to the Matanuska-Susitna Borough.[44] Ironically, the same editorial page twelve months earlier had favored creating a fund, predicting at the time that the idea "will be trampled to death under the stampeding feet of elected politicians running around looking for money to spend on their high-living programs."[45] The *Times* had discovered it liked the permanent fund better in the abstract than in reality, but by the time the paper changed its tune it was too late. The public had accepted the notion that the money from the $900 million lease sale had been wasted and that the fund would rectify the mistake. Jay Hammond himself used that trump card in an opinion piece in the *Times* six days before the election, writing that, "There are, of course, several other reasons to support the Permanent Fund, but off the top of my head, at the moment, I can only think of 900 million!"

On November 2, 1976, Alaska voters approved Proposition 2, the constitutional amendment creating the Alaska Permanent Fund, with a positive vote of 66 percent.[46] But the work had hardly begun. The amendment did little more than divert a flow of revenue. The new fund lacked an institution to preserve its assets, or a mandate to manage the money as an inviolate trust. Without those protections in place, oil income of the future was little safer than it had been before the vote. And in 1976, few people in Alaska politics believed that the permanent fund should be invested prudently, as they would invest their own long-term savings. Instead, most thought they had created a fund for making subsidized loans to constituents and paying for large development projects. The story of how those presumptions changed is the true tale of the creation of the Alaska Permanent Fund. As we shall see, the study, debate, and power politics required to get there took four more tumultuous years.

---

[1]Jack Roderick, Crude Dreams (Fairbanks and Seattle: Epicenter Press, 1997).

[2]Eric Wohlforth, interview by Charles Wohlforth, digital recording, December 23, 2005.

[3]Roderick, 183-189 (leases); 167-172 (selection).

[4]State of Alaska Department of Revenue, *What's Happening to Alaska's Money,* brochure, April 1971, 17.

[5]The Legislative Council of the State of Alaska in association with The Brookings Institution, "A Conference on the Future of Alaska," seminar 1, "The Financial Foundations for Future Alaska, Reports of Policy Planning Sections," typescript document, 1969, statement of Delta Group, part 1.

[6]Tom Fink, interview by Charles Wohlforth, digital recording, January 4, 2006.

[7]Clem Tillion, interview by Charles Wohlforth, digital recording, December 28, 2005; Jay Hammond, *Tales of Alaska's Bush Rat Governor* (Fairbanks and Seattle: Epicenter Press, 1994), 124.

[8]Walter J. Hickel, *Crisis in the Commons: The Alaska Solution* (Oakland: Institute for Contemporary Studies, 2002), 177-179.

[9]Tillion interview.

[10]Keith Miller as told to Joseph Edward Maynard, *Prudhoe Bay Governor: Alaska's Keith Miller* (Anchorage: self-published, 1997), 217.

[11]Sheila F. Helgath and Sarah A. Babb, *Alaska's Permanent Fund: Legislative History, Intent, and Operations,* Alaska State Senate, Rural Research Agency, January 1986, 3.

[12]Miller, 218.

[13]Fink interview.

[14]*The Anchorage Times,* November 16, 1975.

[15]Fink interview.

[16]Kay Brown, *The Anchorage Times,* November 21, 1976.

[17]Alaska Dept. of Revenue brochure, 6-7.

[18]State of Alaska Department of Revenue, *Alaska '75: Facing the Crunch,* brochure, May 1975, 3.

[19]Scott Goldsmith and others, *The Permanent Fund and the Growth of the Alaskan Economy: Selected Studies,* report for the House Special Committee on the Alaska Permanent Fund, Institute for Social and Economic Research, University of Alaska Anchorage, December 15, 1977, IV-11 and 32.

[20]Goldsmith and others, xx-xxi, IV-17, 35.

[21]Goldsmith and others, IV-16.

[22]Roderick; Hickel.

[23]Alaska Dept. of Revenue brochure, May 1975, 4-7.

[24]Brown.

[25]Editorial, *The Anchorage Times,* November 16, 1975.

[26]Brown.

[27]Hugh Malone, interview by Nancy Gross, transcript, circa 2000, 6-7.

[28]Hammond, 247-248.

[29]Clark Gruening, interview by Charles Wohlforth, digital recording, December 27, 2005; Editorial, *The Anchorage Times,* November 16, 1975.

[30]Committee Substitute for HB 324 as amended by the Senate, 1975.

[31]Susan Andrews, *The Anchorage Times,* December 27, 1975.

[32]Helgath and Babb, 41.

[33]Hammond, 248.

[34]Andrews.

[35]Ibid.

[36]Gruening interview.

[37]Helgath and Babb, 5.

[38]Susan Andrews, *The Anchorage Times,* October 24, 1976.

[39]John Havelock, *Anchorage Daily News,* November 24, 1976.

[40]As to Malone: Andrews, October 24, 1976; as to Gruening: his opinion column in *Anchorage Daily News,* March 10, 1975; as to Hammond: his opinion column in *The Anchorage Times,* October 27, 1976.

[41]Gruening interview.

[42]Tom Fink, *The Anchorage Times,* January 25, 1976.

[43]Andrews, December 27, 1975.

[44]Editorial, *The Anchorage Times,* October 24, 1976.

[45]Editorial, *The Anchorage Times,* November 16, 1975.

[46]Alaska Division of Elections. The vote was 75,588 to 38,518.

CHAPTER 9
Fight for the fund, 1976-1980

I n the fall of 1976, soon after he was reelected to the state House for a second term, Clark Gruening received a phone call from Elmer Rasmuson inviting him to lunch. Rasmuson, a man of broad interests and legendary intellect, was a former mayor of Anchorage and the 1968 Republican nominee for the U.S. Senate. His most important accomplishment was building Alaska's largest bank, National Bank of Alaska, which his father had founded in 1916. When Rasmuson died in 2000, U.S. Senator Ted Stevens—who had lost to him in the 1968 primary—said "Elmer was the most talented man I ever knew."[1] Rasmuson was also among the richest and most intimidating men in Alaska. When I was executive director of the permanent fund I went to see him quarterly for a one-hour meeting. The discussions consisted of my listening for fifty-five minutes and thanking Elmer for his advice for the other five, but I gladly endured the lectures in exchange for his knowledge and insight. When he invited Gruening to lunch in 1976, Rasmuson knew that Gruening, who was half his age, would be a key figure in determining the purpose of the new permanent fund. Clark didn't know what to expect. He arrived at the bank and was seated in the opulent board room, where lunch was served to the two men. They were alone.

"He did most of the talking and I did most of the listening," Gruening recalls. "I was resisting it, but I wanted to hear this man, who, certainly in the financial world, knew more probably than I'll ever know. But he certainly had a point of view that I had to respect.... The world of investment is pretty complicated, but it has some simple concepts, and what Elmer was talking to me about was the 'prudent-man rule.'"[2]

Simply stated, the rule requires those who invest on behalf of others to seek the highest-available returns consistent with preserving the safety of the investment. Outside considerations beyond the benefit of the fund itself should not enter into investment decisions. Rasmuson was starting the process of separating spending from investing, pointing out that they are contradictory goals. Low-interest loans for residents or for construction of big projects to develop the economy would not live up to the prudent-man rule (also known as the prudent-investor rule), because they weren't the safest or most profitable investments available.

Rasmuson had similar conversations with Senator Clem Tillion, who also would play an important role in developing the fund. As Tillion recalls, "Rasmuson said, 'You never loan money to somebody who has to have it. You only loan money to people who will use it as a tool to make more money.' Elmer was the guy who said, 'If you make it a loan fund, never loan money to someone you cannot collect on—that you're not willing to utterly destroy them in order to get your money back.'"[3]

Gruening, Tillion, and others came to realize it would be impossible for elected officials or those they oversaw to be tough enough to fulfill the role of prudent investors if they were expected to make loans to constituents. "I could see a real problem of how we were going to protect the investments from political judgments," Gruening said. "You had the chamber [of commerce] and a lot of special interests wanting the loans and pushing for them. 'You've got to get that money out.' At the same time, I could see, 'OK, Elmer's in the business, he should know better.' I could also see the argument, 'How do we administer this? Are we going to let the Legislature administer this? Are we going to let the executive?'"

Besides the risk of politicians making bad loans, some worried that such a huge public bank could become the dominant player in the Alaska economy. Whichever branch of government had control—or if the fund became independent—there would be repercussions in choosing who would hold so much power. The same year the constitutional amendment was adopted, delegates to the original Alaska Constitutional Convention held a twenty-year reunion in Fairbanks and discussed the issues. Some worried that the permanent fund could rupture the system of the three branches of government. The balance of power could tip toward the branch that managed the fund. Or, as appeared more likely, if management were vested with an independent body, those who controlled that agency would become the equivalent of a fourth branch of government.[4]

While these concepts were developing slowly, however, action was moving fast to set up the permanent fund as a development bank to provide private loans and capital for big projects. Hammond assigned the state's Investment Advisory Committee to draft a bill in time for the start of the legislative session the following January, work that was well underway the same week the voters approved the constitutional amendment.[5] The committee was chaired by Eric Wohlforth, who at that time was in private practice as a bond attorney, and included members from a wide range of backgrounds, including Gruening, Anchorage bike-trail advocate Lanie Fleischer, and Republican activist and mortgage broker Jim Crawford. The hearings and meetings became so lively that the staff stopped announcing them publicly to reduce the urge for "grandstanding."

The committee didn't seriously consider making the permanent fund purely a "prudent-investor" savings account, because it appeared from legislative and public sentiment that the decision already had been made in favor of using it as a bank for loans and financing of capital projects. However, they did talk in depth about how to avoid politically motivated lending. Wohlforth suggested using the fund to underwrite loans by other semi-autonomous state entities such as the Alaska Industrial Development Authority, which already existed in state statutes but never had been used.[6] The legislation that the committee drafted and the governor introduced proposed a governance structure with three levels of management—two committees and a staff—to insulate lending from politics. The fund would place at least 40 percent of its assets in investment-grade securities—the "prudent man" savings account—while up to 30 percent could go to development loans and 30 percent to community-development projects and housing.[7] Although the bill would put 60 percent of the fund at risk in soft Alaska-based loans, observers considered it a conservative approach compared to what most had expected.[8] The proposal had the support of bankers, chambers of commerce, and liberal activists such as Jamie Love, a member of the committee and founder of the Ralph Nader-inspired Alaska Public Interest Research Group.[9]

As the session began, the Hammond administration, led by the Department of Revenue, endorsed the committee's bill and pushed for speedy enactment. [10] Before the election, Hammond had been fairly quiet about his desire to distribute fund earnings to long-time Alaska residents—his Alaska, Inc. idea—but now he again focused on that goal, hoping to send out checks beginning in 1980.[11] However, legislative leaders put on the brakes. Gruening, Malone, Democratic Senator Chancy Croft, and others had come to see risks in using the fund as a development bank. Although swimming against the tide politically and in public opinion, they decided to take time to educate themselves, their colleagues, and ordinary Alaskans about the issues. An interim arrangement put the permanent fund's small flow of revenue into the state treasury to be parked in short-term U.S. Government obligations. Meanwhile, Malone, who had been elected Speaker of the House, appointed Gruening to chair a special committee on the permanent fund and Steve Cowper to chair the House Finance Committee. Gruening and Cowper announced plans to hold statewide hearings during the legislative recess in the summer and fall of 1977, putting off action until at least 1978.[12]

At the same time Malone and his pro-fund allies were organizing the House, however, political maneuvers in the Senate took an opposite turn, setting the stage for a long, arduous battle over deciding the Fund's goals. Although Democrats came out of the 1976 election with a twelve-to-eight Senate majority, three crossed the aisle to form a coalition with the Republicans. The defectors were Bob Ziegler of Ketchikan, George Hohman of Bethel, and John Rader, the lone permanent fund opponent who became Senate president. To the further dismay of fund advocates, Rader appointed Hohman to chair the Senate's special committee on the permanent fund.[13] Hohman was a political operator and a good old boy, a reverse image to the gentlemanly and intellectual Gruening. As chair of the Senate's special committee on the permanent fund, Hohman's priority was to deliver capital projects to the Alaska Bush, and he believed a development bank was the perfect vehicle to do so. The House, the Senate, and the governor each worked on their own, each hiring consultants and gathering public opinion separately.

Gruening's committee set about studying the state's finances, its economy, and its potential to absorb fund investments. Committee members delved into macroeconomic theory and investment policy, reviewing how other government investment funds had fared. Jim Rhode did much of this work, and the Legislature also brought in national consultants, including Milton Friedman, the Nobel-laureate economist. The University of Alaska's Institute for Social and Economic Research (ISER) produced a report examining state revenue needs, projecting the permanent fund would receive limited returns from underwriting big development projects, and revealing that the 1970 policy of putting oil money into local banks had done little to spur economic growth.[14]

Among the most persuasive pieces of evidence the House consultants turned up was the poor performance of similar funds around the world that had chosen to invest locally. The unanticipated consequences of investing outsized oil revenues in home economies included corruption, overheated growth, rampant inflation, destruction of the underlying, non-oil economy, and loss of capital through bad loans and politically motivated or poorly planned projects. Among the few successful savings endeavors was in Kuwait, where a portion of oil income was diverted by a single government official who kept it off the books in foreign-investment accounts for the benefit of future generations. Nonetheless, the influx of oil money spent within Kuwait essentially overwhelmed other economic activity and made its people indolent. Examples directly comparable to Alaska were few, however, because our state was a subdivision of a nation and because our expected oil income was so large in relation to our small population. For a time, Alaska oil production, on the basis of barrels per person, would be nearly three times that of Kuwait and four times that of Saudi Arabia. [15]

The closest comparison to the Alaska Permanent Fund was the Alberta Heritage Fund, an oil-revenue account initiated the same year as ours and, like ours, created without a clear goal. Alberta's path diverged from Alaska's, however, when its parliamentary government made quick decisions about how to manage the fund. Albertans had started at the same point as Alaskans, believing they could both save and spend, and organized their fund with four contradictory objectives— saving, reducing public debt, improving the quality of life, and strengthening and diversifying the economy. Later, a study showed little tangible progress achieving the social goals, despite billions devoted to them, although the fund did finance some parks and libraries. The economic-development projects, in general, posted large losses or yielded below-market returns and in the end were poor investments. Alberta invested another large portion of its assets in long-term government loans that could not be liquidated when the money was needed. When the economy hit a downturn due to a decline in oil prices, Alberta borrowed to cover budget deficits, eventually owing as much as it had saved. Moreover, the fund's local investments meant its prospects suffered when the rest of the economy did, so it couldn't counter the economic trend. Deposits of oil revenues were discontinued in 1987, and observers came to view the fund as a failure.[16] In the late 1990s, Alberta reformulated its fund to be more like the Alaska Permanent Fund, but as of 2005, Alberta's account was roughly one-third the size of Alaska's, despite a potentially greater flow of capital.[17] While Alberta's experience was not seen at the time, the potential pitfalls of the Alberta approach were perceptible to Gruening and his colleagues, who traveled to Edmonton to learn about the experiment while considering Alaska's legislation.[18]

Arlon Tussing, an economist with ISER, informally surveyed Alaskan business and political leaders about the need for government loans and summarized his findings in a report that used economic theory to assess their views. While I don't agree with all of his reasoning, it's well worth reviewing his influential comments. Tussing suggested that flows of capital in the United States, including Alaska, were an efficient market: If good investments were available, capital would find them and loans would be made. Tussing's survey found that most of Alaska's lenders and more successful entrepreneurs agreed with that perception. Alaska's remoteness once might have created barriers to information and thus hindered capital investment, but now skilled business people with good ideas knew how to obtain credit. It did cost a bit more to borrow in Alaska, but that made sense because operating costs were higher. The only exception to the rule, Tussing wrote, were business ventures like lodges or fish processors in remote communities where the tiny economic scale and high operating costs made lending unprofitable, and where collateral was difficult to sell in case a loan went bad. In those limited cases, government participation, such as loans from the permanent fund, might help. But for the vast majority of business loans—including rural loans with good collateral, such as standardized equipment or vehicles—Tussing argued that permanent fund investments would interfere with the efficient market. If it made good loans at market rates, the fund would compete with commercial lenders. If it made good loans below market rates, it would displace commercial lenders and subsidize industries that already were doing well, potentially overheating the economy. Only by making soft loans below market rates could the Fund achieve the goal of diversifying the economy, and those were the kinds of loans that most often went bad, because marginal business ventures usually needed more than just a lower interest rate to survive.[19]

In a democracy, of course, academic reasoning doesn't win many votes. Credit was tight nationally, the Alaska economy was in a slump, and business development in rural areas was a challenge. Those demanding help did not want a lecture in economics. Gruening and his House committee faced a daunting challenge. The Alaska Permanent Fund had been sold as a development bank. When the Alaska State Chamber of Commerce sponsored the official election pamphlet essay in favor of the 1976 proposition, its main points were that the fund would remove money from annual appropriation, slowing the growth of state government, and that it would diversify the economy. Hohman continued to push that idea, commissioning a poll that showed overwhelming public support for permanent fund loan programs.[20] His Senate committee worked in private, consulting with the business community, to position the fund as a huge source of loans. Gruening's committee, on the other hand, scheduled public seminars with national experts, issued surveys, and held hearings around Alaska to gather grassroots opinion and help educate the public.[21]

Gruening found plenty of support for loans and projects, but also found strong support for investing the fund safely—the same contradictory pair of goals that had been promoted prior to the election. In response, he posed a common-sense solution: If the principal of the fund were invested according to the prudent-investor rule, then the income would be available for the Legislature to use in any way it chose. Gruening found that most Alaskans understood the concept.

"The public didn't want it spent, but they sure had a lot of ideas about how to invest it," he said. "You know, we had one guy, who pops into mind, in Nome or Kotzebue—we had them all over the state—and he said, 'Well, as long as it makes money, and that includes whorehouses in Nevada, we should do it. But we shouldn't do something that doesn't make money.' That was an inartful way of stating the prudent-investor rule."

When the Legislature returned in 1978, three proposals were on the table. Gruening's House committee wanted to set up the fund as a trust managed by a corporation with an independent board and guided by the prudent-investor rule. In-state investments would be made only if they were as safe and profitable as investing elsewhere in high-grade securities. As a nod to those who wanted a development bank, the House bill also proposed setting aside as much as $100 million for loans and capital projects—a figure critics regarded as too small. The competing proposal advanced by Hohman's Senate committee, which became known as SB1, essentially devoted the entire fund to loans, but with a complex financing mechanism. Hohman wanted to invest the fund's principal on Wall Street, issuing bonds that used those investments as security. The bond proceeds would be loaned to Alaskans for every conceivable purpose, from college tuition to business development. My Alaska Municipal Bond Bank was Hohman's inspiration, but he would carry the idea of leveraging state finances to an extreme, and without the bond bank's mechanisms to make sure the loans were repaid. The Hammond administration opposed both the House and Senate versions. Commissioner of Revenue Sterling Gallagher said Gruening's proposal didn't invest enough money in Alaska and Hohman's proposal invested too much. Hammond stuck with the bill written by the Investment Advisory Commission, allocating 40 percent to safe investments and 60 percent to in-state loans.[22] By the end of the session, the House had passed Gruening's bill, but the Senate had not. The 1978 elections came and went with the fate of the permanent fund still undecided.[23]

My involvement in these issues grew from my role as director of the bond bank. The bond bank had used a modest slice of state resources as leverage to help local communities borrow for capital projects from the national financial markets. The state had a myriad of direct-loan programs as well, mostly administered through the Department of Commerce, which financed fishing boats, housing, small businesses, and resource-development projects. Development banking wasn't new to Alaska. Governor Bill Egan first attempted it with the $12 million Alaska State Development Corporation in 1961, but the track record of the various programs had been spotty.[24] Political loans tended to be poor investments, and management of the portfolio by state bureaucrats sometimes had been lax.

In 1978 I was approached by Eric Wohlforth asking for help with a project that would lead to a new era in the state's economic-development work. I had gotten to know Eric as the attorney for the bond bank, and I came to respect him as a friend as well as a brilliant and enterprising lawyer who didn't cut corners. More than once when I asked for legal advice, Eric gave me ethical advice instead, focusing not just on what I *could* do, but what I *should* do. I came to value highly his integrity and skill. Wohlforth had built his career as Alaska's leading public-finance attorney by creating many of the institutions that would need his services. He came to the state in 1966 at Egan's invitation, leaving behind a solid Wall Street law firm and a comfortable Ivy League background for the uncertainty of a new practice in a new state—a situation made even shakier when Egan, his sponsor, was upset in the 1966 general election by Walter Hickel.

Early in Hickel's term, an opportunity emerged to build a new liquefied natural-gas plant on the Kenai Peninsula. In response, Wohlforth drafted legislation that created the Alaska Industrial Development Authority, a state-controlled entity that could issue bonds to finance the project. The oil company owners would repay the bonds, but AIDA's involvement meant their interest payments would be tax-free for bond buyers, a benefit which would, in turn, lower the interest rate required of project sponsors. As it turned out, the owner companies decided not to use the AIDA. Then, in 1969, a federal tax-law change eliminated much of AIDA's purpose, so it never really existed except on paper.

In 1977, however, Wohlforth and investment bankers from Texas approached the legislature for amendments to the AIDA statute that would allow it to function again under federal tax law. As soon as that legislation passed, three companies stepped forward asking for AIDA to help finance projects. Until he approached me, Wohlforth's firm, the financial advisors, and the Texas bankers had managed the agency with peripheral oversight of three state commissioners who comprised the agency's board. The first deal they lined up was $3.5 million for Alaska Airlines to build a new cargo-handling facility in Anchorage. More deals were in the works. But without someone who represented AIDA full-time, it would be tough to figure out who should sign the papers.[25]

Wohlforth wanted me to step in as the nominal executive director to sign off on deals. I agreed, but suggested that I become a real executive director and run the agency. My board at the bond bank agreed, with the understanding that I would be paid only for one job, not two. We completed the structure by having Hammond appoint the bond bank board to serve also as the AIDA board, so the two entities were practically one in terms of the personnel. This was important because I had earned my board's trust and it understood the issues of bond financing.

I met with Hammond during this time, when I was running both agencies, and learned what a strong and moral leader he was. I tried to explain our work. While he was delighted that we were meeting the need for loans without spending the state's money, he admitted that he didn't really understand what we were doing. However, he still managed to convey the most important piece of direction I could have received. Looking me straight in the eye, Hammond said, "Dave, I ask only one thing. Don't embarrass me. And don't embarrass yourself." I promised I wouldn't, and I kept that promise through the time I served the state with its financial agencies, seventeen years in all.

Once I began directing AIDA, I wasn't interested in being a figurehead who signed papers. As Wohlforth recalls, "All of a sudden he was in the office all the time and deals started happening." We did financing for more Alaska Airlines facilities, in Ketchikan and Juneau; for gas pipelines in Anchorage and Kenai; and for pollution-control facilities for the pulp mill in Ketchikan. By the end of 1979, more than $49 million had been financed, with another $55 million in the works.[26] Without any outlay from the state, we were helping develop industry by lowering the cost of borrowing for large projects. Arlon Tussing's analysis had concluded that the state government should stay out of the lending business. With AIDA, however, we proved there was a role for state involvement because some good loans were too large for the banks and some projects became feasible only when government intervention lowered interest rates. The key was to use the state's access to bond markets, its credit rating, and the reduced interest cost of tax-free financing.

Potential borrowers clamored for more state lending. The Alaska business climate was brutal, having fallen into a slump after the end of pipeline construction in 1977. Nationally, credit was extremely tight, with the prime rate hitting nearly 16 percent in 1979 and topping out at 20.5 percent in 1980.[27] Meanwhile, the state's treasury was growing with oil money. Politicians were in a mood to help. The mantra in every election campaign became "Diversify the economy." The Legislature created the Alaska Renewable Resources Corporation, which put out venture capital but disappeared a few years later due to its losses.[28] Hammond went so far on the "diversification" theme as to pour money into creating a barley-farming industry in the wilderness, with huge agricultural loans made, enormous tracts of land cleared, roads built, railroad cars purchased to carry grain, and a shipping terminal built in Seward to export the barley overseas. The oil-rich town of Valdez built a second grain terminal to compete in this non-existent market. The administration predicted Alaska could provide 20 percent of the world's protein through export of bottom fish, grains, and rapeseed.[29] The rail cars and grain terminals never were used, however, and the barley project turned into a fiasco. A few years later, the federal government began paying the barley farmers not to plant.

This strange economic state of affairs brought people out of the woodwork seeking loans of their own. On one occasion, I was asked by the administration to join Lieutenant Governor Terry Miller in a hearing to listen to the requests. I remember a speaker seeking support to open a waterbed store in Wasilla, then a town of fifteen hundred. [30] Terry leaned over to me and said, "That would be the third waterbed store in Wasilla."

A term for these people — the "loan crazies" — came into common usage among those involved in state finance, as Wohlforth recalls: "Guys would come in the office with a maniacal look in their eyes and say that if they just had five million, or ten million, or twenty, they could finance producing bottled water from icebergs and sell it worldwide, and didn't we know that there was a $100 million business, which would immediately translate into $100 million of profit for them. They could make it easy. That's the way the agricultural guys went nuts and thought the state could be a major producer and exporter of barley, and two barley terminals were built—not one but two—and it just seemed like it struck a chord with all kinds of people, that if they could simply have a large state loan they could produce something that would be of wonderful benefit to them and the world."

Naturally, the loan crazies didn't think they were crazy. They thought bankers and state lenders were unreasonable for denying them the financing they needed. They were mixed in among others who might have good projects but couldn't get money because of tough economic conditions and high interest rates for long-term loans. Politicians, however, made little distinction between the crazies and the reasonable business people. They simply wanted to lend money to stimulate the economy and to make voters and campaign contributors happy.

Arlon Tussing summarized the situation in his report to the permanent fund committee. "Many small businessmen including, it appears, most prospectors, inventors, independent merchants, and operators of hotel, restaurant, and other tourist-related businesses outside of Anchorage, and some contractors, do not ... believe in the efficient markets paradigm," he wrote, adding that many "attributed their cash crunch to the institutional incapacity of financial institutions to serve their kind of business, or to the laziness, ignorance, or malice of particular lenders.... Almost every public official interviewed believed that there was an Alaska capital shortage that could, and should, be treated by application of government money."[31]

The loan crazies, and their relatively sane allies, powered the drive to use the permanent fund as a development bank. We believed that if the state wanted to lend money, AIDA was the program to use. We advanced the idea that the legislature could empower the agency to make development loans for smaller operators. AIDA's first round of projects, such as the Alaska Airlines facilities, had involved no state assets. AIDA contributed only its name and tax-exempt status. To make smaller loans, we would need capital, but we devised a way that the state could provide capital cheaply. The Department of Commerce had a large portfolio of loans it had issued over the years through a variety of programs. As one would expect, the government hadn't collected on the loans as aggressively as a private banker would, but those assets could be used for leverage. If AIDA owned the loans and collected on them, we could pledge the promissory notes as security to back bonds. The proceeds from selling the bonds could be loaned to more borrowers, whose own loan payments would pay off the bonds.

Bringing forward the idea branded me as a fellow traveler with the loan crazies in the eyes of some people, including Jim Rhode, the influential House staffer and aide to Hugh Malone. Their defense of the permanent fund had made them opponents of government lending in general. Rhode had been so skeptical of the bond bank that he had mocked the idea by wearing a beanie cap with a propeller around the capitol. He and Malone thought the plan to expand AIDA into business loans was just another loony scheme. Rhode considered putting the beanie back on.

Jay Hammond understood. Although he lacked a background in finance, Hammond realized that AIDA could help derail Hohman. We could create a development bank out of AIDA rather than allowing Hohman's SB1 to create one using the Permanent Fund. AIDA would become a shield, absorbing the risk of state lending and deflecting the political pressure created by the loan crazies. The governor nicknamed me "the AIDA kid" and helped convince Rhode and Malone. Rhode got it right away. He became so excited about how well AIDA would defend the permanent fund that he nearly oversold it, suggesting that a fund dividend wouldn't be needed—the one thing that might have changed Hammond's mind because the governor was committed to the dividend concept. Malone required more convincing than Rhode, but finally came around to support an expanded role for AIDA as well.

As acting director of AIDA, I gathered allies. Bert Wagnon, the deputy commissioner of commerce, worked to rewrite the AIDA statute and sell it to legislators. Pete Jeans, also working at commerce, pitched in with regulations and underwriting standards. Wohlforth and I met with investment bankers and rating agencies to figure out how the bonds should be structured and to determine what collateral we would need. I joined Tom Williams, the commissioner of revenue, to meet with bankers, measuring their willingness to participate in the business loans. With the banks on board, we would have access to their expertise in loan underwriting. Jan Sieberts of National Bank of Alaska shared many constructive ideas and suggestions.

Williams also helped with legislation to endow AIDA with financial reserves. To our delight, we received a cash appropriation of $15 million during the 1979 session and access to the state's inventory of state loans. Promissory notes were stored in four filing cabinets. AIDA workers picked through the paperwork and selected $166 million in loan receivables that were worth having, leaving behind those that were poorly documented or uncollectible. The loans were collateralized by all kinds of business assets, especially warehouses, shops, and fishing boats. We hired inspectors to check the properties and to survey the vessels, assuring the value of the collateral. Among the notes was one signed by Tony Knowles and me for a state veterans loan, which we had used to refinance the Downtown Deli. I avoided a conflict of interest by directing that the note be left with the state and not selected by AIDA. When we were done, we had nearly doubled our $100 million goal, gathering $181 million in loans and cash. That was fortunate, because we needed 200 percent collateral on our bonds due to the relatively soft loan portfolio we were using as security.

AIDA's tax-free bonds sold at low interest rates, and we began our new business lending program. Banks screened the loans and took on the shorter-term portion of the debt themselves—helping assure they had a stake in the quality of the loans—while AIDA contributed most of the money at lower interest and accepted the latter part of the loan term, which was less attractive to the banks. A committee at AIDA also screened each loan. The program worked. Although AIDA has gotten into some bad projects over the years, the protections we put in place made it far more effective than the direct state lending programs had been. Over time, the authority has paid back $195 million to the state in excess revenues generated by its lending and interest income.[32]

The side effect of AIDA's new role as a lender turned out to be more important than the actual work we did. The authority became a critical escape valve for legislators when constituents requested loans or other state support for private projects. Tillion, Gruening, and Senator Arliss Sturgulewski remember the relief they felt when they urged people with ideas—whether good or crazy—to go talk to AIDA rather than having to give them a straight no. Of course, I still had to say no to plenty of people, including legislators calling on behalf of would-be borrowers, but it was easier for us. If a project didn't make sense, we could request a third-party feasibility study, or point to potential problems with bond-rating agencies and bond insurance standards. Because we did all our business in public, charges of political favoritism or malice wouldn't stick. The AIDA escape valve also changed the permanent fund debate. Proponents of saving the fund as a trust now countered calls for creating a development bank by saying we already had one.

Jim Rhode retired his beanie and became an ardent supporter of the bond bank, AIDA, and similar development agencies funded by the Legislature over the next few years. Eric Wohlforth and I were involved in the legal and political work of most of these initiatives. The Alaska Power Authority supported hydroelectric and other energy projects. The Commercial Fishing and Agriculture Bank mainly financed fishing boats and permits. The Agricultural Revolving Loan Fund put money into Hammond's farm projects. The largest of all was the Alaska Housing Finance Corporation, which used tax-free bonds to lower the interest rates for home mortgages offered through banks. Wohlforth had put forward AHFC's founding legislation in 1971, when he was commissioner of revenue, and it had passed easily with the support of Egan and the legislative sponsorship of Democratic Senator Joe Josephson; only in the late 1970s, however, did the state appropriate any money to the corporation. All these entities were known by their acronyms—APA, C-FAB, ARLF, AHFC, AIDA and AMBBA (the bond bank). Collectively they became known as the alphabet agencies. Without them, the permanent fund probably would not have survived the fate of becoming a development bank itself.

My time with AIDA lasted less than two years. After I requested and received a year-end bonus of $20,000, the board decided that I really did want to be paid for doing two jobs. It assigned me the task of producing a three-year plan for the agency, which then was put into the hands of a new executive director, banker Buzz Hoffman.

Money to fund the reserves of the alphabet agencies came with the completion of the trans-Alaska oil pipeline. When the pipeline started operating, oil prices already had risen dramatically due to the Arab Oil Embargo, then they more than doubled again after Islamic militants deposed the Shah of Iran in January 1979. Money gushed into the treasury at an astounding rate.

Sturgulewski, elected to her first term in the Legislature that year, remembers a money-intoxicated mood in the capitol, with legislators behaving like children who suddenly get their hands on more candy than they can possibly eat. "Young Russ Meekins was chair of House Finance, and I have this vision of him—he was much younger, and he had curly blond hair—running down the hall holding up a piece of paper, which I assumed was a check. I don't know how he got it. It was the first big part of the money coming, $79 million."[33]

Terry Gardiner became Speaker of the House and appointed Hugh Malone to chair the special permanent fund committee. Malone's committee produced a bill similar to Gruening's prudent-investor version, which had passed the House but died in the Senate during the previous session. The new bill was even more conservative, stripped of the concept of a $100 million development fund. AIDA had made that idea redundant and the permanent fund would be focused entirely as a savings trust.[34] Hohman reintroduced his complex concept of using the entire fund for loans, now called Senate

Bill 1. The Hammond administration's position had moved closer to the House. The governor now supported the fund as a trust, to be invested only at market rates of interest, but he would consider allowing the legislature to appropriate money to subsidize loans made by the fund. He also would permit the fund to guarantee debt for large power projects. Fran Ulmer, overseeing policy study in the administration, wrote a detailed paper laying out the proposals, underlining the need for safe investments but including the compromises.

Hammond never had supported a huge loan fund because he didn't support fast, unplanned growth.[35] But the administration's public position on investing the fund vacillated over the years of debate. As the fight neared its climax in the 1980 legislative session, Malone put Rhode to work keeping the governor's position from shifting. Hammond's enjoyment of policy debate and complex ideas, and his respect for different points of view on his staff, could complicate political work when simple power politics would more easily win a fight. As Malone told interviewer Nancy Gross: "Hammond is eclectic and always likes to sample new ideas and can seemingly be distracted at even the most critical phases, and I remember Jim making many visits to the governor's office on the day of the Senate vote on the authorizing legislation, keeping the governor, let's say, contented."[36]

According to Malone, Hammond committed to the House's trust concept in exchange for a House vote in favor of his dividend idea. The dividend long had been Hammond's highest priority, the legacy he wanted to leave behind when he left office. But the legislation had languished in committee year after year, declared dead on arrival by legislators who had no interest in the concept, either philosophically or politically. Three-quarters of the way through his maximum of eight years as governor, pushing the dividend bill through had become increasingly urgent.[37]

To this day, it's debatable whether Malone won Hammond's support or if it happened the other way around. Ulmer says Hammond personally always favored a straight savings version of the fund, as Malone advocated. That makes sense because the savings version best met his policy goals of slower growth, reduced spending, and producing income for a dividend. What seems most likely is that the governor had every intention of backing the House version, but strategically withheld his support from Malone and Rhode until he got their commitment to support the dividend. Sadly, all three men have died, so we'll never know for sure if Rhode was babysitting Hammond in those many meetings in the governor's office, or if Hammond simply allowed Rhode to believe that while, in fact, he was maneuvering Rhode, Malone, and the House.

In 1980, as the issue came to a head, the immense size of the oil-revenue surplus was clear to all. At the same time, interest rates peaked and the pleas of the loan crazies reached a frenzied pitch. But the "savers" in the legislature held firm. At the start of the session, the Senate voted down the House bill, but Hohman never brought up his SB1 for a vote because he could count only nine out of the Senate's twenty votes in favor. Hohman was stymied by two problems: His bill was extremely complicated and difficult to understand, and Hammond would never sign it, because dividends would not be possible with all Fund income going to bond payments.[38] Based on the Senate's negative vote on the House bill, however, Clem Tillion, who was by then Senate president, appointed Hohman to a free conference committee to negotiate differences between the two bodies. But Tillion didn't leave Hohman to his own devices. Tillion also attended the meetings as an observer. Malone represented the House.

Under legislative rules at the time, a free conference committee had complete flexibility in resolving issues between the two houses—it wasn't limited by legislation passed by either body. The pro-savings legislators brought in a series of experts to showcase how ill-conceived the development bank would be. Pro-development legislators brought in loan-hungry constituents who said their businesses were dying under double-digit interest rates—people who desperately needed money, and therefore didn't fit the profile of a good investment, at least under the rule that Elmer Rasmuson had expressed to Tillion. Hohman introduced more legislation pandering to the loan crazies, including a bill that would loan money to nearly anyone and would require loans be given automatically to any small town or non-profit corporation that asked for them.

After three years of making their case, and with the governor on their side, pro-savings legislators had the upper hand. In the conference committee, Hohman agreed to go along with the House version of the permanent fund, but only on the condition that an equal amount of money—25 percent of oil revenues per year—would be made available for loans. No deal. The conference committee dissolved with Tillion's vow to appoint another with members who would approve the House bill without conditions.[39] The new committee, chaired by Tillion himself and by Speaker Gardiner for the House, quickly agreed to a bill that not only accepted the House plan, but doubled deposits to the fund to 50 percent of oil royalties and leases.[40]

Tillion also used the free conference committee to sock a large contribution into AHFC for housing loans.[41] At the same time, the legislature eased lending rules on AHFC mortgages. By this time, the alphabet agencies had emerged as clear and reasonable alternatives to making loans from the permanent fund. Alaskans needed home loans, and the low-interest rates AHFC offered by buying mortgages from banks brought the housing market back to life in a hurry. AHFC ultimately proved itself to be a good investment. Over its life, it received about $1 billion in contributions, almost half of that in 1980 alone; by 2005 it had repaid $1.5 billion to the state treasury.[42]

Tillion hadn't planned on the state making a profit by supporting home loans, only to set aside money so it wouldn't be wasted in the operating budget. For the first time, but not the last, the Legislature was threatening to degenerate into an uncontrolled spending spree. Tillion and other savers grabbed revenue as if saving it from a burning building. In this atmosphere, legislation setting up the fund's management structure proved far less controversial than a bill sponsored by Representative Oral Freeman, a Democrat from Ketchikan, to make a special $900 million deposit to the fund. The figure, chosen for its resonance with the $900 million from the 1969 lease sale, would be enough to "soak up" excess funds, denying Hohman and his allies $500 million they wanted to start another special loan fund.[43]

At the same time, Hammond needed his permanent fund dividend bill to start moving. In the evenings after work, he dropped in on Tillion and his wife, Diana, so the old friends could strategize without other legislators observing them meeting as governor and Senate president. They settled on a plan. Tillion would use a threat from Hammond to break the dividend bill out of committee in the Senate. Hammond would veto budget goodies near and dear to those who bottled it up and, if necessary, would call a special session to force a vote on his bill. After Tillion delivered this message, the bill passed with little discussion in the legislature and little attention from the public.

Getting support for the $900 million deposit proved more difficult. Hohman fought to the finish for his loan fund. When Tillion, Hammond, and their allies had rounded up the votes, Hohman tried to tie up the Senate by arranging a call of the house while making himself scarce, along with Senator Bill Sumner. Under its rules, the Senate could not continue business until all unexcused senators were present. Tillion contacted the Alaska State Troopers and, reminding them he had subpoena powers, demanded that the absent senators be delivered to the floor. A trooper found Hohman and Sumner, handcuffed them, and escorted them to their desks. The bill passed.[44] Later, House Republicans also rebelled against the $900 million deposit and again used the "call of the house" trick, with Representative Ray Metcalfe sent into hiding. Speaker Terry Gardiner sent the troopers after Metcalfe, but they couldn't find him. Hammond issued another veto threat, this time against legislators' favorite capital projects, and the bill finally passed. The permanent fund grew from $500 million to $1.4 billion with the stroke of a pen.[45]

We could hardly imagine it at the time, but the 1980 Legislature, for all its unprecedented spending, was a model of fiscal conservatism compared to the Legislatures that followed in the next few years. Spending went to fantastic heights that have not been equaled since. Legislators had the money to fulfill their constituents' whims, not just their needs.

The fate of the permanent fund owes much to the huge budgets of 1980 and the next few years. As we have seen, when the constitutional amendment was adopted in 1976, little oil revenue was coming in, so legislators hardly gave up anything by agreeing to divert a percentage of it to the fund. On the other hand, when the fund's long-term savings purpose was established in 1980, legislators enjoyed an enormous flow of oil revenue; once again, little political sacrifice was required to help the permanent fund. While they increased fund deposits and dedicated its principal to safe investments, legislators at the same time passed by far the largest capital budget ever, generously funded the state's loan agencies, and more than doubled total state spending in a single year.[46] When money had been scarce, Hohman's development bank scheme offered a unique chance to help constituents with state funds. When there was enough money for everything, his idea no longer mattered.

At the end of the legislative session in June 1980, the most important elements of the fund were in place. Its principal would be a conservative savings trust, with no direct responsibility for economic or community development; investment oversight would be conducted by a board of trustees, not elected leaders; deposits would equal 50 percent of oil royalties and leases (but not taxes) as well as large additional deposits; and half of the income from the fund would be allocated to a dividend paid out to Alaskans, the size of the payment depending on the length of a recipient's residency. Many issues remained, however. Who would manage the money? How would the fund keep pace with inflation since all its income was available for spending? Also at issue was the legality of treating Alaskans differently depending on their years of residency. Over the next two years, each of these issues would be resolved, and the Alaska Permanent Fund would take its final form.

---

[1]Sheila Toomey, *Anchorage Daily News*, December 3, 2000.

[2]Clark Gruening, interview by Charles Wohlforth, digital recording, December 27, 2005.

[3]Clem Tillion, interview by Charles Wohlforth, digital recording, December 28, 2005

[4]Sheila F. Helgath and Sarah A. Babb, *Alaska's Permanent Fund: Legislative History, Intent, and Operations,* Alaska State Senate, Rural Research Agency, January 1986, 42.

[5]Susan Andrews, *The Anchorage Times,* November 6, 1976.

[6]Susan Andrews, *The Anchorage Times,* November 17, 1976.

[7]Susan Andrews, *The Anchorage Times,* January 8, 1976.

[8]Paul Nussbaum, *Anchorage Daily News,* February 28, 1977.

[9]Kay Brown, *The Anchorage Times,* November 21, 1976.

[10]Susan Andrews, *The Anchorage Times,* November 21, 1976 and January 8, 1977.

[11]Brown; also Jean Kizer, Associated Press, *Anchorage Daily News,* May 6, 1977.

[12]Hugh Malone, interview by Nancy Gross, transcript, circa 2000, 4.

[13]Associated Press, *Anchorage Daily News,* March 17, 1977.

[14]Scott Goldsmith and others, *The Permanent Fund and the Growth of the Alaskan Economy: Selected Studies,* report for the House Special Committee on the Alaska Permanent Fund, Institute for Social and Economic Research, University of Alaska Anchorage, December 15, 1977, IV-17, 35.

[15]Malcolm Gillis, "The Effects of In-State Investment: Lessons Learned from Oil-Fired Development in Other Parts of the World," in *Trustee Papers,* vol. 1 (Juneau: Alaska Permanent Fund Corporation, 1981); Thomas R. Stauffer, "Oil Rich: Spend or Save? How Oil Countries Have Handled the Windfall," in *Trustee Papers,* vol. 2 (Juneau: Alaska Permanent Fund Corporation, 1988).

[16]Rögnvaldur Hannesson, *Investing for Sustainability: The Management of Mineral Wealth* (Boston: Kluwer Academic Publishers, 2001); also Peter J. Smith, "The Alberta Heritage Savings Trust Fund and the Alaska Permanent Fund: A Ten-Year Retrospective" in *Trustee Papers,* vol. 2 (Juneau, Alaska Permanent Fund Corporation, 1988).

[17]Alberta Heritage Savings Trust Fund, http://www.finance.gov.ab.ca/business/ahstf/history.html.

[18]Gruening interview.

[19]Arlon Tussing, *Economic Considerations in Establishment of Alaska's Permanent Fund,* report for the Legislative Affairs Agency, State of Alaska, Institute for Social and Economic Research, University of Alaska Anchorage, July 7, 1977, 9-10, 19-20.

[20]Helgath and Babb, 12.

[21]Associated Press, *The Anchorage Times,* August 30, 1977.

[22]Paul Nussbaum, *Anchorage Daily News,* November 4, 1977; Susan Andrews, *The Anchorage Times,* December 30, 1977; Associated Press, *The Anchorage Times,* March 2, 1978; Associated Press, *The Anchorage Times,* March 7, 1978.

[23]Rosemary Shinohara, *Anchorage Daily News,* April 9, 1979.

[24]Brown.

[25]Eric Wohlforth, interview by Charles Wohlforth, digital recording, December 23, 2005; "Securing Alaska's economic future," staff report in *Alaska Industry,* December 1979, 22.

[26]Staff report in *Alaska Industry*, 22-23.

[27]Board of Governors of the Federal Reserve System, http://research.stlouisfed.org/fred2/data/PRIME.txt.

[28]Wohlforth interview.

[29]Terry Miller, "State moves to stop slump," *Alaska Industry*, December 1979, 21.

[30]U.S. Census, http://www.census.gov/prod/cen1990/cph2/cph-2-1-1.pdf.

[31]Tussing, 10, 12-13.

[32]Alaska Industrial Development and Export Authority/Alaska Energy Authority, "AIDEA Declares Dividend to the State," press release, December 8, 2005, http://www.aidea.org.

[33]Arliss Sturgulewski, interview by Charles Wohlforth, digital recording, January 12, 2006.

[34]Shinohara.

[35]Frances A. Ulmer, "Permanent Fund Policy," memorandum of the Division of Policy Development and Planning, Office of the Governor, February 23, 1979; Fran Ulmer, interview by Charles Wohlforth, digital recording, January 13, 2006.

[36]Malone interview transcript, 3.

[37]Jay Hammond, *Tales of Alaska's Bush Rat Governor* (Fairbanks and Seattle: Epicenter Press, 1994, 251; Ulmer interview.

[38]Malone interview transcript, 9.

[39]John Greeley, *Anchorage Daily News*, January 30, 1980; Editorial, *The Anchorage Times*, February 15, 1980; Associated Press, *The Anchorage Times*, March 24, 1980.

[40]Associated Press, *The Anchorage Times*, April 1, 1980.

[41]Wohlforth interview.

[42]Sherrie Simmonds, AHFC corporate communications, personal communication.

[43]Tillion interview; Associated Press, *The Anchorage Times*, April 24, 1980.

[44]Associated Press, *The Anchorage Times*, April 23, 1980; Tillion interview.

[45]John Greely, *Anchorage Daily News*, May 10, 1980; Dave Carpenter, *The Anchorage Times*, May 13, 1980.

[46]Institute for Social and Economic Research, University of Alaska Anchorage, *The Alaska Citizen's Guide to the Budget*, http://citizensguide.uaa.alaska.edu.

CHAPTER 10
Finishing the foundations, 1980-1982

A laska may be known by superlatives—the largest state, the highest mountain, the most wildlife—but since 1982 the fact about our state that has amazed many Americans is that Alaskans, as they say, "get money just for living." Bank accounts swell each autumn with payment of the Alaska Permanent Fund dividend, which distributes half the fund's annual realized income. If the fund were a basic industry and the dividend its payroll, it would be among Alaska's largest—only government substantially exceeds the total amount of dividends paid in payroll terms.[1]

Some recipients blow the windfall on vacations or expensive toys. Others save it for education. Many pay off medical bills or otherwise reduce their debt. The wealthier among us hardly notice the boost, which has ranged over the last fifteen years from $850 to almost $2,000 per resident. In rural Alaska, however, the dividend can make a major difference, providing an essential shot of cash to keep subsistence hunters stocked with ammo and spare parts. As executive director of the fund, I had the pleasure of receiving heartfelt expressions of gratitude from Alaskans for whom the dividend had been a lifesaver.

Thanks to Alaskans' diversity and differing attitudes toward government, we have many interpretations of the dividend's meaning. Through the years, we never have resolved, as a people, why we receive the payment—whether it is a gift, compensation for our citizenship, or profit for exploitation of resources that we own. Nor have we decided whether we want the dividend to be paid annually forever, infinitely growing, or whether we are willing for it to end or to be capped once it has fulfilled the function of helping the state to preserve a portion of its oil wealth. Like the fund itself, the dividend began with many purposes; unlike the fund, those internal contradictions have not diminished, but rather have become more entrenched and complex with time.

For Governor Hammond, the dividend was a primary purpose of the Alaska Permanent Fund itself. Hammond's dividend grew naturally from his political philosophy—distrustful of government and politicians, allied with Alaska Natives and other rural residents, opposed to fast growth, protective of the self-sufficient values of the past, and suspicious of big city fat-cats. Living happily at his Lake Clark paradise, Hammond earlier had opposed statehood because of how it could concentrate power and hasten development. When Congress endowed the new state with an enormous transfer of natural resources, Hammond chose to consider the gift as a possession of the Alaska people, not the government, although the state was necessarily the custodian of the wealth. This belief that the people literally own the natural resources reflects a key difference between Hammond and his pro-development opponents Walter Hickel, Bill Egan, and Bob Atwood, among others. They all saw Alaska's collective resources as the key to building a better Alaska. Hammond didn't buy this. He perceived state wealth as a threat to a way of life that in many ways already was ideal. He thought the money could be used better by individuals than spent on government programs or invested in development projects.

Practically speaking, Hammond was correct in his view that government-inspired economic development and loan programs often come first to urban, wealthy, and politically connected residents. However, rural poverty was horrendous in Alaska prior to the arrival of oil. Alaska Native communities resembled the third world, often lacking basic sanitation, health care, decent housing, communications, education, and transportation. Our government-owned oil revenues did much to address those problems. Prior to oil development, Alaska was a resource colony prone to extreme economic swings and unable to sustain its own government services. Today, Alaska's maturing economy has delivered seventeen years of steady, moderate growth and job creation, thanks in part to low taxes, well-funded schools, economic infrastructure, loans for business and housing, and other worthwhile uses of oil money. Most rural communities have clinics, energy assistance, water and sewer systems, airstrips and telecommunications. Virtually all now have their own schools. These benefits came mainly from collective oil wealth, not direct distribution.

Hammond was elected governor in 1974 and 1978 thanks in part to public dissatisfaction with rapid change and with the political establishment. His charisma and rural roots were entirely authentic, but his success as a populist also relied on skillfully projecting in the media an image of the rough pioneer who had been drafted into politics. In his memoir, "Tales of Alaska's Bush Rat Governor," Hammond described himself as a "reluctant politician." That persona resonated with Alaska's desire to hold on to its vanishing frontier past. When it came to policy, however, Hammond's unique philosophy and conservationism put him outside the mainstream. He sometimes seemed to look for ways to limit development without seeming to do so. He couldn't advocate openly for a permanent fund solely on the grounds of restraining growth or distributing direct payments to residents. In the lead-up to the 1976 vote on the constitutional amendment establishing the fund, Hammond emphasized reducing wasteful government spending and scarcely mentioned the dividend idea.

In his sixth year as governor, with little public or political support, Hammond finally forced the dividend through the Legislature using the power of his office. The 1980 law reflected Hammond's deeply held belief that long-time residents, especially Alaska Natives, had a greater ownership right to the state's resources than newcomers. A prejudice for established residents was common during the oil boom when transients looking for a quick buck flooded the state, sending crime rates skyrocketing, and creating or worsening an assortment of social problems. The legislation provided that adults would be entitled to one dividend share for each year of residency since statehood in 1959. With the first dividend set at $50, the maximum payment in 1980 would be $1,050 for twenty-one dividend shares. The minimum payment, one-twelfth of a dividend share for one month of residency, would be $4. With the passage of years, the disparity would grow—by 2009, the largest payment, representing fifty dividend shares, would be six hundred times that of the one-month payment. At that point, with the annual payout divided into so many shares, each additional year of residency would bring only a tiny increase in an individual's payment. Hammond intended these insignificant dividends to newcomers to deny any incentive for outsiders to move north.

The 1980 legislation's statement of policy, purpose, and findings begins by repeating the Alaska Constitution's declaration that natural resources should be used for the maximum benefit of the people. Next, it lays out three purposes for the dividend—provide an equitable distribution of energy wealth, reduce the rapid turnover of Alaska's population, and encourage residents' interest in the management and expenditure of the Permanent Fund. The findings elaborate on the first two points, but not the third. In support of reducing population turnover, the legislation blames short-term residents for the state's political, economic, and social instability. Of course, the graduated dividend wouldn't address that problem. While large payments might keep old-timers from leaving, greenhorns would hardly be influenced by a tiny, slowly increasing annual check. The only statement in the findings with the ring of conviction is that "the accrual of Permanent Fund dividends ... based on full years of residency since January 1, 1959 fairly compensates each state resident for his equitable ownership of the state's natural resources since the date of statehood."[2]

That finding contains two radical concepts—that individual Alaskans own the state's natural resources, and that their ownership interest increases with time spent living in the state. At first, only the second of those concepts—the longevity preference—was challenged. It was bound to happen. The Legislature was establishing different classes of Alaskans in many ways as it dealt out the oil money: Length of residency would determine tax benefits, employment through local-hire laws, monthly support for the elderly, and so on. From today's perspective, it's easy to see the mistake in creating permanent us-and-them divisions among Alaskans based on when they arrived, but at the time these residency requirements had strong public support. When the constitutionality of the dividend law was challenged by a young law clerk and his lawyer wife, recent arrivals Ron and Penny Zobel, the couple was vilified from one end of the state to the other. They received death threats and were the subjects of offensive t-shirts, bumper stickers, and TV commentaries.

It took courage for the Zobels to make their stand. Ron Zobel's political aspirations never recovered, even decades later. The couple had arrived in 1978 after serving in the Peace Corps and attending law school together. Ron had served two hitches as a Green Beret and had worked as a national park ranger. Yet, under the dividend law, the Zobels each would receive only $100, one-tenth of that paid to some other citizens who had done no public service. The Zobels believed that a law devaluing a certain class of residents—and never allowing them to catch up and become equals—violated both Alaska's frontier spirit and the U.S. Constitution's equal-protection clause. They won their case in Superior Court, lost before the Alaska Supreme Court, and were granted a hearing and an injunction by the U.S. Supreme Court. The injunction put the dividend program on hold pending resolution of the case. The Zobels took the brunt of Alaskans' anger.[3]

Hammond, who eventually came to admire Ron Zobel, in spite of himself, described his attendance at a U.S. Supreme Court session in the fall of 1981 as the worst day in his decades of public life. The justices were openly skeptical of Alaska Attorney General Av Gross's arguments and barely let him speak without interruption.[4] Hammond decided that if the court struck down the residency rule, he would allow the dividend to die and instead support giving half of permanent fund earnings to municipalities. But when his staff reminded him that local governments had spent their oil money on projects he considered frivolous, Hammond decided to work for legislation to create a program giving equal dividends to everyone—a backstop law that would go into effect only if the Zobels won their case.[5]

The Legislature went crazy spending money during this period, 1981 and 1982. Most of the way through the 1981 session, a coalition of Republicans and rural Democrats in the House staged a sudden coup, overthrowing the Democratic leadership and installing Republican Joe Hayes as Speaker. The reasons for the coup were complex and political, but included rural legislators' concern that their areas would not receive an adequate share of oil spending. To keep the old leadership from getting into their offices, the new group broke off keys in the locks of their doors. With much chaos and deal-making, the biggest-spending and longest-lasting session in state history extended well into the summer. In one fiscal year, $6 billion flowed from the Legislature. The public process disintegrated as the capital budget grew. Legislative staffers were able to obtain funding for projects with a word to a finance committee aide. Besides extreme waste, allegations of corruption wafted through the capitol. Two senators were indicted during this period. George Hohman was convicted of bribery, ending his legislative career. Charges that Ed Dankworth attempted to use his position for vast personal gain were dropped due to legislative immunity. The wild spending party promised to go on indefinitely with predictions of oil prices rising continuously and new oil fields to be found. Official state forecasts predicted $140 billion in accumulated revenue by 2000.[6]

Meanwhile, Elmer Rasmuson carefully studied how to avoid losing the wealth that was coming in. Hammond appointed Rasmuson as the first chairman of the Alaska Permanent Fund Corporation's board of trustees after passage of the 1980 legislation that created the corporation and instituted the prudent-investor rule (see the previous chapter). Rasmuson convened the trustees to set up the organization and decide its investment criteria. Three trustees were commissioners of state departments and three, including Rasmuson, were members of the public. None had professional investment expertise. With the wisdom to recognize their shortcomings, the board decided to put off any decisions for a year, during which trustees would study the best way to handle their task.

Rasmuson embarked on trips to the east and west coasts visiting managers of more than ten of the nation's largest pension and endowment funds at corporations, state governments, and universities. He was frustrated that none of the other trustees would join him, convincing him that a trustee's position should be full-time. Rasmuson also brought national experts to Alaska for seminars with the trustees and the public.[1]

Rasmuson and other trustees came to recognize gaps and flaws in the statutes that created and governed the fund. While the 1980 legislation had laid the corporation's foundation, it prevented the fund from investing in equities, an excessively cautious strategy inappropriate for a large fund with a long time horizon. Indeed, the fund's risk-free investments had done so poorly that twice in its first four years it had lost purchasing power due to inflation.[2] Even if the fund performed better, however, its legal structure seemed to make more inflation losses probable for the simple reason that under the law, all income was available for spending. Unless the legislature voluntarily redirected some of the income back to principal, the fund would grow only with new deposits of oil revenues, not from investment earnings.

Finally, Rasmuson saw a problem in the composition and powers of the trustee board. With three members of the governor's cabinet serving as trustees, the board lacked independence. Rasmuson wanted more trustees selected from the public and he wanted them to have more responsibility. He thought trustees should work full-time on the fund, reviewing investment details as well as policy, and that they should receive pay similar to that of the Legislature. His research suggested the trustees should plan the future of all the state's long-term finances, not just the permanent fund.[3] Based on investment theory, that idea made sense—income, savings, and spending should be coordinated— but the idea was naïve. The Legislature would never give up such critical power to a non-elected board, nor should they.

Consideration of the trustees' proposals for statutory changes and the dividend backstop bill came to a head during the 1982 legislative session. This would be Hammond's last session in office, his last chance to make the Permanent Fund strong enough to survive after he was gone. The legislative leadership had changed since the earlier fights creating the Fund. With Hayes presiding in the House, thanks to the coup, permanent fund founders Hugh Malone and Terry Gardiner were in the minority. Clem Tillion, Clark Gruening, and Steve Cowper no longer served in the Legislature. However, my friend and ally from the Anchorage Assembly, Senator Arliss Sturgulewski, a Republican, chaired the Legislative Budget and Audit Committee, which had official oversight of the permanent fund. And Rasmuson himself worked the halls of the capitol, where his imperious style served the fund well. His wealth and accomplishments commanded legislators' respect, and his manner demanded their deference.[4]

The proposed inflation-proofing legislation called for an annual deposit of fund income into the principal sufficient to offset the year's loss of buying power. The omission of an inflation adjustment may have been a simple oversight in earlier legislation, but that didn't mean passage was easy in 1982. Sturgulewski took the lead in the Senate. She says she was known as "Miss Goodie Two-Shoes" for her emphasis on public policy, but Arliss could be an imposing opponent and she had a strong staff, including Steve Rieger, who later became a respected legislator himself. Sturgulewski had worked closely with Rasmuson from the beginning, and Rieger had gone along on one of Rasmuson's fact-finding trips. Hammond supported inflation-proofing, but only if it came after dividends; he believed that if realized income in a year wasn't enough to both pay dividends and reinvest for inflation, then the reinvestment should be reduced, not the dividend. That was bad policy, justified only by Hammond's belief in putting the dividend above all else. But Sturgulewski and Rasmuson had no choice but to go along. Fortunately, there always has been enough money to pay both obligations in full every year.

When the permanent fund bill came out of the Senate Finance Committee, however, the inflation-proofing provision was gone, either because senators didn't understand the legislation or because they didn't want to dedicate more money to savings. Hugh Malone came to Sturgulewski to ask her to fight for the issue with an amendment offered from the Senate floor. The projected vote count stood at a tie, ten to ten. Sturgulewski dispatched Rieger and others to find one more vote—breaking her standing rule not to use staff in this way—and the team managed to turn Senator Brad Bradley from a no to a yes. The amendment to include inflation-proofing narrowly passed, and the bill was approved.[5] Today, inflation-proofing accounts for more of the permanent fund's savings than any other single source—more than either oil revenues or special appropriations, exceeding $9 billion of the $24.6 billion principal in 2005.

The legislation also for the first time allowed investment in stocks, and reconstituted the board of trustees so that a majority—four of six—would be public members. The governor's members would remain the commissioner of revenue and another cabinet member. Rasmuson had achieved three of his four goals but not the higher salaries and expanded responsibilities for the trustees, who would continue to be paid $400 per meeting. Disappointed and feeling his work was not sufficiently valued, Rasmuson turned down Hammond's offer of reappointment to the board later that year and left the fund he had helped shape.[6]

The backstop dividend legislation faced a steeper uphill climb than inflation-proofing. The dividend idea never had strong political or popular support, and without the longevity feature it had lost much of its appeal. Legislators feared a dividend that was the same for everyone would encourage poor people to move to Alaska for the annual check. This probably has happened, to a limited extent, just as low-income residents have been influenced not to leave. The Senate preferred to spend money on big capital projects. And the equal-dividend concept increased moral objections some people had to free money distributions. According to this reasoning, long-time Alaskans deserved payments in exchange for helping build the state, but giving money to those who had done nothing to earn it was wrong. True to this conviction, a small number of citizens gave back their dividends in the program's early years. Representative Ramona Barnes, an Anchorage Republican, tore up a play-money $1,000 bill on the House floor to demonstrate the immoral waste of the dividend.

Cliff John Groh, then a twenty-seven-year-old House minority staffer responsible for the backstop dividend bill, recalls attending a meeting with six to ten legislators early in the session discussing strategy for advancing the legislation. Representative Brian Rogers, a Fairbanks Democrat, asked those in attendance, "Do we have any votes outside this room?" The bill's supporters included the governor, with his intense, emotional focus; a core group of House Democrats; a couple of Republicans; and a Libertarian—it was a tri-partisan coalition, but a small one. With no public groundswell for the dividend and little other political support, experienced observers predicted the bill would die. [7]

Still, the permanent fund musketeers—Malone, Gardiner, Erickson, and Rhode—now with Groh added, prepared for one more fight. As they had in the previous fund battles, they started work with lengthy policy discussions and study. Groh remembers meeting on a Sunday afternoon while his beloved San Francisco 49ers played in the Super Bowl. The record he kept at those gatherings may be the clearest rationale for the dividend ever set down by its creators. The dividend would build a public constituency for the permanent fund; it would hold down government growth by consuming excess revenue; it would deliver the benefits of oil wealth to the public more efficiently than any other kind of spending; it would be the most effective way of stimulating the economy; it would be the most equitable way of distributing Alaskans' oil wealth; it would allow Alaskans to choose how they wanted to spend their share of oil revenue; and it would provide an economic safety net for poor Alaskans when declining oil revenues curtailed state spending and slowed the economy.[8] Hammond had another central purpose for the dividend, which he rarely mentioned and the legislators didn't add to their list—annual help for cash-poor rural Alaskans. It's noteworthy that all of these purposes for the dividend remain operative today except one. Soaking up excess oil revenues hasn't been necessary for a long time.

The policy issues may appear larger in retrospect than they did in 1982. The backstop bill would come into play only if the U.S. Supreme Court ruled in favor of Zobel. Most of the legislative effort concentrated on overcoming constitutional flaws in the original dividend program. Attorney Susan Burke, a law partner to Av Gross, worked with Groh, who then had no legal training, to identify potential challenges to the bill and to work through them with key legislators. Groh even enlisted the help of Ron Zobel to find vulnerabilities. Dealing with each problem meant peeling away an element of Hammond's treasured original concept, with the effect of simplifying the program to its essence. On these grounds, the bill adopted a minimal residency requirement of just six months (much later increased to one year). Anchorage attorney John McKay opined that excluding children might be unconstitutional, and the House hurriedly added language including children in the session's final days, with control of the money to be left to parents.[9]

"We knew it would never pass again if Hammond wasn't in office, and Hammond had to leave office in 1982," Groh said. "You couldn't wait around and go through another round of litigation and then pass it and get another backstop bill. That wasn't happening."

Despite the sour taste of potentially losing his preferred version of the program, Hammond threw all his political weight behind the backstop bill, both publicly and behind the scenes. He underlined the intensity of his position by becoming the first governor ever to testify before a Legislative committee. He employed the same strategy that had worked two years earlier: He threatened to veto capital projects of legislators who stood in the way and he looked the other way on questionable spending by those who went along. He also threatened to call a special session if the bill didn't pass. Senate passage was particularly difficult; senators could only think about pushing more money into construction projects. The previous year, at the absolute peak of oil revenues, the Legislature had approved a $1.8 billion special appropriation to the fund. To obtain Senate votes for the dividend backstop bill, Hammond made a quiet agreement to delay indefinitely payment of part of the $1.8 billion appropriation, leaving more money for senators to spend.[10]

The backstop bill received final passage at the very end of the session. Less than two weeks later, the Supreme Court threw out the original dividend program. Bitterly disappointed, Hammond signed the new dividend bill in private. The first dividend checks, $1,000 each, were mailed almost immediately.

Two decades later, the meaning of the dividend has evolved. No one talks any more about the moral decision of whether to accept the money. The desire to reward longer residency has abated as Alaska's population has become less transient—a consequence of a more stable economy, not the dividend. With most of our real pioneers gone, the concept of paying people according to when they arrived in Alaska now seems strange and ill-advised. Even Hammond came to praise the effectiveness of equal dividends in creating a protective constituency for the permanent fund. He came to see that public support would have been weaker if some Alaskans received larger dividends than others.[11] The dividend built a high wall around the fund and around its income as well.

Indeed, the dividend may have worked too well, transforming the permanent fund into a dividend fund in the minds of many Alaskans. Some residents have come to see the dividend as an entitlement and the permanent fund as a vehicle to deliver it.

Does the record support this belief? In part, the answer must be yes. Recall that the three purposes for the dividend set out in the original 1980 legislation—the only purposes ever expressed in law—begin by saying the dividend would "provide a mechanism for equitable distribution to the people of Alaska of at least a portion of the state's energy wealth derived from the development and production of the natural resources belonging to them as Alaskans." On the other hand, the same document gives support to the concept that a citizenship obligation comes with accepting the dividend. The other two purposes in the 1980 act were to encourage longer residency in Alaska and to motivate awareness and involvement in the management and expenditure of the fund. If the permanent fund were exclusively a mechanism to give people money, then these two other purposes would be redundant, better stated as consequences rather than as goals of making the payments. The third purpose, of buying a constituency for the permanent fund, makes sense only if the fund is assumed to have a function as something other than a source of dividends. It would be absurd to say the goal of paying a dividend is to create a constituency for paying a dividend.

These contradictions came about in the course of political lawmaking. The compromises integral to the legislative process rarely yield a philosopher's logic. The consequences of this ambiguity, however, have been significant. Disagreements over the purpose of the fund and the dividend have contributed to Alaska's inability to address its long-term fiscal problems. Hammond himself ultimately advocated using some fund earnings for government, and even called for a graduated tax on the dividend, which essentially would have made it into more of a needs-based payment than a straight resource rebate. He seemed to have no difficulty reconciling that the dividend could be two things—a return of residents' own resource wealth and a "bribe" of the public to defend the permanent fund.

I tend to think of the dividend payments as a tactic to protect the fund rather than as a way of giving people back their own money. Does anyone really believe that a person gains individual ownership in Alaska's natural resources by living in the state for a year? I don't. Individual ownership would imply that Alaskans have a right to take their portions of all petroleum, hard rock minerals, fish, timber, water and air, not just as cash payments but to carve out of nature. That clearly is not what Congress intended when it made Alaska a state. In fact, the Alaska Statehood Act granted the new state ownership of 103 million acres on the condition that the subsurface minerals could *never* be owned by individuals. These riches came to Alaska as an institution, not as a group of individuals. The endowment was meant to remain attached to the land—unlike people, who come and go—and was supposed to outlast contemporary citizens and serve future generations.

These issues received a fascinating airing in court in the mid-1980s thanks to a clever lawyer, David Shaftel, who was assisted by Ron Zobel. Shaftel tried to use the law's own rhetoric to show that Permanent Fund dividend checks were not taxable by the Internal Revenue Service. Two lawsuits, which were consolidated, advanced two theories. One maintained that the people already owned the state's natural resources, and argued that they couldn't be taxed on what already belonged to them. The Ninth Circuit Court of Appeals flatly rejected the idea that the people owned the state's natural resources, relying on language found in the Alaska Constitution and in the permanent fund statute referring to the state as the owner. Besides, the court pointed out, even if the people did own the resources and the permanent fund, they still would have to pay taxes on their investment income, like everyone else.

Even more creatively, the other suit argued that because the state paid the dividends without expecting anything in return, it constituted a gift, and gifts are not taxable. Shaftel took the case to the U.S. Supreme Court, but it was not heard. "No attempt was made to find out whether the individual applicant did anything positive for the State in return for the dividend," Shaftel wrote. "In fact, the State of Alaska had no legal, moral or other obligation to distribute a portion of the State's energy wealth to Alaska residents." The federal district court and the appeals court both found it more difficult to dismiss this argument, especially because it had found in the other case that the people didn't own the wealth, and that the state owed them nothing. The court used a tortured reading of the 1980 dividend act's statement of purpose to show that, while the state was under no real obligation to pay the money, it thought that it was. Under a legal precedent defining gifts, the intent of the donor was the key. If the state thought the payment was an obligation, not a gift, then it wasn't a gift.[12]

A more persuasive point, barely alluded to in the ruling, was that the state in fact did get something in return for the dividend—a constituency for protecting the permanent fund. It was a good deal, too. At this writing, the state had surpassed $40 billion in its permanent fund thanks in large part to the $14 billion in protection money it has paid out as dividends since 1982.

---

[1] Neal Fried, Alaska Department of Labor, personal communication.

[2] Free Conference Committee Substitute for SB 122 (1980).

[3] Cliff Groh, opinion column, *Anchorage Daily News*, January 30, 2005; Rosemary Shinohara, *Anchorage Daily News*, January 27, 2005.

[4] Jay Hammond, *Tales of Alaska's Bush Rat Governor* (Fairbanks and Seattle: Epicenter Press, 1994) 252-253.

[5] Cliff Groh, "The Permanent Fund Dividend Story," (unpublished manuscript) November 17, 1997.

[6] Groh manuscript; Cliff Groh, interview by Charles Wohlforth, digital recording, December 27, 2005.

[7] Terrence Cole and Elmer F. Rasmuson, *Banking on Alaska: The Story of the National Bank of Alaska*, vol. 2, *Elmer's Memoirs* (Anchorage: National Bank of Alaska, 2000), 176-188.

[8] Sheila F. Helgath and Sarah A. Babb, *Alaska's Permanent Fund: Legislative History, Intent, and Operations*, Alaska State Senate, Rural Research Agency, January 1986, 34.

[9] Cole and Rasmuson, 183-184.

[10] George Rogers, interview by Nancy Gross, transcript, circa 2000, 7.

[11] Arliss Sturgulewski, interview by Charles Wohlforth, digital recording, January 12, 2006.

[12] Cole and Rasmuson, 182.

[13] Groh manuscript and interview.

[14] Ibid.

[15] John McKay, personal communication; other material in the paragraph from Groh.

[16] Groh manuscript.

[17] Hammond, 253.

[18] U.S. Court of Appeals for the Ninth Circuit Opinion, case no. 86-3728, *Greisen v. U.S.* and *Beattie v. U.S.*; and U.S. Supreme Court, October Term 1987, *Beattie v. U.S.*, petition for Writ of Certiorari.

CHAPTER 11
Building the institution, 1982-1984

W hen the job of executive director of the Alaska Permanent Fund opened in the fall of 1982, my qualifications were a remarkable fit. I had earned an MBA and a degree in accounting. I had managed a large government organization with a big budget in the military. I also had started a small government agency—two, if you count AIDA—with only a part-time board for direction. My political experience included working with legislators on complex public-finance issues and interacting with the public as an elected official. The time spent unifying the Municipality of Anchorage showed I could navigate rough political waters. One of my most important qualifications, however, was negative: I was perceived as having little commitment to either the Republican or Democrat party.

As a civil service employee in the military I had maintained my non-partisan status carefully. The Hatch Act prohibited federal employees from running for partisan elected office. Before I could file for my first Anchorage City Council run, I had to obtain permission from my supervisors at Fort Richardson. This wasn't a problem because the council and assembly were authentically non-partisan in those days. My first state-affiliated jobs with the bond bank and AIDA grew out of my experience in local government and my professional relationships. I got no help from a party and I never needed to develop party membership.

In 1982, after seven years at the bond bank under Hammond, the political landscape was about to change. I wanted to continue working on infrastructure and developing the state's economy, but in all likelihood a new governor would choose his own bond-bank director.

The job could be treated as a reward because its duties left plenty of time to work on other issues—in my case, running AIDA and other state and local work. In March 1982, I decided to run for lieutenant governor. If I won, the job would keep me in the middle of things. In order to run, however, I would have to join a party.

I could go either way. My political outlook had four major themes that straddled party lines. My belief in low taxes, small government, and a strong national defense matched with the Republican agenda, while my support for individual freedom and human rights fit better with the Democrats. In terms of style, the Democrats were more appealing to me. The Alaska Democratic Party had shown more respect for public policy and rational debate, while the Republicans generally were more willing to engage in pragmatic, power politics. On state issues, the differences between the Republicans and Democrats were not great. Pro-development attitudes dominated both parties, with hot issues such as the capital move defining candidates more clearly than partisan labels. Republican Hammond stood to the left of many Democrats. In Alaska's open primary system, voters could jump back and forth between parties on the same ballot, voting for their favorite candidates regardless of party. A candidate could win a party primary with more votes from the opposition party than from his own. My choice of which primary to enter would depend on the strategy of the moment rather than on my political outlook or base of supporters.

I met with Democratic gubernatorial candidate Bill Sheffield, who lived in Anchorage. He had made himself a front-runner by campaigning all over the state far in advance of the election, financing his travels with a personal fortune made in the hotel business. Sheffield said he didn't want a running mate in the primary, and hoped to balance the ticket with someone from outside of Anchorage. I had to agree this was a good strategy. In the end, he was paired with Stephen McAlpine of Valdez. Next, I went to see Tom Fink, the ultra-conservative Republican contender. With his deadpan smile, Fink said he would welcome me into the race, promising that if I won, he would be happy to set me up with an office in the basement of the capitol with a candle for light and a walkie-talkie for a telephone.

Some friends and former constituents were shocked to learn I was a Republican when I filed for office that summer. One practical reason for my choice was the large but relatively weak field of candidates on the Republican side. With the vote divided five ways in the primary election, a small percentage would be needed to win the nomination and advance to the general election. A bigger reason for my decision was that I admired Terry Miller, the incumbent lieutenant governor, who was running for the Republican gubernatorial nomination. Miller and I had worked together on state finance issues—he had been a loan advocate—and he impressed me with his ability to execute his ideas despite holding the relatively weak office of lieutenant governor. Unfortunately, he didn't carry his ability to execute into the run for governor. Miller's campaign was lackluster, and Fink surged in the polls. The possibility loomed that Fink and I would be running mates in the general election. Fran said she would move back to New York if that happened. On election night, she was ready to buy her ticket. In early returns, Fink and I both led. However, when all the votes were counted, Anchorage Senator Mike Colletta was the winner in my race. I was second. Fink faced Sheffield for governor.

The outcome of the Republican primary threatened Hammond's legacy. He prepared to leave the governor's mansion amid apprehension that his replacement would be Tom Fink, who had opposed the fund earlier and more consistently than any other established politician. The smoke had hardly cleared from the legislative battles establishing the fund's independence and protecting it from inflation. Citizens were still cashing their first dividend checks. The new laws could easily be changed, and a policy reversal at this early stage could mean losing it all. Fink was campaigning on use of the fund as a source of cash for low-interest loans and to finance building an enormous and unneeded Susitna dam.[1] The administration and trustees worked quickly to solidify the fund as an institution that could defend itself.

Dr. George Rogers was the ideal leader for that work. When Elmer Rasmuson left the board of trustees in 1982, Rogers, who had been biding his time as a trustee, moved into the chairmanship. His record as an economist was second to none in Alaska. His first job, in the 1930s, had involved analyzing North Slope oil prospects for Standard

Oil. He worked as an economist for territorial Governor Ernest Gruening when he came to Alaska after World War II. Hardly an economic issue arose in the territory or the state over the next fifty years without Rogers' keen mind engaged in the solution. He also had compiled a list of academic honors that included many of the world's great universities.[2] Rogers' warmth and good humor made him a pleasure to work with. Rasmuson, for all his brilliance, could treat subordinates with formality and harshness. Rasmuson saw himself as the master of the permanent fund and left when that role was not confirmed by legislation. Rogers had a strong will and many ideas, too, but he preferred to work as part of a team of relative equals.

Among Rogers' first moves, he located high-quality office space in a new Juneau building owned by the Goldbelt Native Corporation. Rasmuson had wanted an independent fund but, always the frugal banker, had kept management in the Department of Revenue while the trustees studied fund management and worked on legislation. Rogers and I, on the other hand, saw an urgent need for the permanent fund to develop its own identity as an institution separate from the administration. He believed, and I agreed, that the fund would gain strength and credibility by standing alone and projecting solidity and an air of corporate success.[3]

Staffing the fund became a priority. Trustees began advertising for lower positions even before hiring an executive director, with the expectation that the newly hired director could choose from among the applicants. Just six weeks before election day, the trustees set standards for the director and decided to advertise only in Alaska. The hiring decision would be made days after the new governor was elected.[4]

For me, the August primary election campaign amounted to a vacation. In order to run, I had resigned from the bond bank—as I had done for the 1978 mayoral race—and lived on my accrued leave. The board took me back when the campaign ended. In hindsight, losing the election was the best thing that could have happened. If I had won, I never would have been considered for the much more important opportunity of managing the permanent fund.

Jim Rhode stopped by my office at the bond bank to suggest I apply for the permanent fund job. I was surprised. Rhode had a lot of influence over the selection. Few had been more active in the fight to create the fund and decide its purpose, and he was employed then as the board's special assistant. But the two of us weren't exactly friends. I could not forget that Jim had ridiculed my beloved bond bank by wearing a beanie around the capitol years before. If he wanted me to run the fund, I could only conclude that he believed I had the qualifications the fund needed. Specifically, I believe he wanted my political background on his side. While Rhode expected to continue in a powerful policy position as special assistant, I would be guard dog defending the fund from Fink and the Legislature.

Hammond said my name was the only one he considered. Many years later, he told researcher Nancy Gross that he was impressed by my run for mayor in 1978, presumably meaning he liked that I stood up for equal rights despite having to pay a high political price. Second, he mentioned my financial background. "Dave was the first thought to my mind," Hammond recalled. "And I really didn't know him that well, but he had a great reputation among those who were more familiar with that sort of thing than I."[5]

Rogers, also interviewed by Gross, knew little about me before the applications came in. "Friends of mine up in Anchorage whom I trusted told me that David is really the man you should get," he said. "And then when I met him, of course, I fell in love with him right away because he's that sort of person that you just can't help but like. He's not impressive looking—he's short and dumpy—but his mind just worked the way mine works and it was a partnership. And so I told the trustees, going through this thing, I said, 'I'm going to short-cut certain things a lot here.'"[6]

I didn't expect an inside track when I went to the interview in Juneau. I didn't know that Hammond admired my political fortitude or that Rogers found me lovable and dumpy, although we had clicked. When I went into the executive session with the trustees, however, the questions quickly revealed the job was mine to lose. They asked pointedly if I would use the job as a stepping stone to higher office. The permanent fund would offer an unprecedented opportunity to build popularity: A successful executive director could claim to have put dividend checks into the voters' mailboxes. I asked if it would help if I promised never to run for office again. The trustees indicated it would. On the spot, I made that promise, ending my political career.

The other issue that came up was how Bill Sheffield would react to my appointment. He had just won the gubernatorial election. During the primary campaign, I had blasted the Democrats, including Sheffield and McAlpine, with standard-issue political buckshot. But it happened that Lance Anderson was present at the trustee's meeting. Besides leading Sheffield's transition team, he had been on my board at the bond bank and was a good friend. "I've known Dave for years," Anderson said. "We always thought he was a Democrat anyway." He offered to give Sheffield the news and assured the board that my selection would be acceptable. Apparently that conversation didn't take place in time. Lance later told me, apologetically, that he simply forgot to speak to the governor-elect. Sheffield learned about my hiring from a newspaper, and reportedly blew his top at having such an important appointment taken away from him—although he says today he soon got over his anger.

After interviewing four finalists—three Hammond administration people and me—and holding a private forty-five-minute discussion, the board reconvened in public session and chose me that same afternoon.[7]

Once again, career advancement required a sacrifice by Fran. She had developed a fascinating occupation as administrator of the village of Akutan, a tiny community with a huge crab fishery out in the Aleutian Islands. Through Fran's efforts, Akutan incorporated as a city, imposed a fisheries tax, and used the money to hire the local Native corporation and its resident shareholders to build needed public facilities. But Akutan would prove too far from Juneau to continue that association. Getting there for monthly Council meetings already was difficult enough, the final leg of the trip from Anchorage having to be made in a float plane because Akutan had no runway. To me, it seemed that every stopover along the way involved a long weather delay and telephone updates from Fran as she whiled away the time eating crab and drinking beer. As it turned out, however, she enjoyed living in Juneau where she owned and operated a women's clothing store there called "Victoria's." We bought a house in Thane, the historic mining area south of downtown Juneau, overlooking the Gastineau Channel on one side and backed up against the rainforest and mountainside on the other.

The advantages of keeping the fund's management in Juneau were significant. In that first year, having George Rogers within walking distance of the office made consultation and decision-making fast and easy. Over the long term, we benefited from our proximity to the capitol, which allowed constant awareness and quick access when political issues arose. One other factor I expected to be important—having less of a time-zone difference from East Coast financial markets— disappeared when a new time-zone arrangement put most of the state in the same hour.

I was happy to have gotten the job, but was far from confident about my prospects. Although the Alaska Permanent Fund had existed in the constitution for six years, that period had been marked by controversy and uncertainty. Although the right laws and the right board finally were in place, a new Legislature and governor were coming into town. It seemed unlikely they would leave the fund alone. Even if they were kind to the fund, I knew Sheffield wasn't happy that I had been hired, and it was possible I would get fired by a new board. When I arrived in Juneau, many people did not expect me to succeed.

My ignorance of the fund's administration up to that date also created anxiety. Staff at the Department of Revenue had managed the fund's investments from their offices in the State Office Building. When I first visited there to size up the operation I was shown into a conference room, empty except for a copy-paper box of files on the table with some yellow legal pads and pens. This was the Alaska Permanent Fund. The box contained lists of assets totaling $3.5 billion, hand-written notes from Elmer Rasmuson, and copies of legislation but no analysis of asset allocation, no meeting minutes, no performance measures, no policies on return objectives or risk constraints. The trustees had made no formal decision on whether to have in-house staff manage the money or to contract with investment houses. Even after six years of debate, the basic purpose of the fund never had been articulated clearly—a prerequisite for designing a rational investment program.

The papers documented incoming revenue and where it had been invested. Prior to the 1982 legislation, the fund had been permitted to invest only in the safest income securities, and the Department of Revenue had carried that direction to an extreme. Eighty percent of the portfolio was in short-term U.S. notes, treasury bills, and bonds, with the bulk of the remaining funds consisting of ordinary bank deposits. Relatively small amounts were invested in mortgages and corporate bonds. Rasmuson had drilled fear of inflation into the staff, calling it "a thief in the night," and as a result the average life of the entire portfolio was less than two years. Next, I checked the internal controls and procedures. Few had been established, and little was written down. However, the numbers worked out, so the money was all there. I began the work of setting up proper safeguards from scratch.

Documents in the box also recorded a large unpaid obligation to the fund. The Legislature had appropriated $900 million to the fund in 1980. In 1981, not to be outdone, the next Legislature appropriated $1.8 billion. I discovered that the state had failed to deposit all the money into the fund. (I didn't know at the time that Hammond had withheld deposits approved by the Legislature to gain support for the backstop dividend bill.) By the end of 1982, the 1981 appropriation was still $700 million short in transfer of money to the fund. I investigated to find out when the state would earn the money to cover the shortfall. Then I went to see acting Commissioner of Revenue Joe Donahue and gave him an invoice for the full amount, breaking it out into an easy-payment plan that coincided with the state's income flow. Donahue politely explained that he would be out the door in a few days, by the end of the new governor's transition period, but he offered to hand over my cheeky invoice to his successor. As it happened, Sheffield was just arriving in town to prepare for his inauguration, and the invoice quickly landed on his desk. Apparently my audacity did not amuse him at all. For the second time in a few weeks, he had to be pried off the ceiling over news from me that had not been presented in the right way.

The governor's anger was a bad omen. I might be fired. To defuse the situation, I drove out to the bookstore at the University of Alaska Southeast in Auke Bay where I bought some postcards that said "Send

Money" in gold on green. They were designed for students to send to their parents. I wrote one to Sheffield, requesting the first $100 million by a certain date based on the payment plan I had devised. The point was to make him laugh while delivering a message of humility—with me in the role of student and the governor as the parent—while keeping the issue of the money alive. Sheffield said he would take it under advisement.

As the legislative session began, a bill went in the hopper to repeal most of the $700 million appropriation.[8] Although oil revenue pouring into the treasury was plentiful by any reasonable measure, oil prices had dropped from their peak, making the spending orgies of the previous few years no longer affordable. By this new definition of poverty, legislators "needed" the $700 million. In other words, legislators saw political benefit in spending the money in their own names, but saw none in fulfilling former legislators' promise to save it. Sheffield took his own shot at the fund. He introduced legislation to repeal the five-year averaging of income, which would severely weaken inflation-proofing, and to do away with the dividend altogether. Instead, he wanted to dedicate the fund's income to community projects, the longevity bonus for elders, and a capital-projects fund.[9] His proposal had ample support in the Legislature, but when the public heard about it, everyone ran for cover as if the governor had stepped in a nest of hornets. Less than six months after the first dividend arrived in the mail, the fund had become politically inviolate.[10]

Sheffield's questionable decision to make repeal of the dividend one of his first initiatives was indicative of his rocky first year in office. Another was a post-election fund-raising trip he made outside Alaska to solicit money from the oil industry. Senator Frank Ferguson, a powerful Democrat from Kotzebue, blasted Sheffield, suggesting the trip made the governor of Alaska appear to be beholden to the oil companies. The flap benefited the permanent fund, however, when Sheffield realized the unpaid $700 million appropriation gave him leverage that was entirely within his control: He didn't need any new authorization to deposit the promised money in the fund, beyond the Legislature's reach. After his spat with Ferguson, Sheffield deposited $100 million, and he reportedly made the threat he would deposit $100 million more every time he was crossed. I don't know how many times he carried out that threat. It may have been a coincidence that while Sheffield's political road remained rough, the $700 million was transferred to the fund faster than the schedule I had suggested. In time, Sheffield recognized the value of the permanent fund in its own right and became its strong advocate. The fund's trustees and management team developed excellent relations with the governor.

In my first days on the job, as I reviewed the fund's investments and scant records, I selected eight staff members to run the operation. One employee had been predetermined—Jim Rhode. Instead of being the trustees' special assistant, he reluctantly accepted the no. 2 position as the research and liaison officer, reporting to me. In practice, however, Jim didn't respect my abilities enough to take a subordinate role, and he continued to operate largely on his own in the political and policy realm.[11] In the transcripts of an early meeting with the trustees, when we were deciding the direction and policies of the new organization, Rhode and I repeatedly are shown contradicting each other's advice, advocating two different visions for the fund. After I stated my opinion, he sometimes spoke up to say the fund was intended to be otherwise by its founders, or to condescendingly explain how things are usually done. Rhode was one of the brightest men I ever worked with, and a chief architect of the permanent fund legislation, so I can imagine it was difficult for him to relinquish his central role. But I was in charge now.

Rhode was used to behind-the-scenes politicking. I struggled to track his invisible moves with the trustees, administration, and legislators. Rhode wanted the trustees to engage the Legislature over the flurry of new bills related to using the fund's income. I said we should speak up only when legislation would affect our trust—the corpus of the fund or the inflation-proofing needed to protect its value—and we should remain silent on any other issue, especially related to the dividend or other uses of the income.[12] Rhode also pushed for creation of an advisory committee of outside experts to help manage investments. He had recruited nationally renowned experts and had letters of appointment ready for the trustees' signatures. Rhode envisioned investment policies being decided by the trustees exclusively in executive session. He believed public meetings would be reserved for educational seminars about the general themes of fund operations.[13] I strongly disagreed. The fund contained the public's money, and I wanted all decisions made in public, with a clear line of authority from the trustees—through me—to the investment staff.

My experience in local government had taught me that openness is the only antidote for accusations of corruption that inevitably arise from controversial decisions. Whenever the assembly would rezone a parcel of property at the request of a developer, some disappointed critic would allege that we were in the developer's pocket. The more secrets we kept, the easier it would be for those allegations to stick. But if our dealings and deliberations were completely open, constituents could follow our reasoning and realize we didn't have a vested interest. This concept was even more important at the permanent fund. It was vital that citizens believe we were handling their money openly and above board. If we lost their confidence, they no longer would trust us to handle these enormous financial reserves—by 2005 exceeding the private financial assets of all Alaskans—and the fund would not survive.[14]

The policy we established made everything public, including the trustees' discussions about particular investments and managers, with the only exception being information provided in confidence by tenants in our real-estate holdings, including sales figures from retail businesses. We issued public notices of all meetings. Later, we began holding meetings in communities throughout Alaska so that more of the public could attend. Our speaker's bureau dispatched trustees and senior staff members to address any group interested in hearing about the fund. Our annual reports and other materials were produced in simple language. We held nothing back. (I was disturbed in 2005 when the fund agreed to keep secret the details of certain exotic investments involving proprietary information. I would have preferred to forego those potential profits in order to maintain a record of complete transparency.)

Trustees and key staff members were required to disclose all their investment holdings and transactions. Whenever I bought or sold a stock, information about the transaction was available to anyone interested. After the fund established a record of success in the markets, members of the public began tracking our personal investment choices as well as the fund's portfolio, and some may have copied our investment moves. This scrutiny made me extra careful in what I bought and sold. I didn't think it would look good if the executive director made off-the-wall choices with his own money. As a result, I fared better with my investments than I would have otherwise.

All of my policy choices for the fund focused on enhancing the institution's credibility, independence, and strength. We would be transparent and non-political, and our dealings would be as simple and straight-laced as possible—quite boring for an intellectual like Jim Rhode, with his taste for political intrigue. After trying to make our relationship work for two years, and after talking it over with the board, I fired Rhode at the end of 1984.[15] I hated to do it. Rhode had helped shape the fund from its earliest conception, his political skill had nursed it through its long legislative birth, and he had assisted in setting up the alphabet agencies that protected the fund. But I couldn't run the fund in competition with a shadow director, one who did not believe in my policies or my ability, and who was constantly dealing independently with administration officials and legislators. Ironically, Rhode never accepted my leadership even though he had been largely responsible for my hiring. To his great credit, Jim made the firing easy on me—whatever he really felt, he said he understood my predicament.

When I first took over the fund, however, Rhode's presence was a given. In addition, almost all the staffers who had managed the fund at the Department of Revenue wanted to move over to the Alaska Permanent Fund Corporation. Career opportunities would be far greater there than in the bureaucracy. Although officially I had my choice of whom to hire, in fact Jim Rhode already had made promises to certain people, including Peter Bushre, the state's chief fiscal officer. Bushre had been a finalist for my job, which he essentially had been doing from within the revenue agency. We had butted heads when I was at the bond bank when I had pushed for speedy payment of our appropriated funds. I went along with Bushre's selection as comptroller of the fund, however, and as it turned out his work and commitment were impressive.

I accepted most other people from the Department of Revenue, including a terrific administrative staff and a knowledgeable investment officer, Bill Means. Bill's extreme caution was right for the fund in our formative years, but later I came to the conclusion that he wasn't willing to take enough risks or able to bend to new circumstances. When the fund expanded into equity investments, I asked Bill to find an assistant to handle the stock portfolio while he concentrated on the income securities. He made an unorthodox choice— Bob Storer, who worked for Los Angeles County. Although highly recommended, Storer's credentials were weak. He didn't even have a bachelor's degree. I offered him the job on the condition that he would get his bachelor's at University of Alaska Southeast, even offering to pay his tuition as long as he got As or Bs. The hire proved to be one of my best. Storer was tall, shy, and cautious—my opposite in appearance and personality—and he was loyal, smart, and capable. He contributed much to the fund's success. Later, he became executive director himself. Bob got his college diploma while working for me with all credits paid for by the permanent fund except one—he got a C in music appreciation.

The group I worked with at the Alaska Permanent Fund Corporation grew into a second family, and performed far better than I ever could have hoped. Juneau was a small town, not the kind of place you would expect to recruit the staff for a multi-billion-dollar investment fund. Our growing staff probably had credentials far below those required by similar institutions headquartered in larger cities. I tried to stretch them with as much responsibility and authority as possible—often, more than they felt ready for—while I alone was accountable to the board. My people proved worthy of the trust I placed in them, and I let them know it frequently. We ran a fun, casual office, too, with humor and personal warmth always evident. As the Fund gained value, our collective confidence grew. We evolved into a close-knit team of highly capable professionals, sought after for our skills but loyal to one another. As I frequently counseled, we tried to be confident but not arrogant.

From the start, I tried to establish our independence from the state government. For example, I insisted on having an able staff member, Joyce Sinclair, keep tabs on the oil revenue flowing into the state treasury so we would be sure of getting our correct share. This caused consternation among officials who always had been trusted to deposit the right amount without oversight. We faced a test of our independence when it was time to sign a lease for our offices. The best choice was obviously the space George Rogers had found and the board had approved in the Goldbelt Building, but the Department of Administration insisted I follow their procurement procedure. This required advertising, receiving proposals, and so forth. I thought that as an autonomous corporation we didn't need to observe all the state's rules, particularly so because we had reviewed carefully the available space and rental costs. Rogers backed me up. I rented the Goldbelt space and ordered furniture and equipment.

The furniture had not arrived when the time came to sit down with the trustees to discuss investment and management principles that would guide the Permanent Fund for decades to come. We couldn't meet in our own offices, and I didn't want to meet in a state office, either, because we needed to underline our autonomy, especially in these formative discussions. A meeting room at the Cape Fox Hotel was available for only part of the time we needed it. So my wonderful office manager, Melanie Wilhelm, helped me set up folding tables in the boathouse basement of my house in Thane—an unfinished room with large doors that would allow a boat to be winched in from Gastineau Channel. Partway through the meeting, the trustees left the Cape Fox and gathered in the boathouse for a work session. The meeting agenda was simple but crucially important:

> Determine the objectives of the Fund
> Establish investment policy by
>> Defining return objectives
>> Defining risk constraints
>> Special investment needs
>> Construct asset allocation formula
> Fund management structure
>> In house management
>> Outside management
> The Role/selection of national advisors
> Legislative activities

The first decision for any investment program is its objective. Individuals invest differently depending on whether the goal is income for retirement, capital for a major purchase or college tuition, or speculation for wealth accumulation. But the founders of the permanent fund avoided stating any single goal; they gathered political support by allowing everyone to imagine their own purpose for the fund. One universally accepted goal was to prevent wasteful expenditure of a portion of Alaska's oil wealth. Yet, as Elmer Rasmuson had observed, that was a negative goal: It told what the fund was *against*, but not what it was *for*. Years of legislative debate had considered and discarded a series of other potential goals, such as in-state lending, economic development, or community projects, but that process of elimination had left no single positive objective remaining. Without knowing the ultimate purpose, we had no external guidance to make decisions about the term of investments, the degree of acceptable risk, the desired return, and the desired amount of annual income.

At our work session, trustee Steve Cowper—no longer a member of the Legislature—declared the fund's goal should be to provide recurring income for state government when our oil fields were depleted. If that were the goal, then a relatively straightforward equation could help define the fund's policies. Variables would include the annual income needed for state spending, the time left until the oil was gone, the size of deposits to the fund, and the rate of return on investments. In reality, however, adopting such a strategy lay well beyond our capabilities because the most important variables were unknown or beyond our control. Besides, at that time, the fund appeared unlikely ever to grow large enough to replace oil revenues. Through the discussion, the trustees were able to agree only on the original "negative" goal. Rogers finally moved the meeting on to the second item of the agenda with no resolution of the first. To this day, the fund's income is mandated for dividends, inflation-proofing, and whatever else the Legislature chooses to spend it on—it has no clear objective.

Next, I gave the trustees a tutorial on investment policy choices, the most important of which was setting a target rate of return. Based on that decision, we would decide how much money to invest in stocks, bonds, and real estate. The greater the investment in stocks, also known as equities, the greater the potential gain, but also the greater the possibility that the fund could lose money in volatile markets. After a bit of circular discussion in which the trustees grappled with the question of what kind of fund we really were, I suggested a 3 percent rate of return after adjusting for inflation. I recommended we place $100 million in equities, $50 million in real estate, and $125 million for in-state investments such as certificates of deposit or Alaska-issued bonds. The trustees were surprised. This plan was far less ambitious than they had expected.

"It represents my timidness with respect to equities," I said. "I think it is essential that if we do it, we do it right, with a feel for entering gingerly into that field."

"This is very cautious and timid," Rogers said. "I was going to go for the 4 percent."[16]

My thinking centered on how the public would perceive our fledgling institution. If we went heavily into the stock market and posted a loss, even on paper, the public response could be negative far out of proportion to the size of the downturn. Many people thought stock investing akin to casino gambling. Stock investors must be prepared for volatility, which routinely can bring short-term losses in excess of 10 percent. If we lost only 1 percent of the fund, that would equate to $35 million—a figure large enough to make newspaper readers gasp. You could build several schools for that much money. The popular belief in the "waste" of the $900 million from the 1969 lease sale came about in large part due to a stock market loss of $6 million, less than 1 percent of the total. Our fund's survival might depend on avoiding that kind of publicity. Earning 3 percent rather than 4 percent annually would mean, over the long run, foregoing much more money than we would lose in a hypothetical 1 percent stock decline, but the opportunity cost was a reasonable price to pay for the strength that the fund would gain as an institution through stability and steady profit. We knew we could make 3 percent, and probably a good deal more. When it came time to report our results, we could be heroes, soaring over the low hurdle rate we had set for ourselves. That kind of success would build confidence, allowing us to be more daring later.

The strategy proved successful. We phased in an allocation of stocks as 15 percent of our portfolio over a two-year period. Three-quarters of the stock investments would be in indexes, with the rest actively managed in specialized areas of the market. The *Anchorage Daily News* editorialized in favor of our cautious approach, remembering the "loss" of $900 million received from the 1969 lease sale: "Alaska mineral royalties and lease fees have not always fared well in the stock market, but they also have not always enjoyed the sophisticated and successful management given the permanent fund in recent years."[17] Already the fund had gained some credibility for success that had been the result of our caution.

Even with our low-risk strategy, we dramatically out-performed our goal of a 3 percent real rate of return. Within a few years, Alaskans began to think of the permanent fund as a success, one of the few lasting legacies of the oil boom. I received personal credit as an investment wizard, credit which I did not deserve. Financial markets rose steadily during those years, buoying the permanent fund despite our conservative strategy. As Elmer Rasmuson said, "Any turkey can fly in a strong wind."

I can take some credit, however, for policies that helped build public confidence, allowing us to be daring enough later to make the fund fly under its own power.

---

[1] Hal Spencer, *Anchorage Daily News*, March 13, 1986.

[2] George Rogers, interview by Nancy Gross, transcript, circa 2000.

[3] Rogers interview transcript, 6.

[4] Alaska Permanent Fund Corporation Board of Trustees, minutes of the annual meeting of September 17, 1982 (amended).

[5] Jay Hammond, interview by Nancy Gross, transcript, circa 2000, 9.

[6] Rogers interview transcript, 8.

[7] Alaska Permanent Fund Corporation Board of Trustees, minutes of the special meetings of November 4 and 5, 1982.

[8] SB 92, introduced by Sackett and Mulcahy, January 1, 1983. The bill would repeal all but $1.2 billion of the original $1.8 billion.

[9]HB 316, introduced by the governor, April 4, 1982.

[10]Editorial, *Anchorage Daily News*, February 16, 1983.

[11]On Rhode's respect for my abilities: Cliff Groh, interview by Charles Wohlforth, digital recording, December 27, 2005.

[12]Alaska Permanent Fund Corporation Board of Trustees, transcript of the work session of February 18, 1983, 35.

[13]APFC Board of Trustees transcript, February 18, 1983, 29-33.

[14]Scott Goldsmith assisted with this calculation in personal communications. The permanent fund contains $50,000 per capita; Alaskan adults' mean per capita net financial assets are about $36,000.

[15]Annette Taylor, *The Anchorage Times*, December 14, 1984.

[16]APFC Board of Trustees transcript, February 18, 1983, 24.

[17]Editorial, *Anchorage Daily News*, April 1, 1983.

CHAPTER 12
The permanent fund matures, 1984-1992

In 1990 Walter Hickel won the governorship by defeating two of my good friends—Tony Knowles and Arliss Sturgulewski—and for the first time, Alaska had a chief executive who lacked enthusiasm for the permanent fund. Hickel paid lip service to the fund, but its concept ran counter to his philosophy. Hickel believed in big, bold projects and surely would have preferred spending the money on bridges, dams, roads, railroads, and other great notions that would stand as monuments to the Alaska spirit. His opposition to the dividend was outspoken as late as 1988, and resurfaced after he left office in 1994. But while he was governor, Hickel couldn't afford the political price of going against the fund or the dividend. He wanted to fire me, and sent an intermediary with heavy hints that I should clear out. I saw no reason to comply, and he took no action against me. Hickel told trustee Oral Freeman that I had become a "monarch."[1] I had delivered good returns and healthy dividends for eight years, and the governor apparently regarded me as untouchable.

I don't deny occasionally putting on a regal air, but not for my own benefit or to enhance my political career. I had made a solemn and unconditional promise never again to seek elected office. Instead, I played the role of king of the permanent fund to strengthen the fund itself. I avoided testifying before the Legislature too often, and when I did go to the capitol, I contrived to have metaphorical trumpet flourishes announce my arrival. The point was to develop the psychology that the permanent fund was too important to be tampered with—that it stood apart from and above the political fray.

By the time Hickel returned to the governorship, legislative attacks on the fund had become rare. But in my first few years on the job, new proposals were made more frequently than we could evaluate and respond to them. It was then, in protecting the fund, that I contrived to become a monarch—and coincidentally became impossible for Hickel to fire.

In 1984, even though the Legislature still had plenty of oil revenue to work with, the permanent fund was a constant target. Eleven House Republicans, led by John Cowdery of Anchorage, introduced a bill to reverse the fund's savings concept, repealing the prudent-investor rule, and mandating that half the principal be invested in Alaska.[2] The fund at that time contained $5 billion, so the proposed loan program would amount to $2.5 billion—or about six times the net worth of all the banks in the state. The Alaska economy was too small to absorb that much money, and the banks would have been forced out of the lending market. As I testified, the bill would destroy the banking system, the economy, and the permanent fund.[3]

Governor Sheffield helped kill that bill. He also resisted a Senate plan the same year to use about $600 million of accumulated fund earnings to pay for Southeast Alaska hydroelectric projects and to make a partial payment on the proposed Susitna Dam, a massive project north of Anchorage. A supporter of that idea, Democratic Senator Bill Ray of Juneau, argued that the income should be spent before the Alaska Permanent Fund Corporation could waste it. "Possibly they're using that money as a contingency fund while they dibble and dabble in the stock market," Ray said. "I don't know whether it's their mad money, play money, or what. Somewhere along the line, that money should be used."[4]

Although I had usually kept silent when the legislature discussed use of fund earnings, the trustees and I decided to speak up on this issue. We believed it was too soon to consider tapping the fund's earnings for government.

Politicians were slow to recognize the fund's popularity. In 1984 Sheffield still was talking about getting rid of the dividend, perhaps during his "second term."[5] But slowly it dawned on him and other politicians that Alaskans cared about the fund—and their dividends—

far more than they cared about grandiose projects such as the Susitna Dam. Sheffield began the 1985 session calling for an additional deposit into the principal of the fund. The fund's principal is the portion safeguarded by the constitution—the core holdings that can never be spent—while the earnings reside in other accounts that the Legislature can use at its discretion. Sheffield's proposal was to deposit money from the undistributed income account into the principal, setting it aside forever. The idea initially ran into hostility from the Legislature, which was focused on spending. However, Sheffield's proposal caught on publicly and won strong editorial support from the newspapers. The proposed special deposit grew as income built up in the reserve, and legislative support grew at the same time. The House approved a $400 million deposit in 1985, but the Senate failed to go along. I favored the deposit. Although oil prices were falling steadily from the highs recorded after the Iranian Revolution, the state budget remained double what it had been in 1980. I thought needs should be much greater before permanent fund earnings were spent by the Legislature, and the best way to assure that the earnings weren't used would be to add them to the principal.

That summer, meanwhile, a grand jury called for Sheffield to be impeached for trying to steer a Fairbanks office lease to a campaign supporter. Although impeachment hearings ended without Sheffield being removed from office, his reelection prospects for 1986 looked poor. Then, as that year's legislative session started, oil prices went into freefall, dropping by half in four months. Due to Sheffield's political weakness, however, and the Legislature's excessive spending habits, the state prepared no meaningful response to the crisis. Budget cuts amounted to only 8 percent; the Legislature dipped into reserves and continued planning an ever-larger permanent fund deposit.[6]

Senator Rick Halford, an Anchorage Republican, took the hardest line in favor of the fund, based on his small-government philosophy. He pushed for moving the entire undistributed-income account into the principal, regardless of how much the income account contained. The legislation passed. On the last day of the fiscal year, the income reserve held $1.24 billion, and all of it automatically went into principal. Halford attended a trustees meeting, suggesting they cash out all the rest of the fund's paper profits before the end of the fiscal year—more than another $1 billion—so that those funds would flow automatically into the principal as well. (We could buy the same securities back the next day.) But the trustees retreated from the idea, which sounded too much like playing games.[7]

Steve Cowper, my friend and a former chair of the board of trustees, slaughtered Sheffield in the Democratic primary for governor that summer and beat Sturgulewski in the general in November. As soon as the votes were counted, however, he found state finances to be in shambles. Cowper appointed me and six others to develop a plan to cut the budget. Oil prices stood at the lowest levels seen, in real terms, since the start of the Arab oil embargo in 1973. Sheffield already had cancelled the year's capital spending, laid off three hundred state workers, cut wages, and reduced payments to cities and school districts. Still, the deficit that remained equated to roughly 40 percent of the budget, and some predicted the state would run out of cash in February. The size of the shortfall depended on how you counted it and what revenue estimate you used, but it approached $1.2 billion.[8]

The irony of this number did not escape fund critics. The budget shortfall equated to the $1.2 billion that recently had been removed from possible use and deposited into the permanent fund. As the Alaska economy spiraled into a catastrophic crash, legislators, commentators, and economists questioned the earlier decision to save rather than spend that lump of fund income. A Canadian economist who lectured the trustees in 1988 found it simply "inexplicable," suggesting the deposit was evidence that the popularity of the dividend program had made any other expenditure of the fund's income politically impossible.[9]

However, I defended the $1.2 billion deposit. If the money had been plugged into the budget, we could have softened the blow a little, but after those funds were gone we soon would have been back in the same fix. In twenty-five years, oil prices have never returned, on a real basis, to the high they set in 1981. Except for a brief spike during the Gulf War, oil traded in a range of $10 to $20 a barrel for ten years after the crash. Spending had to be reduced. Although that thankless task was going to be tough to do in such a short time period, the fault wasn't with those who made the cuts. The fault lay with the legislators who had vastly over-inflated state spending and the economy in the first place. During the years of high oil prices the state had spent $17 billion above a maintenance level—well over $30 billion in 2005 dollars—forcing the economy into hyper-speed growth.[10] Even if we had liquidated the entire permanent fund, we could not have sustained that unrealistic level of economic activity for long. The state government had taken us to the top of the cliff; once we were there, we had only one direction to go. Thousands of jobs disappeared, the population shrank, the real-estate market collapsed, bankruptcies went through the roof, the construction industry dried up, businesses closed, and storefronts stood empty.

Desperate business people and real-estate owners looked to the permanent fund to bail them out. Thousands of broke homeowners walked away from their mortgages, leaving the Alaska Housing Finance Corporation an inventory of abandoned houses and condominiums, primarily in Anchorage and the Southcentral region. As the crisis peaked, AHFC owned 4,653 foreclosed homes and was repossessing 230 more a month.[11] (Because AHFC had required mortgage insurance on its loans, its own losses were manageable—another lesson in spreading investment risk outside the state.) Thousands more empty and unneeded units were held by the federal Department of Housing and Urban Development (HUD), the Federal Deposit Insurance Corporation (FDIC), the Federal Savings and Loan Insurance Corporation (FSLIC), and the surviving banks and thrifts. Agencies liquidating foreclosed properties at outcry auctions drove prices still lower. Condominiums sold for as little as $10,000. Commercial property stood empty. Realizing that some low-quality shopping centers never would be occupied again, lenders paid to have them cut apart and hauled away on trucks.

Tom Fink ran for Anchorage mayor in 1987 promising to "blast money out of Juneau" so he could "jump-start the economy." Besides propping up the real-estate market, he wanted a New Deal-style jobs program, quite a reversal for Alaska's most conservative mainstream politician. Of course, the state's only remaining source of money for such a program was the Alaska Permanent Fund. Fink began his campaign by targeting the fund, but switched to other issues as election day neared and he realized how unpopular his idea to raid the fund was.[12] Yet, even without expressing a clear way to pay for his bail-out, Fink struck a chord with voters who were hurting economically. He beat Dave Walsh in a run-off to succeed Tony Knowles as mayor. One of Fink's first moves was to call for the permanent fund to buy foreclosed properties to take them off the market.[13]

In Juneau, we would be on the receiving end of any "blasting" from Fink. We needed a plan of our own. My mind turned to the model of the alphabet agencies that had defended the permanent fund before—the "blockers," as I called them—such as AIDA and AHFC. I floated the idea of forming a "bridge bank" to coordinate the selling of institutional inventories of real estate. If FDIC, AHFC, and HUD competed for buyers, they would drive prices progressively lower, but if they worked together to control supply, demand might start to catch up. The state would pitch in $15 million to run the bank and maintain the properties. I also suggested destroying low-quality housing to reduce supply. Further, I thought AIDA could make money by acquiring abandoned commercial properties, bulldozing them, and then holding the raw land for sale after the market recovered.

Among the many schemes floating around the capitol, mine became the leading contender, backed by Senator Tim Kelly, a powerful Anchorage Republican.[14] However, the truth was that I agreed with other administration officials, including Hugh Malone and Gregg Erickson, that state intervention in the real-estate market made little sense. No matter what we did, we would be picking winners and losers. Besides, the Legislature's track record of managing the economy did not inspire confidence. When asked about my bridge bank, I said that it was the best of a bunch of bad ideas. The movement for state intervention died, ultimately replaced in 1988 by a sensible package of AHFC programs to assist homeowners and demolish substandard housing.

At the permanent fund, we had a program to buy certificates of deposit from Alaska banks, fully backed by collateral. I had started making the deposits before the crash to help ease shortages of capital, even though our requirement for a market rate of return would not lead to cheaper money for the banks or borrowers. We planned to invest

$300 million, but we never reached that goal before the banks started to fail and we cut off additional deposits. Time and again, always on a Friday, a struggling bank or savings and loan would find the grim reapers from the FDIC or FSLIC on their doorstep, locking their entrances for the last time. We never lost access to our deposits, however, because the grapevine always let me know the day before a bank was going down, and I made withdrawals or seized collateral in time.

The FDIC regularly informed the administration about its activities in shuttering the state's insolvent banks. Cowper asked to have me attend those meetings, but FDIC officials steadfastly refused to allow it because the fund had so much invested in the banks. Early in 1987, federal banking regulators advised the governor that they planned to close four banks at one time. Cowper immediately let me know. I blew my top, urging the governor to call back FDIC officials and demand them to reconsider. Losing so many banks at once would be a severe blow to an economy that already was on the ropes. Cowper made the call and work began to find another way to deal with the problem.

The deal that resulted had some resemblance to my bridge bank plan, but without state involvement. Instead of closing all four banks, the FDIC merged two of the largest—United Bank Alaska and Alaska Mutual Bank—into Alliance Bank, and injected $360 million to make the new bank solvent. An outside investor, the Hallwood Group, took over management. By the end of 1987, eight Alaska financial institutions had gone down, but Alliance Bank was born as Alaska's second largest. The move created some confidence in the banking system and reduced the competition among downward spiraling institutions.[15] We knew Alliance Bank probably wouldn't survive, but it lasted through sixteen months of the worst of the downturn, dying once and for all in April 1989—ironically, just after the *Exxon Valdez* oil spill, which brought the economy back to life with clean-up spending that summer.[16]

Governor Cowper had more than one reason to involve me in major economic issues. On a personal level, we worked well together. Steve had been an excellent chair of the permanent fund board of trustees, taking over from George Rogers in the summer of 1983. The position had helped him run for governor. Cowper and Sheffield were frequent adversaries and, while Sheffield was still in office, I fell into the role of mediating their conflicts. After he became governor, Cowper sometimes showed up at our house in Thane without any particular purpose. If I was digging a hole in the yard, he would grab a shovel. I knew he was having trouble in his marriage and was happy to have his companionship.

I also was useful to Cowper because the success of the fund and my studied role-playing as fiscal royalty had made me into something of a financial guru. He appointed me to the Alaska Housing Marketing Council to help manage the institutional sales of repossessed properties. I was asked to comment on whether the state should build the Susitna Dam, and pointed out the questionable economics and timing of the project. I was an important witness in a court case about huge losses in the state employee deferred-compensation program. In each case, the issues had little or nothing to do with the permanent fund, but my position and profile there made me an honest broker.

Success was my biggest ally in building that profile. The fund consistently beat its goal of a 3 percent real rate of return, usually by large margins. I made sure the news media knew when the fund made a good move or passed a milepost—$5 billion, $6 billion, and so on— and I spoke to groups all over the state to tell them how their investments were doing. Among the facts I reported was the fund's sheer size, which took some getting used to. In 1987 I announced that we were larger than any college endowment, larger than any private foundation, and larger than any union pension fund. If we had been a Fortune 500 company, our net income would have ranked us at number fifteen.[17]

Jim Rhode, whom I had fired in 1984, said that I was enjoying a "halo effect" that would attach to anyone associated with the Alaska Permanent Fund because it was one of the few successes in Alaska's fiscal history. There was some truth to that. However, my prestige reached its peak thanks to media coverage of investment decisions I made in 1986 and 1987, and for which I did deserve some credit.

The period was volatile in the markets. In 1986 the value of some of the fund's government securities spiked. I didn't believe the levels were sustainable, so we sold, realizing profits of $280 million. Under the ungainly system written into state law for calculating the fund's income, that realized gain then became available for expenditure by the Legislature. I was accused of making a political move by providing spending money when state finances were in the dumps and by pumping up the dividends.[18] Those charges were way off track. In fact, I was committing a much more serious offense in the eyes of institutional fund managers—market timing.

The theology of fund management holds that institutional investors should choose a long-term strategy and then hold to it, ignoring temporary ups and downs in the market. All other permanent fund directors have hewn closely to that doctrine. In general, I agree. A large trust with a long-term outlook never should speculate on short market fluctuations because quick moves undermine the overall strategy and, besides, quick moves are often wrong. Rare is the manager who consistently out-guesses the market in the short term. On the other hand, there *is* such a thing as judgment, and it makes no sense to check it at the door when you are managing a fund. If fundamental measures indicate that assets have risen in price well beyond their historical underlying value, a manager should sell those assets. To do otherwise is to pay an unnecessary price for obedience to a hands-off doctrine. Many funds, including ours today, do pay that price, holding on to securities even in the face of strong evidence of coming losses.

It turned out our decision to sell the government securities in 1986 was the right one. The *Anchorage Daily News* reported that the move "in hindsight has the look of a masterstroke."[19] In late winter of 1987, I made an even more controversial decision. In January the stock market had made a wild upward run, well beyond any fundamental drivers of value. The situation looked like an example of market volatility caused by investors moving assets into stocks for reasons beyond intrinsic value—in this case, bonds were going down and investors needed a place to put their money. I anticipated a crash and developed a plan to sell one-third of our stock, primarily from our unmanaged, index-based investments. Although those assets had outperformed our managers, I preferred to have real people selecting stocks during the downturn I expected.

Before I could act, I needed permission from the board of trustees. Its goal had been a 20 percent allocation to stocks; I was asking to reduce that to 12 percent. Once I had made my decision, I didn't want to wait three weeks for the next meeting, given the possibility a market correction might take place before we acted, so I asked for a special meeting by telephone. After an hour's discussion, the board approved my recommendation, and we began selling the shares over a span of about a week in late February and early March. We had to take it slow because our sales, if carried out all at once, would represent 10 percent of all of a day's transactions on the New York and American stock exchanges, a large enough sell-off to cause a drop in the market.

Over the next seven months, the Standard & Poor's 500 gained dramatically, although with alarming volatility. I came in for heavy criticism. The *Daily News* ran an article in August headlined "Stock sale costs permanent fund $220 million" because we would have gained that much if we had not sold our stock.[20] In September, the *News* quoted one of our own investment advisors as saying we were "leaving a lot of money on the table" by our cautious stance toward stocks.[21] Then, on Monday, October 19, the stock market collapsed in a storm of panic selling, without any triggering external event—the speculative bubble simply popped. In a single day, the Dow Jones Industrial Average lost 22.6 percent of its value—more than 500 points, taking it below the level where we had sold. Trading was suspended for the rest of the week. Bill Means reached me at poolside in Phuket, Thailand, where Fran and I were on vacation, to tell me about the crashing market.

The next day, the *Anchorage Times* led coverage of the crash with the headline "Fund looking like a genius."[22] We finished that fiscal year in the top 9 percent of all public investment funds.

After that, our investment judgment never faced serious challenge again. Concerns were raised, however, about the ethical content of our portfolio. In 1985 House Democrats Jim Duncan and Don Clocksin introduced a non-binding resolution calling on the permanent fund to divest stock of companies with business activities in racist South Africa.[23] While I sympathized, I viewed South Africa divestment as a first step onto a slippery slope. Only by remaining completely non-political could the permanent fund ward off the many political claims placed on us. Over the years, we would be asked to divest tobacco stocks and, after the *Exxon Valdez* oil spill, to unload stock in Exxon Corp. If we caved in to any of these pressures, it would be difficult to say no to any other political use of the fund, including unwise in-state investments. We had avoided political investments such as Fink's idea to buy distressed real estate only by clinging to the prudent-investor rule. We couldn't afford deviations from that standard.

When other large investment funds began voting their proxies or supporting shareholder resolutions for social purposes, I decided to avoid those entanglements as well, even though to do so would cost the fund nothing and would not violate the prudent-investor rule. Voting our proxies would mean assuming political power, and I hadn't been hired for my political values—except for the politics of defending the fund. The purpose of our investing was to make money for the people of Alaska. We had no business trying to dictate social values to the CEOs of America's corporations. Keeping a clear, simple role made our job possible. Breaking any of its sharply defined boundaries would put at risk the magnificent money machine the state had created. Today, the fund continues on this path. Although the fund may vote on corporate governance issues, with the goal of protecting its investments, the trustees take the position that only the Legislature can direct proxy votes on social issues.

As word of the fund's success spread, I was invited often to speak on these issues around the country. I debated bright, socially conscious representatives from California's and New York's vast pension funds, which were using their investing power for good causes and, in New York's case, for local development. I argued for a clean division between the corporate world and investment trusts, pointing out that public money could be used to spur development much more efficiently by leveraging the financial markets as Alaska had done with its alphabet lending agencies.

Later, I was invited to serve as a director on some large public companies. I was intrigued by the challenge and attracted by the offer of director fees, but when I discussed this with the board of trustees, I was reminded of my own words about keeping a solid wall between our trust and the companies in which we invested. Of course, the trustees were right: The concept worked both ways, whether the issue was voting proxies for social causes or sitting side by side with other board members. The Alaska Permanent Fund should remain aloof from every outside influence.

The most significant opportunity of this kind came from Fouad Jaffar, general manager of the London-based Kuwait Investment Organization, who invested its Future Generations Fund. It was one of the few successful oil-wealth savings accounts in the world. The Kuwaiti fund came into existence thanks to a single official in that nation's non-democratic government who set aside the money. While transparency and openness defended the Alaska Permanent Fund, secrecy was the Kuwaiti fund's best defense. Prior to the Iraqi invasion in 1990, this fund was the biggest in the world, containing assets roughly estimated at $100 billion. Only Jaffar and his colleagues knew the real value.[24]

I liked Jaffar and invited him to visit Juneau. He suggested he stay at our home, and I was inclined to agree. But first I conferred with Fran. It would be simple, I told her: We could move into the basement and give Jaffar and his retinue the upper level of the house. She was amenable to this arrangement until the matter of security came up. Jaffar's pilots, who also were his bodyguards, carried machine pistols at all times. A good Jewish girl from Queens, Fran couldn't accept the idea of a bunch of Arabs running around the house with heavy-duty automatic weapons.

Later, Jaffar approached me with a big idea. He suggested that his Kuwait fund, the Alaska Permanent Fund, and the California public employee pension and teacher retirement funds should pool their proxies to take control of British Petroleum. Originally I had met Jaffar through real estate our funds jointly controlled, but we'd never considered anything like this. I have to admit, for a moment it was an appealing idea. BP was one of the two largest producers on Alaska's North Slope, as well as one of the world's greatest oil companies. The idea of controlling its board from my office in Juneau briefly went to my head. I told Jaffar I'd think about it. But not much thinking was needed before I realized the move would violate our principle of separating politics, corporate governance, and our trust responsibilities. Besides, if Alaska controlled BP, with whom would we negotiate—

ourselves? The people of Alaska never gave me that job. I tried to explain all this to Jaffar, but he kept saying, "You haven't given me a good reason." Finally, frustrated with his insistence, I said, "My reason is, I just don't want to." He laughed heartily and told me the pension fund heads in California had given him the same reason. Later, Britain passed a law limiting foreign ownership in BP. Sadly, Jaffar lost his job over legal troubles related to dealings in Spain,[25] and the Kuwait fund was depleted in rebuilding the country after the Iraqi invasion.

My decade running the Alaska Permanent Fund was an era of learning and maturing for me, the fund, and the state. When I arrived, the fund existed as an arm of the state government, essentially a pot of $3.5 billion invested in the most basic fashion, attracting the covetous attention of legislators looking for money to spend. Ten years later, when I left, the fund contained $13.3 billion and had become Alaska's safest sacred cow. Investment success and growing dividends had made the fund virtually immune from criticism, and woe to the politician who thought otherwise.

When I started, I had been cautious to an extreme. Perhaps the risk aversion I'd learned from my father's early death still was part of my psychology. Yet, at the time, caution made sense. We needed the public's confidence before showing too much confidence ourselves. As the years passed and the public grew more comfortable with our management, the fund worked into ever more sophisticated investments with higher risk and greater potential for return, including foreign securities. For example, our real-estate portfolio started out with baby steps into pooled investments. After we got our feet wet, we began buying into particular projects as junior partner with other funds, such as Kuwait's. Finally, we began taking the lead. The Tysons Corner Center was one of my most rewarding projects. We bought the mall in McLean, Virginia, and remodeled it into a thriving attraction with 290 stores. Interestingly, we had to keep some stores open during construction to fulfill the Alaska Constitution's mandate that we invest in only "income-producing" properties.

I may have become a monarch of sorts by the time I left the permanent fund, as Hickel said, but if so it was for the benefit of the institution. By then, however, the fund no longer needed royalty in charge. Subsequent directors have not become as personally identified with the fund, nor have they received such close attention from the media. The Alaska Permanent Fund matured into a normal part of Alaska life, its ups and downs accepted by the public.

Are we happy with what we created? By and large, yes. During the course of research for this book, most of the leaders who participated in the early debate expressed pride and satisfaction with the mature organization. I am among them. However, in looking to the future, it may be useful to look at the misgivings of those few who see risk and potential disaster for the fund. Tom Fink, who never believed in the concept, expects the Legislature to go after the income and eventually the principal as well before instituting new taxes on Alaskans. In Fink's view, the fund owes its survival to Jay Hammond's popularity and the twenty-three years Hammond devoted to defending it after he left office. "I really think it has a lot to do with personality. The fact that Hammond is now dead means it is no longer as sacred," Fink said. "It's a matter of time."

Hugh Malone, one of the fathers of the fund, also took a pessimistic view when Nancy Gross interviewed him a year or so before he died in 2001. Malone could be forgiven for taking a dark view of the politics of wealth after his experience in the Legislature in the early 1980s. He had watched legislators engage in a frenzy of wasteful appropriations—spending that eventually caused the crash of the mid-1980s—without any consequences for those who used public money to destroy the private economy. In today's context, Malone feared that a single financial scandal at the permanent fund could provide the pretext to again flood the Alaska economy with money that would devastate it.

"If you can shake the Alaskan public's confidence in the present investment scheme of the fund," Malone said, "then you can make the argument, 'It's foolish to have this money invested in Europe, Japan, and, for that matter, Wall Street. We need to invest it right here in Alaska.'" Such a change would take only a vote of the Legislature. But Malone feared that dumping the $40 billion fund into Alaska's economy, or even a significant portion of it, could lead to an economic catastrophe as bad as the 1980s, or worse. The larger the fund, the greater the risk, was his view.

"I guess I think now that the creation of the permanent fund—at least allowing it to grow apparently to unlimited size—may have been a mistake," Malone said. "I don't know what to do with the fund as it continues to grow and this black beast gets bigger and bigger and is hiding in the closet. ... If I had my druthers, I'd say, 'OK, everybody, line up here and get ready. Here's your last dividend, because next year we're going to give the fund away. We're going to give it away to somebody else and it will be their headache after that. ... It's not going to be a part of the Alaska debate or political scene or economic activity anymore. Goodbye.' Because the risk is too large that it will make people's lives worse instead of better."

Although I disagree with Malone's pessimism, Alaskans should note that one of the fund's most thoughtful founders came to see such enormous risk in misuse of the savings account that he wished it had never been created. I'm sure Malone knew that giving away the fund—and he meant giving it to non-Alaskans—would be impossible. I believe he cited a real risk, but the solution is to keep the fund strong and transparent institutionally. The fund's success and Alaska's economic future depend on maintaining public confidence in the trustees, staff, financial managers, and investments.

In the next chapter, I'll explore the structure of the fund—why it works, how to maintain its integrity, and how this model can be replicated elsewhere.

---

[1]Hal Bernton, *Anchorage Daily News*, April 26, 1992.

[2]Mark Baumgartner, Associated Press, *Anchorage Daily News*, February 15, 1984.

[3]Dave Rose, legislative testimony of March 8, 1984 (in personal archives), 5.

[4]Andy Ryan, *The Anchorage Times*, March 18, 1984.

[5]David Ramseur, *The Anchorage Times*, June 27, 1984.

[6]Hal Spencer, *Anchorage Daily News*, May 14, 1986.

[7]Bill White, *Anchorage Daily News*, June 10, 1986.

[8]John Tetpon , *Anchorage Daily News*, November 9, 1986.

[9]Peter J. Smith, "The Alberta Heritage Savings Trust Fund and the Alaska Permanent Fund: A Ten-Year Retrospective" in *Trustee Papers*, vol. 2 (Juneau, Alaska. Permanent Fund Corporation, 1988), 27.

[10]Scott Goldsmith, "ISER Fiscal Policy Working Paper #3," Institute for Social and Economic Research, University of Alaska Anchorage.

[11]Alaska Housing Finance Corporation, *Accomplishments of Alaska Housing Finance Corporation by Fiscal Year,* http://www.ahfc.state.ak.us/iceimages/about/ahfc_accomplishments.pdf.

[12]David Postman, *Anchorage Daily News*, November 1, 1987.

[13]John Lindbeck, *Anchorage Daily News*, February 20, 1988.

[14]*Alaska Legislative Digest,* January 29, 1988; *The Alaska Economic Report,* February 12, 1988.

[15]Bill White, *Anchorage Daily News*, December 30, 1987.

[16]George Frost, *Anchorage Daily News*, April 29, 1989.

[17]Alaska Permanent Fund Corporation, "The Permanent Fund and Alaska's Future...A Long-Term Perspective," April 11, 1987 (manuscript in Rose personal archives).

[18]George Bryson, *Anchorage Daily News*, April 26, 1987.

[19]Ibid.

[20]Hal Bernton, *Anchorage Daily News*, August 28, 1987.

[21]White, *Anchorage Daily News*, September 25, 1987.

[22]David Foster, Associated Press, *The Anchorage Times*, October 20, 1987.

[23]Bruce Scandling, Associated Press, *Anchorage Daily News*, March 9, 1985.

[24]John T. Haldane, "Rebuilding Kuwait," *The Washington Report*, 1991, http://www.washington-report.org/backissues/0491/9104081.htm.

[25]*Al-Sabah v. Grupo Torres SA*, February 11, 2000, http://www.ucc.ie/law/restitution/archive/englcases/al-sabah.htm.

CHAPTER 13
The permanent fund model

A laska may not be the only place in the world where a small population lives on top of rich natural resources, but economists and political scientists have a hard time finding another place where a significant portion of mineral wealth has been transformed into an endowment-like fund similar to Alaska's. Due to my role in that transformation, I have been invited often to lecture and present ideas for other nations and political subdivisions as they consider following Alaska's path. In the 1990s, the U.S. Agency for International Development, through the University of Alaska, sent me to Russia and republics of the former Soviet Union, and more recently I worked with leaders in Iraq. The history of the Alaska permanent fund doesn't serve as a perfect road map for those governments because their circumstances inevitably differ from Alaska's strange and bumpy ride to riches from 1969 to 1982. But we can draw some broad lessons from the Alaska experience that can apply anywhere, regardless of the shape of history.

What follows are my thoughts on the essentials for creating a permanent fund under three main themes—ownership, institutions, and operations—and conclusions on applying these ideas elsewhere.

Ownership

The first prerequisite to saving is wealth, and for collective savings to accumulate, wealth must be owned in common. In the context of capitalist societies, commonly owned wealth usually consists of natural resources controlled by the government. Alaska's late development in the course of American history assured government ownership of underground resources. Through the nineteenth century, the federal government gave away subsurface energy resources through homesteading and other land laws. In 1906 President Theodore Roosevelt began a long political struggle to stop privatization of the subsurface, and, by 1920, federal law retained ownership of oil and gas when it disposed of land.[1] Because virtually all of Alaska was federally owned at that time, the subsurface would remain public unless Congress specified otherwise, as it did in the 1971 Alaska Native Claims Settlement Act. The 1958 Alaska Statehood Act gave the new state of Alaska the right to 103 million acres on the condition the subsurface never would be privatized: If the state disposed of minerals other than by lease, the federal government could take the land back.[2]

Certainly I believe in private property, but privately owned oil— the stereotypical image that comes to mind is the lucky rancher becoming a billionaire when a gushing oil well is discovered on his property—is not a model worth copying. Luck alone shouldn't determine who gets to take immense wealth from the earth. However, public ownership by itself cannot assure fair distribution of petroleum wealth. If we think of the land as a bank containing finite resources, then the generation that withdraws and dissipates those deposits derives an inequitable benefit, like the rancher with his gusher. What gives that generation a greater right to the wealth than those who come later? We accept in theory that those living now have an obligation to leave the natural environment livable for our descendants. A similar obligation should attach to people in a small political subdivision suddenly endowed with fabulous resource wealth. Citizens should recognize a broader collective ownership that crosses generations.

At first glance, ownership by people who haven't been born yet might seem paradoxical. After all, if democracy is based on a social contract in which members are tied to a community through what each can contribute and receive in return, then the citizens of the future have no way of compensating us for what we give them. Two arguments overcome this lack of a *quid pro quo*. First, it is a basic human impulse to provide for institutions we treasure. How else to explain legacies bequeathed to colleges and other charities? More practically, saving is not a benefit strictly for the future. A regional economy can get more benefit from wealth spread over time than from an overwhelming pulse of money that is spent all at once. Saving can multiply the value of finite petroleum revenues for today as well as for tomorrow.

Many examples exist of economies damaged by fast consumption of finite mineral wealth. Alaska in the 1980s is one example. The tiny Republic of Nauru is an even better model of the phenomenon. Lying just south of the equator, northeast of Australia, Nauru is an island one-tenth the size of Washington, D.C., where indigenous people subsisted for millennia on fruit and fish. Beginning early in the twentieth century, colonial powers exploited valuable phosphate deposits for use by Australian farmers. In 1968 Nauru gained independence and took over the mines. The profits were enormous relative to the small population, creating excess income, but a poorly managed savings program lost most of what was put aside. Meanwhile, islanders used one-time wealth to fund a lifestyle far richer than that found on neighboring islands, abandoning fishing, fruit collection, and any economic pursuits other than importing goods using phosphate revenues. When the phosphates gave out, the remaining savings were depleted to continue this spending. Today, 90 percent of the island is a mined-out wasteland. Unemployment stands at 90 percent. The bankrupt government is sustained by foreign aid from Australia. Facilities are deteriorating, including the desalinization plant that provides the island with fresh water. The 13,000 residents face a grim future.[3]

Nauru suffered an extreme case of an economic disease that commonly afflicts resource-rich regions. Out-of-proportion mineral revenues damage the underlying economy by forcing up prices, distorting business decisions, importing population, over-inflating real-estate values and the construction industry, overextending government, and creating a demand for unsustainable services. When the flow of funds is cut by lower commodity prices or resource depletion, the resident population can be left far worse off than if the income from minerals never was received in the first place. The bubble bursts, investment values crash, and unemployment rises. The economy that preceded the boom may take many years to recover.

As I have explained, the Alaska Permanent Fund was founded with several contradictory goals. That confusion created a multi-part constituency. The most influential leaders focused on the dangers of unsustainable growth when they set aside petroleum revenues from the North Slope—the "negative goal" banker Elmer Rasmuson cited. By slowing the rate of spending, the fund did protect Alaska somewhat from the fate of Nauru, although we went through a crash nonetheless. Yet the idea of simply slowing down spending would not make ownership intergenerational. Indeed, many conceived of the permanent fund simply as a rainy day account from which money could be withdrawn after oil revenues were depleted, essentially smoothing out the ups and downs of oil income without permanent savings. That approach would postpone the day of reckoning, but would not prevent it because no other industry appeared likely to replace oil.

Our fund, in its unique form, is more of an endowment containing investments that are never intended to be used except for the income they spin off. Although its founders didn't expect the fund would grow so large that its income would replace oil revenue, their efforts to make it politically secure created this opportunity. To their surprise, the income of the permanent fund began to exceed Alaska's oil income in 1998.

Non-renewable mineral resources can be made into reliable, renewable financial assets by investing enough of the proceeds of development so that, when the mineral deposit is depleted, an identical value has been saved in a trust account yielding a sustainable income in perpetuity. The portion of non-renewable revenues that must be invested in order to save 100 percent of their value depends on how long exploitation lasts and the rate of return on the investments. A longer span of time and higher rate of return reduces the percent of non-renewable revenues that needs to be set aside annually to meet the goal.[4] In Alaska's case, as of 2005 we had reaped about $100 billion in oil and gas revenues and we had diverted $11.3 billion of that amount to the permanent fund. Thanks to successful investing and reinvestment of earnings, the fund's principal balance had surpassed $40 billion in 2007. By setting aside 11 percent of our revenues, we had accumulated more than one-third of our petroleum income in financial reserves.[5] The longer the petroleum lasts, the greater our chance of capturing its full value in our investments.

Economic calculations could determine the optimum savings rate to achieve this goal, but in reality, the messy process of politics determines how much money is set aside. Rarely is a single person powerful enough to dictate the transfer of wealth from the present to the future, and in those rare cases when this happens, another leader just as powerful may emerge later who will reverse the decision or even steal the money. An authoritarian regime saved massive oil wealth in Kuwait thanks to a benevolent subterfuge to keep some income off the books. The country's rulers didn't have to worry about political pressure to break into the fund for Future Generations, but after Iraq occupied their territory, they chose to spend the savings on rebuilding.

A democracy may have a harder time creating a savings fund than an autocrat would, but the distributed power in a democracy also makes the account more difficult to raid once it has been established. Alaska's structural barriers to change, including the constitution and a bicameral Legislature, act as defensive barriers. The Alaska Constitution is the most important key to the fund's permanence. The fund cannot be altered without a super-majority of the Legislature and a vote of the people. I doubt any government-owned trust could be truly permanent without constitutional protection to place it beyond the reach of contemporary needs and wants. Leaders in a parliamentary system without a constitution would face constant temptation to dip into a savings fund.

Even with its constitutional protection, Alaska's fund might have been destroyed by misguided investment policies if not for the checks of the bicameral Legislature, with its committee system, and the governor's veto power, which stymied many attempts to make unwise changes in the early years. The policy inertia inherent in the American system, which makes progress slow and incremental, created a systemic bias in favor of saving the fund. By foiling decision-making in the present, options were reserved for the future.

Creating a savings fund in this political system is as hard as raiding one. Adding to the challenge, American democracy encourages free spending: Power in the Capitol is distributed among many actors, creating an incentive to compromise; in budget writing, compromise almost always means spending more. How can politicians overcome the barriers to change—and the urge to spend—to build a fortress-like savings fund? I've traced the exceptional historical circumstances in Alaska—a first burst of money that was perceived as wasted; a period of low revenues when leaders could create a structure for saving without the sacrifice of actually setting much money aside; and finally a large flood of wealth that could provide for all reasonable needs, leaving substantial funds to flow into the savings structure that had been previously created. Nations can hardly count on this sequence of events to create their own permanent funds, but they can address certain elements needed for success.

First, the government must have excess revenues. Until basic needs are met, such as education and public safety, the government has no business saving for the future. Besides, citizens in a democracy are unlikely to tolerate savings deposits if essential services are lacking. Defining basic needs can be difficult, however, because our standard of living sets our perceptions of what we need: Once we're accustomed to receiving goods and services, they become essential to us. The phrase "basic needs" means something very different in Alaska compared to Nigeria. Practically, the public's perception of needs may dictate that savings can begin only as income rises; voters probably won't stand for cutting services in order to start a savings account.

Experience also suggests, however, that citizens will recognize the readiness to save before their elected leaders do. Individual consumers of new services receive only the marginal benefit of those services, while the personal career boost to politicians acting as benefactors can be much greater. One measure of when the threshold has been met is when taxes are cut or eliminated. Government services that aren't worth paying for may not be worth spending one-time resource money on, either. One thing is certain: A government that waits until all needs are met before saving will never save. At the height of Alaska's most outrageous spending, legislators still didn't have enough money to buy everything they wanted.

Elected leaders have incentives for short-term thinking. A long-term transfer of wealth to future generations requires deferred spending in the present. Politicians can always pander to greed instead, a temptation that easily spills over into corruption, which was seen in Alaska when oil prices were at their peak. Corruption consumed immense fortunes in some resource-rich underdeveloped countries. To start a savings fund, the government must be led, at least temporarily, by men and women of exceptional principle and intelligence. Unless wise, honest leaders acquire power and stand firm, economic disaster and colossal waste are the most likely outcome of natural-resource wealth.

Idealism is not enough, however. Success in the political arena, for good or bad ends, requires skill and occasional dirty hands. Good public policy wasn't enough to create Alaska's fund. Leaders also had to use misdirection, deal-making, and raw power. The misdirection began with the contradictory goals that sponsors stated prior to the fund's inception. Those who wanted to use oil money entirely for fast growth in the economy went along because they were led to believe the fund could issue soft loans and pay for capital projects. After passage of the constitutional amendment, pro-savings legislators used it as a beachhead to fight for laws dedicating the fund to prudent investing. Meanwhile, Alaska created separate institutions to meet economic development needs. Finally, Hammond executed a grand compromise to solidify the fund. He allowed profligate spending temporarily, withholding his veto in exchange for the passage of key savings legislation.

The meaning of all this maneuvering is simple: A deal was made between the present and the future. Give the people of today what they need—and more—in exchange for saving a fraction of resource revenue for tomorrow. A permanent fund is a time machine for wealth. If its savings are secure and its investments are profitable, it eventually may deliver the full value of mineral resources to unborn generations.

Institutions

Nothing manmade is truly permanent, especially in the realm of money and politics, but we can do our best. For a governmental entity to set aside money with the intent of saving it permanently, the assets should be separated from day-to-day politics and managed by a self-contained entity. Clark Gruening, one of the fathers of the Alaska permanent fund, wanted this institutional structure to be "insulated but not isolated" from the people. The fund needs to be left alone, but it cannot survive without public support. Ordinary citizens need both a vested interest in preserving the fund and ways of raising capital so they won't covet the fund's wealth.

To accomplish this complex mission, one institution may not be enough. A savings fund deserves an institution that has as its sole purpose protecting and increasing the endowment. But there are other legitimate investment purposes that the public may demand from its collective wealth, too, such as capital improvements or loans for economic development, education, and housing. Mixing these functions with savings is a mistake. A savings fund dedicated to the prudent-investor rule is obliged to seek the best investments to attain its goals of risk and return. A development bank or loan fund invests to attain a social or political goal. Few investments meet both goals.

Why? First, the marketplace finds the best investments while government investment is usually the option for projects that can't obtain capital or can't pay market interest rates. By definition, those unmarketable investments are not the best selection for a prudent investor. Second, prudent investing requires diversification—spreading risk broadly so that losses in any one set of holdings will be offset by gains in others. Placing a large portion of a savings fund within the borders of the region it serves violates this rule by concentrating too much money geographically. Finally, local investments tie the fund's success to the same economy that it relies on for deposits. If the local economy declines, the fund takes a double hit, in both earnings and new deposits. In fact, the local economy can gain more if the fund is invested elsewhere. Linking the financial system to the global marketplace of investing and borrowing reduces economic volatility, because outside links spread risk and provide counter-cyclic balance to business ups and downs.

From a political perspective, setting up a savings fund with a single, prudent-investor purpose also helps prevent the manager from becoming too powerful. As long as the fund observes the prudent-investor rule, it operates as a money machine, with the range of the manager's discretion limited to selecting among the best investments on the market. If, however, the fund has two or more inconsistent goals—such as saving combined with economic development—the manager may become an economic czar, choosing when and how far to deviate from a profit-driven philosophy, and deciding to whom the fund's largesse should be granted. If this manager is chosen in a political process, the fund is liable to be plundered by allies helping keep the manager in office. If the manager is a benevolent dictator, isolated from the political process, like a judge or the chair of the Federal Reserve, he or she could become a powerful, undemocratic force in society.

None of this means a resource-rich government should not pursue economic development and other local investments. In fact, such efforts are probably a practical and political necessity. But a government need not consume resource wealth for these purposes. Instead, it can use the wealth to leverage the importation of capital for housing, municipal facilities, power, education, economic development, and infrastructure. Debt financing makes a better source of funds for several reasons. A smaller portion of resource wealth can be magnified into larger projects. The money goes further. The total investment portfolio remains more liquid. Risk is spread beyond the local economy. In the United States, state and local governments can borrow at low rates with tax-free financing, but get to invest their own cash in taxable securities that pay higher rates without having to pay taxes. Perhaps most important, the credit markets demand a degree of caution in lending that a purely political loan fund might not observe. That discipline can protect a government program from losses. By bringing in commercial lenders as partners, another layer of expertise and care can be added.

I have called these alternative financing institutions "blockers" because they block raids on the savings fund. In Alaska, a constellation of blockers surrounded the permanent fund. The Alaska Municipal Bond Bank Authority used a small state appropriation to establish reserves that helped local governments borrow for capital projects. Interest earnings on the reserves paid agency expenses. In the same fashion, the Alaska Industrial Development Authority leveraged state assets to borrow on national credit markets, creating a pool of funds for low-cost business loans made through banks. The Alaska Housing Finance Corporation used this concept to offer low-rate financing for housing. Other blockers provided funding for fishermen, farmers, students, inventors, and power companies. In each case, the state established an institution to meet the legitimate needs of citizens and to develop the economy. Alaska did diversify its economy, although not to the unrealistic extent that some may have hoped. We also lost money on bad projects. Losses are inevitable in the inherently speculative business of economic development. The important point, however, is that the blockers shielded the permanent fund from these kinds of losses, allowing it to concentrate on its one, overriding purpose of saving according to the prudent-investor rule.

Governor Steve Cowper created a final blocker with a different structure. The Constitutional Budget Reserve received windfalls coming to the state from the settlement of tax disputes with the oil companies. Money from this reserve cannot be spent except when revenues fall short of the previous year's appropriations, or with a three-quarters majority of the Legislature. Withdrawals are supposed to be replenished when revenues recover.[6] After Cowper left office, legal settlements over oil-tax disputes deposited enormous balances into the CBR. As oil revenues declined over the following decade, the legislature steadily drew on those funds to cover budget gaps. Thanks to Cowper, the windfalls were not spent as soon as they came in, and Alaska's fiscal situation remained fairly stable. The permanent fund and its earnings weren't needed. However, the Legislature so far has failed to replenish the CBR, so it might not be available for the next decline in oil prices or production.

While surrounded by blockers, the Alaska Permanent Fund Corporation itself stands as a fortress of savings with its own formidable defenses. I've already touched on how the constitution and the checks and balances of the bicameral Legislature defend the fund. The structure of the corporation also kept it strong as an institution. Other resource-rich governments have attempted to manage their investments using an existing bureaucracy, even when their savings funds have a distinct name and function. That's a mistake because it leaves a fund without its own distinct voice. The Alaska Permanent Fund Corporation speaks for the fund, not for the state administration. It can even raise an alarm with the public when the trustees perceive danger from the governor or Legislature. Conflicts have arisen now and then—such as when I sent the invoice for $700 million to Governor Bill Sheffield. A fund director working directly for the governor would shrink from those conflicts.

As conceived in the 1982 legislation, the six trustees were intended to be appointed with overlapping four-year terms, assuring continuity and shielding the fund's managers from gubernatorial transitions. The new governor had two automatic board members—the commissioner of revenue and another commissioner—but would have to wait for terms to expire before replacing the rest of the board. In violation of that concept, Walter Hickel fired everyone but John Kelsey from the board of trustees when he returned to the governor's office in 1990. Tony Knowles acted similarly upon his election in 1994. I was pleased that the Legislature finally amended fund statutes to clarify that trustees could be removed only for cause, restoring the intended continuity.

The strongest defense of all is the Alaska Permanent Fund dividend. Its most important function is to create a public constituency opposed to political meddling with the permanent fund. After the first dividend was paid, it took a couple of years for the political establishment to recognize the strength of the voters' protective urge. After four dividends, the permanent fund became the third rail of Alaska politics. Candidates swore to protect the fund and the dividend at all costs, fearful that being soft on the dividend would end their political careers.

The dividend's impact on the permanent fund has been good and bad. On the good side, the dividend served its defensive purpose, and then some. Unlike public owners of funds elsewhere in the world, Alaskans know about their permanent fund and care what happens to it.[7] Legislative moves to force the permanent fund to invest in loans within Alaska died out a few years after the annual dividend payments began. The prudent-investor rule is safe as long as the dividend is being paid.

A less-anticipated result was that the dividend defended the income of the fund, preventing the Legislature from spending it and eventually tripling the size of the principal. The general public made little distinction between the income and principal, but the constitutional design of the fund treats them separately. The principal, which represents appropriations and contributions to the fund, essentially the cost basis of the investments, cannot be spent by the Legislature. But interest, dividends, and capital appreciation are available for spending once realized. By the end of 2005, the principal stood at $25 billion and with earnings totaling another $8 billion, of which $4.5 billion was unrealized.[8] The principal had accumulated from three roughly equal sources—automatically dedicated oil revenue, special appropriations, and earnings that were reinvested to counter the effects of inflation. More than one-half of the money began as fund income that was returned to principal, thanks to legislative action.[9]

Legislators tried and failed to tinker with the 1982 law that reinvests a portion of fund income to counter inflation. In the short-money year of 1987, first they considered scrapping inflation-proofing, and second tried forcing the fund to "repay" money appropriated to principal that the Legislature now sought to recategorize as loans or as "advance payments" on inflation-proofing. I spoke out against the first proposal and flatly refused the second; thanks to the dividend, I had a bully pulpit from which to speak to the public.[10]

Most of the special appropriations to principal also came from income. Of roughly $7 billion in these deposits, only $2.7 came from the general fund—the special appropriations in 1980 and 1981, which preceded the first dividend. The larger special appropriations, which came from fund income, probably wouldn't have occurred without the dividend. Voters equated more money for the permanent fund with more dividends. Legislators could score major political points by putting the income into the corpus, even when the short-term impact on dividends would be small.

Unfortunately, at times the dividend has come to eclipse the fund itself. Some Alaskans call their savings account the "permanent dividend fund," exposing their belief that paying the dividend is the sole purpose of the fund. Elected officials suggesting any use of earnings have suffered slams from negative campaign ads accusing them of being permanent fund raiders. In the early years, when budgets declined from historic peaks but remained unsustainably high, I joined those who said it was too soon to use fund earnings. However, if the permanent fund is ever to realize a public purpose, the income cannot be off-limits forever.

As Alaska's oil revenues shrank through the 1990s, the Legislature became a chronic deficit spender, raiding accounts of one-time revenues in order to avoid for one more year having to impose taxes or spend permanent fund earnings. In inflation-adjusted, per-capita terms, spending from the general fund declined year by year, from a peak of $19,700 in 1982, to $5,800 in 1992, and to $3,600 in 2002—when it stood below the level of 1976, the year before the pipeline started flowing.[11] Alaska paid a significant cost for allowing oil production and prices alone to determine its spending: Roads and bridges deteriorated; schools lost staff and programs; University of Alaska facilities fell into disrepair; and aid to local governments evaporated, forcing small cities to disband or face bankruptcy. Although we had ample income to cover our needs, legislators preferred to let our infrastructure fall apart rather than be perceived as raiding the "dividend fund."

Anyone familiar with recent history in Alaska is weary of the term "fiscal gap." The state government has wrestled repeatedly with its unsustainable finances, failed, and then seen its fortunes improve in the nick of time with improved oil prices. In the most recent attempt to address the problem, Governor Frank Murkowski in 2004 convened a Conference of Alaskans in Fairbanks, with fifty-five members, similar to the Constitutional Convention in 1955. The entire state listened in on the thoughtful debate of the delegates as they adopted a reasonable fiscal plan for use of permanent fund earnings under the Percent of Market Value concept, or POMV as it was called. A constitutional amendment would change the pay-out of fund income from the unwieldy "realized earnings" model to a simple 5 percent of the total market value. Under the conference plan, one-half of the 5 percent would be used for dividends while the other half would go to state spending. I didn't agree with every aspect of the plan, but it represented a reasonable compromise. The Legislature was unable to agree. But no longer could the blame be placed on the public and hunger for dividends. One statewide poll showed 60 percent of voters supported using fund earnings for government—a dramatic change from earlier polls. Of those who understood the POMV plan, most supported it as well.[12] The Conference of Alaskans was successful; when Alaskans heard reasoned debate on the issue, they understood what was at stake and changed their thinking. The dividend wasn't the problem. The legislature was.

Operations

Government savings funds should be measured against two standards—profitability and public confidence. These standards sometimes conflict. Occasionally the most attractive investment available raises potential public questions. Most often, these concerns relate to risk, but sometimes, if secrecy or perceived conflicts of interest are involved, an issue of integrity can arise. Even when such concerns are completely unfounded, public confidence must come first. Profits rise and fall, but if the managers and trustees of a large public savings fund lose the faith of the public, the existence of the fund itself will be at stake. Regardless of the institutional framework protecting the fund, it can be dissolved if the public believes management is corrupt or incompetent. That response might be reasonable. The size of a petroleum fund easily can surpass any other single pool of wealth in the economy. In Alaska's case, the permanent fund exceeds individual financial assets of all the residents combined. Who would invest such a sum with a manager he or she didn't trust?

Operating procedures should be designed to meet every conceivable challenge to the fund's honesty. During my years at the fund, we observed a policy of total transparency, even concerning the personal financial dealings of the senior management and trustees. Every time one of us bought or sold a stock in our personal investment accounts, we entered the information about the transaction on the public record. We put out notice of every meeting of the trustees and permitted comment whenever possible. Executive sessions rarely occurred. The only business information we would not disclose were trade secrets of tenants in buildings we owned. We refrained from accepting trips, meals, or free seminars from investment advisors who wanted our business. We paid our people well and gave them recognition for their work, but we required as a condition of employment that our employees not to go to work for investment vendors after leaving the fund. Unfortunately, this rule and some others were relaxed after my departure. The fund has accumulated a deep reservoir of public confidence, but the trustees and management should be careful because a single slip could spill that good will.

Public support of the fund also depends on avoiding entanglement in the political or corporate worlds. The very existence of the permanent fund represented a compromise among people with vastly different perspectives and personal values. Regardless of these differences, all agreed to transfer resource wealth to future generations. As long as the fund's management focuses solely on that single point of agreement, the compromise is safe. But if the fund begins using its political weight or business influence for any other purpose, some part of its constituency is bound to become alienated. I came to believe the permanent fund should resist any activity outside the core function of meeting its investment goals.

The public really does own the fund and has final control over how it is used. I tried to keep that in mind in communications with the public and with trustees. I wanted the trustees ready to answer any question from an ordinary citizen, so I reported to them frequently in writing and on the telephone. I spread information directly to the public as often as possible with talks, reports published in plain language, and through news media contacts. These efforts enhanced the fund's public image, and, even more important, exposed our owners to investment concepts and debate as to why we bought certain asset classes and excluded others. Rather than portray ourselves as investment wizards with magical money-making ability, I wanted the public to grasp the reasoning behind our decisions. That way, when our choices went bad—as they did occasionally—we would be forgiven.

Winning public confidence in an investment manager's competence is harder than maintaining belief in a fund's integrity. Our honesty is always within our own control, but investment losses cannot be avoided with absolute certainty. After the fund had a track record spanning years, a down year or an occasional bad investment was not particularly alarming. But as the fund was starting out or expanding into new kinds of investments, the public could be uneasy with the uncertainty of having their dividends affected by our investment decisions. A significant loss at that point could have crippled public confidence in the very idea of entrusting vast wealth to a small group of managers.

The founders of the Alaska permanent fund wisely began with an extraordinarily low-risk strategy, investing only in income-producing securities, the great majority of them U.S. government issues with short maturities. The fund barely broke even and sometimes lost ground slightly against inflation, but no investment losses were posted. Before I came on board in 1982, the legislature broadened the fund's allowable investments to include some domestic equities. Still, we moved slowly. Our first purchases came entirely from the S&P 500 Index, which at the time represented 83 percent of the stock market and whose performance was covered widely in the media. Citizens could understand the index and didn't have to worry about our stock-picking decisions.

Over the years, as the fund became more ingrained in Alaska's culture, the Legislature and trustees moved gradually to expand its investment holdings to reflect a more sophisticated investment philosophy. By using more asset classes, we diversified our portfolio, increasing our opportunity for success and reducing our risk. First, the fund retained a growth-stock manager and a value-investing manager—stock pickers more likely to find good buys in the portion of the market not covered by the index approach. Second, we expanded into foreign stocks, with the Legislature's approval. We moved into real estate in the same gradual way. First, we bought into pools of real estate offered by reputable managers. The pools offered diversification within the asset class, holding commercial, residential, and industrial properties. As the pools performed well and the public got comfortable with real-estate investments, we began selecting individual properties. At first, we joined other investors as minority partners. With greater confidence, the fund took controlling positions in real-estate investments and eventually adopted a policy of participating only when we had control. The fund had matured as a real-estate investor when other funds began signing on to join us as minority partners. Rather than our piggybacking on the expertise of others, now others were relying on our experience.

Another sign of success came when the Legislature entirely deleted the list of allowable investments in 2005. Now, the Alaska permanent fund is free to invest in any income-producing asset so long as the trustees observe the prudent-investor rule and keep the portfolio diversified. In contrast to the noisy battles over investment policies in the 1980s, the elimination of restrictions in 2005 received little media attention and not much legislative debate.[13] That's a sign of the public confidence the fund now enjoys, but it also represents risk. Lack of public interest could allow the trustees to stray into dangerous territory, but that doesn't mean the public won't wake up angry if something goes wrong.

With the loosened investment rules, the trustees recently began keeping some of their records and meetings confidential so they could participate in more "alternative investments," which include unregulated securities and outfits making exotic, speculative moves far beyond the understanding of all but the experts.[14] As I wrote this, the fund was using its new, broader authority to consider a multi-billion-dollar investment in a trans-Alaska gas pipeline—a decision that would violate several of the principles I believe are crucial to the fund's long-range success.

The fund is entering a new phase of its existence. It may find a safe course through uncharted waters, creating new principles for the safety of its basic function. Every institution must learn and grow. However, the trustees' first instinct should be caution along with the awareness that, thanks to openness and risk-avoidance, the institution they are responsible for has already survived longer and grown larger than any other of its kind.

Conclusion

In the decade after my departure from the Alaska Permanent Fund Corporation, worldwide admiration grew for Alaska's approach to saving, but replicating the fund's success has not proved easy. The Alberta Heritage Savings Trust fund now emulates the Alaska model to some extent, although public awareness there is far lower than in Alaska, likely because Alberta does not pay a dividend.[15] My travels to Russia to share Alaska's experience with members of the Duma and with other resource-rich republics of the former Soviet Union yielded some fascinating experiences, but I am not aware of a long-term savings fund that has been created, despite immense resource wealth.

After the U.S. invasion of Iraq, I became involved in advocating for an Alaska-style fund there. We received support from the president, secretary of state, and U.S. ambassador to Iraq, as well as interest from leaders in the Sunni minority. I gave a briefing at the Pentagon on options for creating a fund. However, the country's on-going internal warfare made it difficult to take the idea further. Iraq's new constitution included language assuring that natural-resource wealth would be owned in common by all citizens, but the sectarian violence and developing civil war split the country. Regionally, oil resources lie with the Kurds in the north and Shi'a in the south. The Sunnis' central region lacks much petroleum wealth, which may explain why this sect supported our collective-wealth model.

Alaska was lucky when it created our fund. We were lucky that the public perceived—whether accurately or not—that our first pulse of oil money had been wasted, and we were lucky again to have the time to address the problem before most of our petroleum income arrived. Yet we still suffered "the resource curse" that nations around the world have endured—excessive spending that distorts politics and the economy and leads to dislocation and losses rather than sustained prosperity. Perhaps the curse is unavoidable. But we avoided the far worse fate of seeing our wealth lead us into poverty. Iraq received more oil wealth than Alaska, but ended the Baath Party era with a wrecked economy and deeply in debt. In Nigeria, some $300 billion flowed through the treasury, but the oil boom left behind little but a record of theft and waste and a people worse off than before.[16] Developed countries went through this affliction even when free of corruption or dictatorship—democracy is no antidote. The term "The Dutch Disease" was coined in the 1970s for the phenomenon seen in the Netherlands, where petroleum-powered social spending undermined the real economy.[17]

The black magic behind the resource curse is free money. Resource wealth is like an addictive drug for politicians and the people they represent, nearly impossible to forego even when the spending becomes self-destructive. Conventional governments are limited by the amount of broad-based taxes they can levy. Taxation brakes spending and keeps the size of government in proportion with the economy. With the discovery of a big oil field, the brakes are off. In Alaska, we anticipated this fate and labored to avoid it, yet we were able to save only 11 percent of our oil income. Fortunately, the investment of our permanent fund increased those savings three-fold, with the numbers still rising. While history suggests this outcome was less than ideal—why didn't we save more?—the context of worse results in other resource provinces argues we may have done as well as we could.

The essential lesson of the Alaska model lies in the many layers of security needed to achieve any level of success in saving oil money. Like a series of bank vaults within bank vaults, we had the protection of our constitution, our blocker institutions, our prudent-investor statute, our independent corporation, our board of trustees with staggered terms, our conservative investment strategy, our transparency, our public information efforts and, on top of all that, our dividend program. The use of so many different defenses might seem to reflect a level of paranoia on the part of the fund's founders, or at least severe pessimism about the wisdom of elected leaders to keep the savings secure. The record shows, however, that every element of protection eventually was needed to prevent the loss of the fund.

The goal of truly permanent savings of resource wealth is just short of impossible. We have achieved it for thirty years through constant vigilance and an interlocking institutional structure sturdy enough to block the intense temptations of powerful people. Whatever form these precautions take in other, similar situations elsewhere in the world, they cannot be made too strong.

---

[1]Walter J. Hickel, *Crisis in the Commons: The Alaska Solution* (Oakland: Institute for Contemporary Studies, 2002), 39-40.

[2]Alaska Statehood Act: Public Law 85-508, 72 stat. 339, July 7, 1958; section 6(i).

[3]Rögnvaldur Hannesson, *Investing for Sustainability: The Management of Mineral Wealth* (Boston: Kluwer Academic Publishers, 2001); also Central Intelligence Agency, *The World Factbook,* http://www.cia.gov/cia/publications/factbook/geos/nr.html.

[4]Hannesson.

[5]Scott Goldsmith for $100 billion figure; Alaska Permanent Fund Corp. for year-end FY 2005 figures. The $11.3 billion diverted to the fund includes $8.6 billion in mineral revenues and $2.7 billion in special appropriations from the general fund, but not special appropriations from fund earnings.

[6]Alaska Constitution, article 9 section 17.

[7]Hannesson.

[8]Alaska Permanent Fund Corporation, monthly financial report.

[9]Alaska Permanent Fund Corporation, "Historical Totals," October 19, 2005. End of FY 2005, deposits of income were 54 percent of principal.

[10]Sue Cross, *Anchorage Daily News,* February 10, 1987.

[11]Institute for Social and Economic Research, University of Alaska Anchorage, *The Alaska Citizen's Guide to the Budget,* http://citizensguide.uaa.alaska.edu.

[12]Joel Gay, *Anchorage Daily News,* March 27, 2004.

[13]Larry Persily, *Anchorage Daily News,* May 8, 2005.

[14]Gregg Erickson, *Anchorage Daily News,* September 28, 2005.

[15]Hannesson.

[16]Fawaz K. Saraf, oil dividend paper presented February 14, 2005, to the Iraq Foundation, http://www.iraqfoundation.org/studies/2005/11_oil.htm.

[17]Philip Revzin, *The Wall Street Journal,* December 5, 1977.

CHAPTER 14
Life after the fund, and final thoughts

I n 1991 Walter Hickel cleaned house as few other new governors had done before, firing staff deep from within the ranks of all departments. The Alaska Permanent Fund's board of trustees was no exception. To the dismay of fund founders such as Clark Gruening, Elmer Rasmuson, and Arliss Sturgulewski, Hickel fired all but one board member. Since the corporation's inception, twenty-two trustees had served on the board and none ever had been dismissed. The law allowed the governor to remove trustees with a written notice stating a reason, but Hickel didn't fulfill even that requirement.[1] Why he failed to give a reason appeared obvious: His true objective was to clear out the board so he could give the seats to friends and campaign supporters.

Hickel automatically got two representatives from his cabinet on the board—Millett Keller, commissioner of administration, and Lee Fischer, commissioner of revenue. He fired three of the four public members—Byron Mallott, Marc Langland, and Charlie Parr. All were distinguished members with strong public records. Mallott had been a trustee under Hammond, Sheffield, and Cowper. In their place, Hickel appointed Oral Freeman, who became chairman; Carl Brady Jr., and Ralph Seekins. John Kelsey alone was allowed to remain. Besides eliminating many years of experience and continuity, Hickel had for the first time politicized permanent fund management.

Within a month of the new appointments, Lee Fischer approached me to say, "The governor wants to know if your bags are packed." I understood the message clearly enough, but I simply replied that they were not. I was determined to do my best to prevent the fund from being politicized down to the executive director level. I would not resign without a reason, or at least a credible excuse. Fischer repeated the question from the governor on several more occasions, but he never asked for my resignation directly or suggested that I resign. Much later, I learned that Hickel felt I had become too popular to fire.

As it turned out, I lasted longer than either Fischer or Keller. Ten months into his term, Hickel fired them both following publication of a newspaper article alleging a procurement violation (Nancy Usera and Darrell Rexwinkle took their places). The firing was a disservice to these bright, hard-working men whose only fault had been lack of familiarity with the public process. Internal politics offered the best explanation for the purge. Hickel had won election by promising to make drastic budget cuts and had put Keller in charge of delivering on the promise. A tough fiscal conservative, Millett welcomed the assignment and became known in Juneau as "Millett Scissorhands." However, Hickel and his closest advisors and aides quickly lost their taste for unpopular budget cuts and decided not to follow through with their promise. Smearing Keller and Fischer offered a convenient escape from that policy and a chance to move on to something else.[2] I didn't know Fischer as well, but I respected Keller as a man with a keen mind, leadership ability, and unimpeachable integrity. I remember standing by his side on a rainy spring day while his daughter Lisa and my son Mitch competed in East High School track events. He didn't deserve this shabby treatment from Hickel.

The new governor's propensity for abrupt firings caught up with him more than once, including an amusing incident affecting Fran. Under Cowper, she had been a special assistant in the Department of Commerce, and it was no surprise that Hickel's initial round of dismissals put her out of a job. Fair enough. We were more concerned at the time about a project that threatened our home in Thane, the reopening of the AJ Gold Mine. Fran fought the mine. That spring, she appeared with her picture on the front page of the *Juneau Empire* criticizing the Bureau of Land Management's handling of the project. The pro-development Hickel crew was so incensed that they called the Department of Commerce and ordered her to be fired—again. An item about Fran being fired twice from the same job appeared under the headline "Wally World" in the Alaska Ear gossip column in the *Anchorage Daily News*.[3]

Hickel sent word through Oral Freeman for me to stop criticizing the mine project as well. I complied, even though the governor's pressure was entirely inappropriate. At the time, without knowing Hickel's thinking—we never developed the face-to-face relationship I had with the other governors—I thought that the AJ Mine controversy was the reason he wanted me fired. In fact, later I learned that Hickel thought I had too much influence. He wanted to use the fund's earnings for spending in the operating and capital budgets. I thought that was unnecessary, and said so. My defense of the fund was a potential political problem for the governor.

Recognizing that my time at the permanent fund was drawing to a close, I began to make plans for the next phase in my life. In April 1991, with Hickel still new in Juneau, I filed paperwork to establish Alaska Permanent Capital Management Company, Inc. The company would be Alaska's first in-state money manager for fixed-income securities. When I left the fund, I would set up the new organization as sort of a mom-and-pop investment business. I applied later that year to the Securities Exchange Commission and to the state for registration as a financial adviser and received approval.

Around that time, I was approached by a head-hunter attempting to recruit a chief investment officer for the Washington State Retirement Board. As one of two finalists, I traveled to Olympia for an interview. I may have been the throw-away candidate; in any event, the other finalist was selected. The significance of the event for me was that it was covered by the Associated Press, and the news reached the trustees. Oral Freeman made much of the article, suggesting that perhaps I should leave the fund if I no longer was interested in serving it. By then Oral and I shared mutual dislike, but I continued to have good relationships with most of the trustees, particularly Carl Brady Jr. and John Kelsey.

In January 1992, I heard from the chief financial officer for the North Slope Borough, Dan Fauske, asking for help in setting up the borough's own permanent fund. With property taxes from Alaska's Arctic oil fields, the predominantly Inupiat borough banked enormous per-capita revenues. In the early years, hasty spending and corruption had consumed much of the income, but now the borough had decided to establish a savings program. Fauske and I spent many hours on the phone discussing how such a fund could be created, maintained, and protected and outlining the necessary regulations. The next month, Fauske called to ask me to review draft documents and to consider serving as his financial consultant for the borough's new fund.

This opportunity seemed a perfect fit with my yet-to-be started investment-management business. Besides, I had reached my fifty-fifth birthday on February 15, 1992, making me eligible for full state retirement. I was ready to move to the private sector. Enough time had passed since Hickel's arrival for my departure to be an independent and largely non-political event. I informed the trustees of my intent to retire. Some of Hickel's hand-picked trustees were overjoyed that his wishes finally would be granted, and there may have been one or two bruised bodies in the great rush to get out the door and call the governor. A series of executive sessions followed in which we discussed a departure date. Once I expressed intent to leave, the trustees wanted to rush me out the door as fast as possible, cutting three months off the transition I planned. Finally we agreed that I would leave April 15 but would stay on the payroll until my leave was used up on June 30, the last day of the fiscal year. Fran and I sold our Juneau home and shipped our household goods to Anchorage, settling in an apartment while we looked for a house.

I was moved by the warmth of goodbyes from friends, coworkers, and colleagues in the banking and finance industry. Besides a number of memorable retirement parties and gifts, my announcement brought a flood of congratulatory mail and newspaper coverage. Two questions came up constantly. Was I interested in running for governor? Was I available to manage money? The answer to the second question was an enthusiastic yes, but I said I had no interest in running for office. Not everyone believed this. Tom Fink, then mayor of Anchorage, confronted me on a TV panel saying he was sure that I would be a candidate. Mike Doogan, popular columnist for the *Anchorage Daily News*, thought I should run for governor. "While Rose has been running things, the Permanent Fund has been handled in all the ways public money usually isn't—professionally, non-politically, successfully," Doogan wrote. "Rose has had his critics, people who questioned his motives and decisions. Who knows? Maybe he did sell too soon or buy the wrong thing once in a while. But, considering his overall record, that's like criticizing Babe Ruth because his home runs didn't go farther out of the park."[4]

Whether intended as criticism or praise, the suggestions about my potential strength in a gubernatorial race served chiefly to puff up my ego, not to make me seriously consider running. In my 1982 job interview with the fund trustees, I promised never to run for office again. That pledge contributed to my success because it assured my focus would remain on the fund and its security and success. I had bolstered my reputation and courted positive publicity, but not for my own benefit— the fund needed public support. Confidence in our management was a critical ingredient to that support. Besides, after thirty years in government, I was ready to try making money on my own.

Our new company began operations in early July 1992. With a staff of three—me, Fran, and the talented Jane Cuddy—we set out to establish ourselves as a low-cost, Alaska-based alternative for institutions investing in bonds. Our first client was Jake Lestenkof, administrator of the Aleutian and Pribilof Islands Restitution Trust, a fund created by Congress to compensate Aleuts terribly mistreated by the U.S. military during World War II. Next were Dan Fauske at the North Slope Borough and Bob Jettner at the Aleutians East Borough. By the end of 1992, I was well on the way to fulfilling my dream of creating of a new financial institution in the private sector. I was sure we would succeed, but I knew that if we didn't we could still eat at Downtown Deli, which we still owned in partnership with Tony and Susan Knowles. Clients kept coming in, often thanks to local leaders whom Fran and I had worked with in many Alaska communities over many years, and who trusted us and knew we cared for their welfare.

As this book was being written, early in 2006, Alaska Permanent Capital Management handled about $2 billion, all from institutional clients in Alaska. My son Evan now runs the business. Fran and I have moved our offices out of the building to avoid seeming to look over his shoulder. He doesn't need our help. As CEO, Evan has surrounded himself with a young, vital staff and the latest communications and analytic technology. It's not a mom-and-pop investment outfit anymore. Fran and I sold our interest in the Deli, although we still eat there and own the building. We are far better off financially than we ever expected to be. Although I have faced challenges with my health, I enjoy looking back on my life and keeping in touch with our many friends.

The future looks promising from where we sit. Our children are grown and married and have successful careers in business and government. We have five amazing grandchildren. We plan to devote our time and resources to them and to our philanthropy. On the other hand, I have concerns about the future of the Alaska Permanent Fund.

In 2005 the fund contained assets in excess of $33 billion. At a sustainable 5 percent real rate of return, the fund can spin off $1.5 billion a year indefinitely while continuing to grow. Such a large sum of money is a big target and cannot escape the attention of anyone in Alaska politics with good or bad aims.

Three constituencies support the fund based on differing priorities for the use of the earnings. The delicate balance of these three political forces helps maintain the fund's health. The three groups (whose memberships overlap) and their priorities include the inflation-proofers, who say "protect the purchasing power of the fund for the future;" the dividend hawks, who say "earn as much as you can and give it to me"; and the government spenders, who say "support my program, taking the money from permanent fund earnings if you have to."

The inflation-proofers include those leaders whose wisdom and foresight gave us the fund in the first place. Their motivation is the disinterested desire to transfer the fund's value to the future. The dividend hawks see the direct payment of fund revenues to Alaska residents as a sufficient end result. This group includes reasonable people with good economic arguments as well as those who are simply motivated by greed. The government spenders see the fund's earnings as one of the few sources of revenue large enough to continue public services when oil production or prices turn downward. While some attempts to spend fund earnings on government have been frivolous—including trying to further bloat capital spending in the 1980s—Alaska someday may find itself with a legitimate need for the earnings to pay for necessities such as education and public safety. One of these three constituencies may have the upper hand at any one time, but my "delicate balance theory" suggests that all three must have hope of fulfilling its wishes in order to retain wide public interest in the fund's preservation. If the politics surrounding the fund fall critically out of balance, then I fear the two losing constituencies may abandon their support for protection for the fund. If that happens, and the prevailing constituency is not strong enough, the fund could be lost. For the fund to survive, I believe it must meet all of the constituency needs.

For a quarter-century, the dividend constituency has been the big winner. Those seeking to inflation-proof the fund have been successful as well, and those who advocate government spending of the earnings have been the consistent losers. Each time the price of oil drops and a fiscal crisis looms for state government, leaders simply hope for an upturn the next year. So far, we've been lucky. Prices have recovered and spending has continued unabated, or even risen, without substantial surpluses set aside in our budget-reserve account to provide stability for the next decline in oil revenue. We have been through the cycle enough times that the patterns have become familiar: The alarm is sounded, cuts are identified, affected groups mobilize, politicians criticize anyone suggesting touching the dividend, and the Legislature does little but trim around the edges and spend reserves while backing away from hard decisions and long-term planning.

In 2004, however, an alliance between the inflation-proofers and the government spenders proposed giving both uses a higher priority for access to a portion of fund earnings. That year, the Legislature came closest to adopting a concept originally advanced by the fund's trustees simply to modernize the formula for calculating income, known as Percent of Market Value, or POMV.

When the Legislature originally drafted the constitutional amendment in 1976 that enabled the permanent fund, it focused on diverting oil revenue and making those dollars immune from spending but left open the question of how to use earnings. That's where things stand today. Inflation-proofing, dividend payments, and any other use of income are at stake whenever the Legislature is in session. The constitutional language has the advantage of being easy for the public to understand, since it resembles the way a retiree might handle finances—avoid spending capital while living off interest and dividends. At the fund's creation, when it owned only government bonds, the system made some sense, but it doesn't work well with investments such as stocks and real estate that earn money primarily though appreciation. Capital gains—earnings from the rise in the value of assets—become available as income only when "realized" by the sale of the underlying securities. In a buy-and-hold operation like the permanent fund, those gains can remain unavailable for many years, later flooding the earnings account all at once when the trustees sell to take profits. Another flaw in the constitutional amendment is that it overlooks inflation. While an individual's retirement account may be needed only during one's lifetime, a truly multigenerational fund must reinvest earnings to offset inflation or it will lose its value over time.

Inflation-proofing and dividend legislation passed in 1982. The system for allocating fund income since then has been as follows: First, pay as dividends half the annual average realized earnings over the previous five years; next, if money is left, calculate the impact of inflation on the Fund's value and reinvest to compensate for it; and finally, if any more money is left, hold it in a reserve account available for expenditure by the Legislature or for payment as future dividends or inflation-proofing. Between the fund's inception and 2006, dividends have consumed about $14 billion of earnings while inflation-proofing has totaled about $9.5 billion. State general fund spending from the earnings has been miniscule in comparison.

Even without considering how we spend the fund's earnings, however, our current system for calculating and paying out the income is outmoded and unwise. First, treating capital gains in the same way as dividends and interest creates a potential conflict of interest for trustees. If the state needs money, trustees might be asked to sell securities for the express purpose of realizing income, but such a sale might not be the right move in their role as prudent investors. Second, the system has the potential of leaving the fund short of income to meet its obligations. The five-year averaging rule for paying the dividend can require large payouts when the fund's income is down; it's possible for the earnings account to go dry before paying the entire dividend, leaving nothing for inflation-proofing or anything else. If that happens, the trustees could be forced to sell securities unwisely to raise money. Finally, treating inflation-proofing as lower in priority than the dividend payments betrays the constitutional purpose of the fund, which is *permanent* savings. The real, unrealized rate of return—that is, the change in the fund's value after inflation—is the appropriate measure of the fund's income, not a realized payout that may have more to do with passing investment decisions than how the underlying fund is actually faring.

These reasons led trustees in 2000 to recommend the POMV concept, which is used by other large endowment funds. Under POMV, a fund's long-term real rate of return becomes its annual payout. If the anticipated real rate of return is 5 percent, then the annual income is simply 5 percent of the value of the entire Fund, regardless of how much investments gain or lose in any given year. To determine the payout percentage, investment experts estimate the anticipated rate of return and subtract inflation—yielding a projected real rate of return. If they expect the fund to make 8 percent annually and inflation to take 3 percent, then a 5 percent payout is sustainable with no loss of purchasing power in the principal.

The proposal makes inflation-proofing foremost and unlimited while providing a relatively stable flow of earnings for dividends and state spending. It also promises a far more predictable payout than under the current system because the fund's total value changes less than the amount of money accrued year to year from capital gains, interest, and dividends. The critical safety factor in the POMV proposal is that the real rate of return, which determines the percent of market value that can be spent, must be set according to rational economic considerations and enshrined in the constitution, not subject to upward revision at the whim of a Legislature. Unless the percent of market value is beyond legislative control, the principal could be vulnerable to those hungry for additional state spending, either to pander to voters through pork-barrel projects or by making direct payments.

The higher the POMV set for spending, the greater the risk to the fund. Anything over 5 percent may put the fund in peril because reaching for higher returns requires greater risk. I support putting a maximum 5 percent POMV in the constitution. Of course, the fund will sometimes have losses. Under the POMV plan, the principle will sustain the payout through the bad years, more than making up those reductions in value during the good years.

Instituting the POMV in the constitution will mean the fund's inflation-proofing constituency no longer needs to compete with the dividend hawks and the government spenders for its annual income. At that point, the fund's savings function will be as safe as government can make it. However, I do not support taking the next step of dividing up the POMV income constitutionally. The Legislature should decide annually how much income should go to the dividend and how much can be spent on government services or reinvested. The original drafters of the constitution had good reasons for prohibiting dedicated funds. Savings is a special case: It conserves funds for future use and thus does not foreclose decisions. But all the reasons other states came to regret dedicating revenue streams still apply to putting the dividend into the constitution. It's easy to imagine circumstances under which the citizens of the future could decide they had a better use for the money. Suppose Alaska faced a catastrophe and needed revenues to address emergency needs? Perhaps even the dividend hawks would be willing to concede to the greater good at that point. Today's Alaskans have no right to take those decisions out of the hands of future generations.

One of the hallmarks of the Alaska Permanent Fund in the early years was simplicity, which assured citizen understanding, trust, and acceptance. Over the years, operations and investments have become more complicated. Care must be taken to inform Alaskans fully about the fund's activity and to teach each new generation why the fund was not set up as a development bank. The trustees are responsible for this. Without understanding there is no trust, and without trust, the fund may be imperiled.

The Fund's long-term strength depends in part on the constituency built by its public-information program. Communications must bedesigned both for the narrow, well-informed elite and for the broad population of Alaskans, with each message pitched at the right level for those on the receiving end. The trustees should carry the message to civic, community, and professional groups, and the fund should maintain an active program of lectures to encourage an informed public discussion. Citizen information should be published in general terms and by providing historical information in detailed statistical charts and tables. A newsletter would be helpful in explaining the latest changes in investment policy and pursuits, as would posting details on the fund's Web site.

The fund must attend to its credibility in other ways as well. Trustees should use care in projecting future returns. The public is unimpressed and often unaware when projections are made, even if they call for double-digit earnings. Failure to reach those projections, however, attracts public attention and undermines confidence in fund management. Losing confidence in management may mean losing confidence in the very concept of the fund, especially among individuals already feeling disempowered or cynical about government. The fund should keep expectations at a reasonable level. If low expectations are exceeded, fund managers may look like heroes. More important, the modest forecasts are in effect insurance in fund credibility.

The trustees have a duty to hold down operating expenses. This, too, can help bolster an image of good management. The fiscal year 2006 budget for the thirty-five positions on the corporation's organizational chart and other in-house costs is $7.8 million, while outside contracts cost another $50 million. The fund retains twenty-six outside management firms for its equity portfolio alone. In FY 1984, with about a dozen staff, my first full-year budget totaled $2.3 million, including in-house and contractual costs—equivalent to $4.5 million in 2005 dollars. As a percentage of funds under management, a ratio that is independent of inflation or fund size, costs now are almost four times what they were in 1984.[5] Of course, the investment program is much more complex today, but economies of scale should have helped the cost-to-investment ratio. The point is that budgets can creep upward beyond need, especially in an environment lacking competitive pressure and with an easy source of funding. The trustees should carefully examine proposed increases in budget, personnel, and contracted money managers.

The Legislature has work to do as well. Statutes should define the role of the Legislative Budget and Audit Committee in providing the fund with checks and balances. The Legislature should consider having the committee engage external auditors reporting to lawmakers rather than continuing the current practice of having auditors report to the trustees. An objective, third-party review can strengthen the credibility of the fund.

Finally, the legislature must protect and nurture the blockers, institutions that run interference by providing for capital needs that otherwise it might be asked to support. The so-called alphabet agencies are tempting sources of cash when legislators face budget shortfalls. Rather than raiding them, however, legislators should make sure they are funded with all the reserves they need to continue making loans for municipal infrastructure, housing, economic development, and education. Besides producing benefits for Alaskans who need this help, the agencies relieve political pressure for spending from the Legislature and deflect attacks on the permanent fund. Over time, the state general fund has received significant dividends from these investments. Agencies such as the Alaska Housing Finance Corp., the Alaska Industrial Development and Export Authority, and the Alaska Municipal Bond Bank Authority are successes just as important, in their own ways, as the permanent fund itself.

Another entity that blocks raids on the fund is the Constitutional Budget Reserve created by Governor Cowper to retain windfall payments from settlement of oil-tax disputes. The balance can be used when revenues drop, or with a three-quarters vote of the Legislature. This idea has worked. The CBR provides critical protection by providing a buffer between decreasing natural-resource revenues and increased fund earnings. It has, in fact, bridged general-fund shortfalls. However, those expenditures had not been replenished as I wrote this book. To keep the CBR as a useful tool in the future, it should be refilled in years when surplus revenues are available.

A large deposit into the CBR now would create the potential for a second long-term investment fund with management similar to the permanent fund but with fewer restrictions on spending. This clone fund could generate annual income that would continually refill the CBR when its funds are used to supplement the general fund. Those revenues would keep the needs of state government another step away from use of the permanent fund earnings.

Former Governor Frank Murkowski's idea of state equity ownership in a trans-Alaska gas pipeline, a project projected to cost between $20 billion and $30 billion, would make a much better investment for a CBR-supporting fund than having the permanent fund buy into the line. The fund's history and prudent investor philosophy teach that it should be fully diversified, resisting an overload of in-state or single-sector investments, and should separate its trust responsibilities from social or political goals. A large partnership share in the gas line would violate these principles, as well as reverse the fund's basic function of converting non-renewable resource wealth into renewable financial assets. A non-trust fund, such as the CBR, could be used for development because such investments would not affect the permanent fund's balanced portfolio. The CBR is not intended to be a permanent fund, and has no prohibitions against social and political investing, so it could hold an equity position in the gas line and thereby receive a steady stream of income. With a strong CBR providing revenue for state government, another of the permanent fund's constituencies would be satisfied, allowing continued and increasing dividends.

There is good reason for optimism about Alaska's future. Until success was achieved by our Alaska Permanent Fund, little evidence existed anywhere that a government could turn a large petroleum discovery into meaningful, long-term benefits for its people. Now we know that nothing about human nature prevents us from transforming mineral wealth into financial assets, investing for the future, and passing our good fortune on to unborn generations. With a combination of exceptional leadership, smart politics, and good luck, we made it happen here. With vigilance and an eye toward history, Alaskans can extend their success indefinitely and perhaps see the Alaska Permanent Fund used as a model worldwide.

---

[1]George Frost, *Anchorage Daily News,* January 30, 1991; Terrence Cole and Elmer F. Rasmuson, *Banking on Alaska: The Story of the National Bank of Alaska,* vol. 2, *Elmer's Memoirs* (Anchorage: National Bank of Alaska, 2000), 182-183.

[2]Ralph Thomas, *Anchorage Daily News,* October 2, 1991 and October 17, 1991.

[3]*Anchorage Daily News,* April 7, 1991.

[4]Mike Doogan, *Anchorage Daily News,* April 14, 1992.

[5]FY 84 budget $2.3 million, FY 83 total ending market value $4.429 billion; cost-to-investment ratio .05 percent. FY 06 budget $57.2 million, FY 05 total ending market value $29.962 billion; cost-to-investment ratio .19 percent.

By Fran Rose, as told to Charles Wohlforth

My husband, Dave, died May 27, 2006. After three awful months in a Texas hospital, this was hardly a surprise. He had finished work on this book while breathing through a tracheotomy tube, his condition steadily worsening until his body seemed to be shutting down, even his hearing. Finally, the physical collapse overpowered David's unwavering optimism, and he asked us to let him go. That was the right decision, and it ended the long nightmare of watching him suffer.

Two days later, on Memorial Day, Temple Beth Sholom in Anchorage filled with hundreds of friends and politicians gathered to pay their respects. Afterward, they exited past me into the freshness of an early summer evening. Thinking of how Dave would have enjoyed such an outpouring of affection and tribute, I was able to smile and accept their condolences.

Over the next weeks, I gathered the many published memorials with the knowledge they would have pleased him. As time has passed, however, and my hours alone have piled up, I've felt his absence with profound pain. David and I shared our entire adult lives together—two complementary halves of a partnership in love, family, politics, and business.

I recognized David's charisma from the first moment I met him in the basement office of the Queens College student newspaper, *The Crown*, when he came to pitch a story. Even then it was obvious he was going places. I was attracted by his energy and the positive feelings he created. People wanted to be around him because of his attitude: He always anticipated good things happening and, with a friendly smirk, seemed to invite others to join in.

I assumed his self-confidence came from his higher station in life as the son of a factory owner. I didn't know then that the factory was a shoestring operation. My own background was strictly working class. My father was an electrician, our apartment was small, and I was the first in my family to go to college. I never could have attended without free tuition and the ability to continue living at home.

In some ways, we were opposites, but we enjoyed our differences—two strong wills in tension while appreciating the other's strengths. I've never known how to turn on that warm beam that David used to make connections with complete strangers. I grew up with practical parents and my outlook tended toward realism. His can-do attitude brought us further than my skepticism ever did, but he placed great importance on a few milestones in our life when, as he saw it, I made life-altering sacrifices to support him in his career. For example, I turned down a hoped-for job offer from the Smithsonian Institution so we could live in Alaska. I never regretted the decision, and I didn't consider it as much of a sacrifice as David did. I didn't have his ambitious drive, which matched his optimism. I would have preferred work involving my interest in history, but it was obvious that Alaska was where we belonged, so I looked for other work.

While I was willing to compromise, David's personality drove him toward his goals with the intensity of a competitor. It certainly helped that he had brains to match. He ran circles around a few of the less-talented generals for whom he worked in his military career. Working for the army as a member of the federal civil service, he attacked each task with vigor and took to heart every commendation and performance review—he preserved all of them—until he had reached the top and could go no higher. At that point, with the climb completed, he moved on to a new career. Again, he believed I created a great turning point in our lives when I encouraged him to take his time finding a new job while I supported the family—but it wasn't such a big deal. He didn't understand that, to me, a job was a job. It simply made sense that I earn the money while he decided where next to invest his heart and competitive spirit.

Dave found a way to add something new to every job he took on. The answering machine he installed in our home after he was elected to the Anchorage City Council made him a one-man troubleshooting bureau. While serving simultaneously on the Anchorage City Council and the Anchorage Borough Assembly, and working for the army during the day, he managed to remain active at Temple Beth Sholom and in the Lions Club, and even prepared taxes on the side to earn extra money. Time was his only limitation—not only his fear of living a short life, but also the lack of hours in the day.

David didn't have many free hours for typical father-son activities like throwing a ball in the backyard, and that became one of his regrets. But the boys, Evan and Mitchell, don't feel as if they missed out on anything. Mitch remembers going to assembly meetings and listening to planning and zoning cases rather than attending baseball games.

"There wasn't a lot of staring out the window and wishing Daddy were there," Mitchell recalls. "When we were young we would be going out and passing out brochures or nailing down yard signs, and when we weren't doing that for Dad, we were doing it for Tony [Knowles]."

Mitchell says those experiences were exciting. His father's life was interesting and, if he didn't have time for playing catch, he did come home and share the intrigues of city hall—which Mitch probably enjoyed more. His fascination with his father's political activities helped shape his future. Although Mitch doesn't consider himself to be the natural politician David was, he made a career as a congressional staffer and lobbyist in Washington, D.C. David greatly enjoyed Mitch's political successes.

Mitchell was fifteen when David ran for mayor of Anchorage in 1978, exposing the boys to a sordid, ugly side of politics. I had influenced my husband to take his strong stand on equal rights for homosexuals, but I never expected him to be pilloried by the religious right and abandoned by much of the community. For Mitchell, it was a formative experience. Until that time, he had believed Anchorage was a classless society. He never had encountered prejudice and thought the synagogue could remain in a separate world from the rest of his life. Suddenly, the phone rang constantly with hateful, anti-Semitic attacks, and Mitch was on the receiving end of some of those calls.

"That hurts, and it was wrong," Mitch recalls. "It was morally wrong. But we all lived and grew, and got stronger, and it made us realize that Anchorage—very much of an idyllic place until then . . . I guess that kind of ripped the cover off it."

Evan, as the older son, related to his father more through work than politics. As a teen he washed dishes at the deli, worked at a car wash, and cleaned offices to make money. When he finished high school, Evan resisted going to college—he wanted to go to sea as a merchant seaman or become an electrician. David applied gentle pressure to keep Evan in school for a couple of years until Evan's own motivation took hold and he earned his degree. David and our friend Eric Wohlforth exposed Evan to the benefits of a career in investment banking. This included an impressive night out to hear classical music at Lincoln Center in Manhattan. Through business connections, David helped Evan get a job in municipal investment banking with Dean Witter Reynolds in San Francisco. At David's advice, Evan started in the back room and learned the business from the bottom up, working his way into responsibility and financial success.

By the time we moved to Juneau, both sons had left for college. Mitchell thinks of our departure as repudiating Anchorage after the bitterness of the mayoral race. I, too, remain angry about what happened—and I was even angrier back then. David, however, simply wanted a new challenge, and the Alaska Permanent Fund represented a terrific opportunity that fit his skills perfectly. I had to quit my job as city manager for the Aleutian village of Akutan, but I, too, was ready for something new. I worked as a deputy to Lisa Rudd, the commissioner of administration, but I wasn't happy there. When David saw an advertisement for the sale of a dress shop, he encouraged me to buy it. I had enjoyed shopping at Victoria's and decided to give it a try. David knew far more about running a business than I did, and he guided me through many steps of learning my new responsibilities—he negotiated the sale contract and he helped count socks at inventory time. I loved every moment of the experience as a Juneau retailer, attending chamber of commerce meetings and such.

One day in 1988, driving to a chamber meeting, I was stunned to see David lying on a sidewalk being tended by paramedics. He had been walking to the bank from the permanent fund offices in the Goldbelt Building and was struck in the crosswalk by a contractor's van, whose driver smelled of alcohol and whose explanation for the accident I did not buy. David was conscious and nodded to reassure me, but when we arrived at the hospital, the situation was very serious. He had twelve to fourteen broken bones, including both sides of his pelvis, his right arm, and ribs. But the most long-lasting damage wasn't as obvious. David had been diagnosed with diabetes eight years earlier, but drugs and diet had kept it under control without insulin. That meant his pancreas still worked somewhat. After the accident, however, his blood sugar shot up and massive insulin injections were the only solution. I steeled myself to administer the injections. His casts prevented him from doing this for himself. The result: David's pancreas shut down, he became dependent on insulin for the rest of his life, and we took the first step on the long road of his physical decline.

Meanwhile, David rallied with a vigor that made him the star at Juneau's physical rehabilitation facility. The physical therapy went on for months. He couldn't manage the stairs at home, so we put a bed in the living room. The permanent fund migrated to his bedside little by little—a desk, computer, telephones—as our house became a branch office, with a steady stream of staff and board members, and the daily delivery of mail and papers that needed signing.

In the absence of David's active help, I made a business mistake moving my dress shop to a new location with less traffic. Within a year, I had to close Victoria's. I worked briefly for the state again until Walter Hickel was elected governor. By then, our time in Juneau was winding down. We started our institutional-investment business, expecting it to be a mom-and-pop operation. I restricted myself to administrative duties to avoid disagreements with David over investments. As the company grew, it became clear that Juneau wasn't the right location. When a mining company offered to buy our house, and thus remove our opposition to its project on the mountain above us, we sold out and moved back to Anchorage.

In the investment business, your product is the skill of your people and the trust your clients place in them. David succeeded at the permanent fund and at Alaska Permanent Capital Management by finding strengths in his employees and shaping them into a team. He didn't hire stars. Like a baseball scout trolling the sandlots for hidden talent, he could identify potential where no one else recognized it. When he placed an employee in a position, he stepped back and gave that person autonomy to perform without interference. Employees appreciated his confidence, and as they grew in the job so did their loyalty to David. He led by example, relying on his own optimistic spirit to infuse others. It did. These were happy workplaces with employees who loved their boss and would do anything for him. The financial results soon followed. David's faith in his people was rewarded by excellent performance.

By the mid'90s, business was booming but David's health problems worsened. His eyesight, always poor, deteriorated with diabetic retinopathy and macular degeneration. Laser surgery was only a stopgap. He lost the ability to drive but kept functioning at work thanks to reading machines that enlarged small text to headline size. He often found errors that sighted people missed. His kidneys began to suffer, too, despite a strict low-protein diet. The symptoms of kidney failure include a lack of energy and excessive sleep, but David's spirit kept him going, leading the business through its busiest period of growth. I didn't recognize the seriousness of the problem until we traveled to Greece. In Athens, I wanted to climb the steep hill to the Acropolis. David fought his way up, panting and stopping every few yards, but he wouldn't give up. Later, he paid for his persistence with pain and vomiting. I was scared. I didn't know what was happening, and we were alone in a foreign country.

David went onto dialysis in 1998 and asked Evan to move back to Alaska to help with the business. For Evan, the move wasn't easy. Settled in San Francisco's North Beach with his future wife, Barbara Saenz, and her two boys from her previous marriage, he had become a success in his own right. He would be sacrificing career opportunities, but would gain the opportunity for a better environment for the children, an easier lifestyle, and the chance for he and Barbara to go back to school for advanced degrees. The main factor, however, was David's health. "I felt a certain amount of obligation to try to continue the legacy," Evan says.

Patients at the dialysis center sat twenty at a time in rows connected to noisily beeping machines, their blood visibly and audibly churning through tubes, for four hours three times a week. Besides the tedium, the place was deeply depressing—a harsh medical environment filled with people in pain, short on hope. We got to know the other patients, but sometimes they disappeared because they'd chosen death over continuing dialysis. This infuriated David—he would never give up. He fought back by trying to brighten the place. He played practical jokes on the nurses and technicians. One young tech fell into depression over his sad work, and David sent him to an Oakland Raiders football game. For his own mood, he listened to books on tape. He began work on this book by dictating his memories, filled with humor, to Nancy Gross—a friend he had known since his days on the assembly. Nancy sometimes drove David to dialysis so I wouldn't have to go every time. So did several other friends. No one ever heard him complain. Nor did anyone at the office, where he still managed to work effectively. Nor did he ever complain to me, not even in private moments.

I complained plenty. I was the one who wept and wailed over his pain. He would say, "Don't be ridiculous. Stop it. Oh, Franny, stop it, it will be OK."

One spring, just before Easter, he asked me to drive him to a costume shop so he could rent a bunny suit to wear to the dialysis center. I flatly refused. I can't think of a clearer example of the difference in our personalities: I hate dress-up stuff, but I have many pictures of David as a bunny, a leprechaun, and so on. He insisted, and the Saturday of Easter weekend here was a Jewish Easter bunny being wheeled around the dialysis center, delighting the patients and staff.

David intended to get better and put his focus on getting a kidney transplant. To become eligible, he needed heart surgery—a quintuple bypass to deal with clogged arteries. That was successful, but no kidney became available. Other patients had been waiting a decade. So he began researching overseas sources. This frightened me. However, a friend stepped forward and offered a kidney. At first David refused, but when his health worsened, she repeated the offer and he accepted. The magnitude of the gift is hard to imagine—the donor not only made a gift of life from her own body, but also accepted the burden of extensive medical testing and the surgery itself plus psychological testing intended to assure that the donation was voluntary. The transplant, performed just after the events of September 11, 2001, was a success. David was free of dialysis.

With a kidney transplant comes the lifetime need for drugs to prevent rejection. David broke down a year after the operation due to a reaction of one of these drugs with his cholesterol medicine. His muscles were damaged, and it took months for him to learn to walk again. He never returned to normal. Hospitalizations became more frequent and problems came up, all made more serious by the transplant, the drugs, and the combinations of issues. Illnesses befell his system like falling dominoes.

In 2005, when David needed a new heart valve, his Anchorage doctor said the risks of surgery were too great. David might not be strong enough for the operation, and post-operative infections were likely because his immune system had been suppressed due to the transplant. However, the doctor recommended a doctor at the Texas Heart Institute, where many cardiac surgical techniques had been pioneered. We went to Houston and met the doctor who would do the surgery, but I had terrible misgivings. The risks seemed too great. David himself told Charles Wohlforth that the probability of survival was "slim." The alternative, however, was to succumb slowly to congestive heart failure, and it wasn't in David's make-up to wait for decline and death when there was a chance, however remote, for a better life.

Before the operation, David went on a final trip with his sons. Mitchell used his business connections at the Walt Disney Company, where he had worked, to get luxury tickets for the Super Bowl. The game was in Detroit that year featuring the Seattle Seahawks and Pittsburg Steelers. Long-suffering Seahawks fans from Alaska were disappointed by the outcome, but Evan, Mitchell, and David took the opportunity to be together and talk. Mitchell knew his father was proud of him for taking the plunge to form his own lobbying practice in Washington. Evan knew that David was proud of him, too. David had entrusted Evan with the business he had built in Anchorage, which Evan had taken over by that time.

The Houston heart operation took place on February 20, 2006, an eleven-hour marathon, and David's recovery was slow and uneven. A breathing tube filling his mouth, he lay sedated and essentially unconscious for three weeks. I whiled away the time at his bedside and at a Holiday Inn. Houston was one of the few cities where we had no friends, and the heat and solitude were almost unbearable. Watching David reliant on machines and showing little improvement was torture. After a month, he was transferred out of the recovery room, but it was several more weeks before he could talk.

David's earlier work on this book had stopped when Nancy Gross died in 2001. He restarted the project in early 2005 with Charles Wohlforth. They completed most of the manuscript over the next twelve months, the pace growing intense as the surgery approached early in 2006. Finishing the book became David's driving interest. When he became lucid and able to speak after the operation, he was crazy to review the final chapter and make corrections, but he wasn't well enough to do this until late April. On May 4, he was satisfied, giving approval to send the manuscript to friends and associates who had agreed to read it for accuracy and possible revisions.

David wasn't getting better. Infections set in that couldn't be controlled without destroying his transplanted kidney, and he had to go back on dialysis. He lost his hearing, suffered a perforated bowel, and infections invaded his body. Although his brain remained active, he was dying. His system seemed to be breaking down.

"I want you to pull the plug," he told me. "I've had a good life and done all the things I want to do." He listed his accomplishments—the kids and grandchildren, our long and happy marriage, the business, the permanent fund. It was a long list. I arranged for an air ambulance to take him back to Anchorage, where friends could visit him at Providence Hospital. David told his doctor there to discontinue dialysis. The treatment stopped. Sedated, he died within a week.

After watching David suffer for three months, his death was a relief to us. As of this writing, we've had most of a year to try to get used to his absence.

At the end of his life, David had plenty of chances to settle his relationships and look back on his life, with its long road from Jamaica Avenue, Queens, to becoming one of Alaska's financial pioneers. A park was named for him—the former Conifer Park, which occupied land David had saved from development when he was on the assembly. He attended a committee meeting of old friends who gathered to bestow the honor. Many of his kind and good acts came back to him in that last year, and he always enjoyed the recognition and the warm feelings that came with them. For example, a woman contacted us to tell us the outcome of a story we had forgotten. Decades earlier, she had approached David for help bringing back home to Alaska her daughter, who was on drugs, was broke, and was pregnant. David raised the money from among members of the Lions Club to send the daughter a plane ticket. She flew to Anchorage, had the baby, and handed off the child to her mother to raise before returning to her degenerate lifestyle. That woman—the grandmother—called to let us know that the child had become a successful accountant. She believed he would have turned out very differently—or never would have been born—without David's being willing to get involved. This woman's story illustrates so much of what David was about—kindness and compassion.

"He will never probably get as much credit as he should get," Mitchell says, "because there's not a lot of credit put in this world for just being a really decent, good, honest, solid citizen. Sometimes you've got to be other things to be great—or to get to use that moniker of 'great'—but I think if you can have an unbiased view of a life, he would be right up there."

Dave Rose's
ACKNOWLEDGMENTS

Writing one's first book is a daunting task, particularly when you are not sighted. The late Nancy Gross performed the yeoman task of organizing more than fifty cases of memoranda, meeting notes, minutes, and news clippings. Before her death, she interviewed with the late Governor Jay Hammond and the late Representative Hugh Malone. She also taped interviews with Dr. George Rogers, the first chairman of the Alaska Permanent Fund Corporation, and with me. Nancy was a friend who is sorely missed. I recall her interest in Anchorage planning and zoning and the many times I returned from an assembly meeting to find her on the steps of my house, waiting to tell me why I had voted incorrectly on a particular issue.

Charles Wohlforth spent more than a year reviewing Nancy's files, doing original research, conducting interviews, and drafting and redrafting this text. I appreciate his keen insight and understanding of the many events that shaped my character.

Each of us tends to recall historic events differently, and I have relied on historians, economists, and leaders who were there when history was made to review my manuscript. My thanks go to historians Jo Antonson and Dr. Terrence Cole; to former commissioners of revenue Tom Williams and Eric Wohlforth; and to Senator Arliss Sturgulewski and Representative Clark Gruening.

Alaskans owe a great deal of gratitude to Jay Hammond, Hugh Malone, and Jim Rhode, who are no longer with us. Without them, we would not have a fund today.

I am grateful for the patience of my family—Fran, Evan, and Mitch—and for their encouragement and their help to me in telling my story.

I have had many mentors. I have learned much from so many friends and associates. Foremost among these·have been Eric Wohlforth, with his high standard of ethics, his humility, and his wise counsel; John Kelsey, both a gentle man and a gentleman who served as chairman of the Alaska Permanent Fund trustees; Byron Mallott, who also served as a chairman and as executive director of the fund, and who was a constant champion for Alaska's Native people and for humanity as a whole; and Marc Langland, a good friend who served as chairman of the fund's board of trustees, and whose cheery demeanor and positive outlook strengthened me in my darkest hours.

Members of the Fiscal Policy Council contributed greatly during the past two decades and should be recognized for their superior oversight. All of them have influenced me in different ways. They are Langland, Sturgulewski, Scott Goldsmith, Jim Cloud, Lee Gorsuch, Cheryl Frasca, and Dan Fauske.

Charles Wohlforth's
ACKNOWLEDGMENTS

Taking Dave Rose's comments and voluminous files and turning them into a written narrative was one of the most enjoyable tasks of my career as a writer. Dave was a skilled storyteller. Our many mornings of interviews were a pleasure, and he was an easy collaborator, making few changes to the text, and then only with thoughtful intent. I always shall treasure the role I was invited to play in his last year and the privilege of passing on his thoughts and memories to readers.

I thank Fran Rose for her strength and thoughtfulness and Laurie Ford, Dave's assistant, for support in many forms. Karen Datko transcribed many hours of interviews with Dave. Bruce Merrell of the Z. J. Loussac Library and Sharon Palmisano and Lynn Hallquist of the *Anchorage Daily News* library were especially helpful, as always. Dr. Scott Goldsmith assisted me with nailing down facts and finding economic information. Jack Roderick, George Sullivan, Eric Wohlforth, Arliss Sturgulewski, Clark Gruening, Clem Tillion, Bob Dupere, Cliff Groh, Don Hunter, Fran Ulmer, and Tom Fink consented to lengthy interviews to complement Dave's memories and material. Fortunately, the late Nancy Gross had interviewed Jay Hammond, Hugh Malone, and George Rogers. Wohlforth, Groh, Gruening, and Sturgulewski, as well as Dr. Terrence Cole and Jo Antonson, reviewed the manuscript and provided comments and corrections.

I regret that Dave's death will prevent him from holding this book in his hands, but I feel certain he was pleased with the text and with the final gift to Alaska that it represents.

INDEX

ABOUT THE AUTHORS

DAVE ROSE (1937-2006) was the first director of the Alaska Permanent Fund, the first chairman of the Anchorage Assembly for the unified government of Anchorage, and possibly the first Jew to open a kosher New York-style delicatessen in Alaska. Rose was a charming, self-effacing, and charismatic spinner of tales whose personal warmth helped him overcome a wide range of challenges in government, finance, the military, family, and community service. When he died at age 69, Rose left his wife and lifelong companion, Fran, and sons, Evan and Mitch, and their families, as well as a rich legacy in business, politics, and friendships.

CHARLES WOHLFORTH is the author of numerous books and articles, and winner of more than two dozen national and regional awards for writing, including the 2004 *Los Angeles Times* Book Prize. A family friend of Dave Rose's since childhood, Wohlforth followed Rose's footsteps to the Anchorage Assembly, where he represented the city's downtown area from 1993 to 1999. Wohlforth's previous books include *The Whale and the Supercomputer: On the Northern Front of Climate Change* (North Point Press-Farrar, Straus and Giroux), and assistance rendered to former Governor Walter J. Hickel in the writing of *Crisis in the Commons: The Alaska Solution* (ICS Press). He lives in Anchorage with his wife, Barbara, and four children.

Recommendations for readers interested in
MEMOIRS & BIOGRAPHIES ABOUT NOTABLE ALASKANS:

ACCIDENTAL ADVENTURER:
Memoir of the First Woman to Climb Mt. McKinley
Barbara Washburn, hardbound, $19.95

ARCTIC BUSH PILOT:
From Navy Combat to Flying Alaska's Northern Wilderness
James "Andy" Anderson & Jim Rearden, paperback, $17.95

GEORGE CARMACK:
Man of Mystery Who Set off the Klondike Gold Rush
James Albert Johnson, paperback, $14.95

KAY FANNING'S ALASKA STORY
*Memoir of Pulitzer Prize-winning Newspaper Publisher on America's
Northern Frontier,* Kay Fanning with Katherine Field Stephen,
hardbound $24.95, paperback $17.95

ON THE EDGE OF NOWHERE
Jim Huntington & Lawrence Elliott, paperback, $14.95

ONE SECOND TO GLORY:
The Alaska Adventures of Iditarod Champion Dick Mackey
Lew Freedman, paperback, $16.95

RAISING OURSELVES:
A Gwitch'in Coming of Age Story from the Yukon River
Velma Wallis, paperback, $14.95

SISTERS:
Coming of Age & Living Dangerously in the Wild Copper River Valley
Samme Gallaher & Aileen Gallaher, paperback, $14.95

TALES OF ALASKA'S BUSH RAT GOVERNOR
*The Extraordinary Autobiography of Jay Hammond,
Wilderness Guide and Reluctant Politician*
Jay Hammond, paperback, $17.95

These titles can be found at or special-ordered from your local bookstore.
A wide assortment of Alaska books also can be ordered directly from the
publisher's website, www.EpicenterPress.com, or by calling 1-800-950-6663.

Alaska Book Adventures™
Epicenter Press Inc.
www.EpicenterPress.com